The *Breakthrough* Depression Solution

The *Breakthrough* DEPRESSION Solution

A *Personalized* 9-Step Method for Beating the *Physical* Causes of Your Depression

James Greenblatt, MD

Sunrise River Press
39966 Grand Avenue
North Branch, MN 55056
Phone: 651-277-1400 or 800-895-4585
Fax: 651-277-1203
www.sunriseriverpress.com

Edit by Karin Craig and Karen Chernyaev
Layout by Monica Seiberlich

ISBN 978-1-934716-15-1
Item No. SRP615

Library of Congress Cataloging-in-Publication Data

Greenblatt, James.
Breakthrough depression solution : a personalized 9-step method for beating the physical causes of your depression / by James M. Greenblatt.
p. cm.
Includes index.
ISBN 978-1-934716-15-1
1. Depression, Mental--Diet therapy--Popular works. 2. Depression, Mental--Nutritional aspects--Popular works. I. Title.
RC537.G724 2011
616.85'270654--dc22

2010042413

Printed in USA

10 9 8 7 6 5 4 3 2 1

Contents

Acknowledgments

I would like to thank my wife, Judy, and my three children for their patience and understanding during my many morning and weekend disappearances to work on this project. I also want to thank my parents, who have provided a lifetime of unwavering support and encouragement. Finally, this book could never have been written without the research, writing, and editing help of Lee Yuan, Virginia Taylor, and Suzanne Stoterau, MD.

Most importantly, I would like to thank the thousands of patients who have led me to think about what truly helps rather than what is supposed to help.

Introduction

Another book about depression? You've probably summoned enthusiasm before about the promise of a new therapy or the advertised benefits of the latest drug. You have good reason to be frustrated and cynical, especially if you are still depressed.

I understand. I have been treating patients with depression for more than twenty years. In that time I have talked to young children who claimed that they would rather die than live with their "sadness." I have treated adolescents who cut themselves to relieve the emotional pain of depression. And I have helped adults who can no longer function at work and have had relationships destroyed by the ravages of depression.

But I urge you to restore hope once again and to read on. In this book I am not promoting a particular therapy or a new drug. In fact, I am not hyping any one treatment for the complex phenomenon of depression, a disease so prevalent that it threatens to become the major cause of disability worldwide by the year 2020.

Depression has myriad causes. Unless treatment targets the particular causes that underlie an individual's case of depression , it is doomed to fail.

In this book I offer a method designed to ensure personalized treatment for depression.

Personalized Medicine

We recognize early on in life that a vast array of differences in appearance and personality exist among those we know. It shouldn't be hard to realize then that we are also biochemically unique, meaning that our bodies function differently from one another. For example, your body requires different amounts of vitamins and minerals for optimal function than your mother's or father's or a complete stranger's body. These biochemical subtleties affect our brains, our moods, and our recovery.

My approach to treating depression is grounded in personalized medicine. The fundamental premise of this approach is that just as your personality and appearance are unique, so is the constellation of factors that contribute to your depression. Through identifying and treating these factors—many of which have long been ignored in conventional psychiatric treatment—you can get well.

Conventional treatment methods are based on the results of research studies. These studies derive statistics from large populations. But we can't reliably infer the particular treatment that will work for you from generalized statistics based on a large population.

Personalized medicine, on the other hand, seeks to identify all the factors that may be relevant to your depression. It is an integrative approach, focusing on nutrition, genetics, stress, and, when needed, a technology to ensure that medications are targeted toward your individual biochemistry. The goal of personalized medicine is a treatment approach designed especially for you.

As a way to help you remember each component within this method of personalized medicine, I've devised a mnemonic: THE ZEEBrA. Beginning in Chapter 1, I explain what each letter stands for but now just a word about the animal itself that inspired the acronym.

Since childhood, I have been fascinated by zebras. I learned that zebras are sensitive and alert, they move in a zigzag pattern to avoid their predators, and because of their stamina, they can usually outlast them. Zebras have excellent eyesight and hearing as well as an acute sense of smell and taste. But the most interesting feature of zebras to me—both then and now—is that each member of the species has a unique stripe pattern. Zebras may all look alike to the untrained eye, but closer inspection reveals that some zebra stripes are brown, and others are black. There are even some black zebras with white stripes. Each zebra's stripe configuration is unique.

The uniqueness of each zebra's stripe configuration symbolizes this book's message about depression. While the illness of depression has enough common features to be considered a diagnostic category, each person's version of depression is unique. Therefore, to be effective, treatment for depression must take into consideration the particular mix of factors that contribute to each person's disease. We cannot assume that people, any more than zebras, are of the same stripe.

I am not interested in pinpointing the blame for depression on your past, your parents, and, most of all, you! I want you to recognize that what happens in the brain is not separate from the body. The health of the brain or what we might call the mind depends directly on the health of the body. A complex mix of factors—nutrients, hormones, genetics, stress—interweave to affect how the mind works and how the individual responds to life events. The slings and arrows that beset us in the world, in other words, are only one set of factors that determine whether we will be mentally healthy or suffer from depression.

Let me mention just a few of the major factors I address in this book.

Nutrition

After twenty years of practicing psychiatry and seeing thousands of patients, I have come to believe that feeding the brain well is fundamental to the effective treatment of depression. Yet this simple truth is often overlooked. Physicians tend not to think in terms of nutrition, partly because they do not learn about it in medical school. Graduates of U.S. medical schools receive inadequate training in nutrition, according to a study conducted by the National Academy of Sciences. A follow-up survey in 2006 yielded the same conclusion: Physicians lack the training they need both to understand the importance of nutrition and to counsel their patients.

If nutrition is critically important in treating depression as well as other diseases, why has the medical community been slow to accept simple, inexpensive nutritional interventions? Partly because they are simple and inexpensive! Companies fund research studies to test drugs that will generate profit. The sophisticated, glossy advertisements for antidepressants that come across your doctor's desk or the TV commercials our children are watching tout drugs that will bring a profit to the pharmaceutical companies. Physicians choose treatment options that are familiar to them, like the ones they read about in their medical journals. These medications are considered standard practice because a research article (usually funded by the company making the drug) supports their use.

The medical profession has been slow to see the light in regard to nutritional interventions in general. In a study on spreading the word about health innovations, Dr. Donald Berwick tells the story of Captain James Lancaster, a British sea captain who discovered in 1601 that lemon juice prevented scurvy. The British government did not adopt this simple and inexpensive intervention right away—but 264 years after its effectiveness was definitively proven. Just because physicians largely ignore the benefits of nutritional interventions does not mean these interventions are ineffective.

A phenomenon called "the tomato effect" helps explain the reluctance of the medical community to recognize the benefits of nutritional therapies. The tomato effect was identified by Dr. James Goodwin in 1984 in the *Journal of the American Medical Association.* He wrote, "The tomato effect in medicine occurs when an efficacious treatment for a certain disease is ignored or rejected because it does not 'make sense' in light of accepted theories of disease mechanism and drug action."

The rejection of a potentially useful treatment because "everyone knows it won't work" is named for Americans' stubborn belief—from the sixteenth to the nineteenth centuries—that tomatoes were poisonous.

Understanding this human tendency to reject a treatment outside one's frame of reference—even in the presence of contradictory evidence—helps explain the medical profession's persistent resistance to using nutritional interventions to treat depression. Still, we can no longer accept a glacial pace of progress in identifying remedies for depression. The costs of depression—in terms of joy, energy, opportunity, relationships, even life itself—are legion. Physicians owe it to patients and their families to break free from long-held but mistaken assumptions.

Medication

Instead of looking first at a patient's nutritional status, psychiatrists today are much more likely to prescribe a medication. Individual psychiatrists tend to favor particular drugs; one may tend to order Prozac first, another Lexapro. Sometimes the first prescription helps; more often, however, the patient's depression lingers. Usually, another drug is prescribed, and sometimes a third, often to medicate the side effects brought on by the first or second. Doctors continually prescribe more medications partly because they don't fully understand how antidepressants actually work, although it appears that chemicals in the brain called neurotransmitters are affected by these medications. If these drugs were completely without risk, all the patient would waste during this trial-and-error sequence would be money and time. But living with depression itself brings risk, and the longer one suffers, the more difficult it is to recover. Moreover, we probably do not yet fully appreciate the potential risks of prescription medication, especially to children and the elderly.

Recognizing the over reliance of the psychiatry profession on prescription drugs, Dr. James Watson, winner of the Nobel Prize in Physiology or Medicine for determining the structure of DNA, has urged the medical profession to focus research and funding on better understanding psychiatric disorders. Speaking in 2010, he insisted that we need breakthroughs to determine the origins of psychiatric disorders and to develop treatments based on their results.

One promising technology, called referenced-EEG (rEEG), is already available to help guide psychiatrists' prescription choices based on patients' biochemical individuality. The technology, which is simple and noninvasive, will be described as part of THE ZEEBrA approach. This book will guide you and your physician in how to use the technology to greatly enhance the likelihood that a medication prescribed to treat your depression will actually be effective.

Using nutritional and metabolic testing and assessing the potential effectiveness of prescription drugs, we can understand the nature of depression within each individual sufferer. Only then can treatment be tailored to the patient. Until you know the stripes, you can't know the zebra.

Overcoming Stigma

Even today, despite advances in educating the public, mental illness is shrouded in stigma. Patients, in addition to suffering from depression, tend to live in the shadows of guilt and self-blame. I believe the stigma is due in part to our culture's tendency to explain depression in vague, psychological terms. One patient is ashamed that he hasn't been able to get over a divorce, and another laments that it has taken her too long to recover from having been raised by a preoccupied mother. Or, still another may be hopeless about his ability to recover because his own father languished in undiagnosed depression.

Of course, our life experience influences our moods. Our genetic blueprints are the gift or curse we inherit from our ancestors, and they have an impact on our biological potential for health and illness. Yet we are not determined by our life experience, and genetics is not destiny.

Our culture's lack of attention to other concrete, biological factors that may influence depression makes it easier to fall into the trap of self-blame. People are not likely to feel guilt about a diagnosis of celiac disease, a deficiency of zinc in their blood, or a low thyroid level.

This book offers you a guide to the array of potential factors that could be making and keeping you depressed. Everyone has a unique biochemistry, and so this book cannot give you the one treatment that will end your depression. This book can, however, provide you with the tools to ask the right questions.

As you begin to address the biological causes of depression, you will find hope, motivation, and strength for recovery. A patient of mine likened his sense of depression to being in a dark hole. He was at the bottom, and although there was a ladder that extended up to the light, it had no rungs, and he was powerless to climb out.

The tools defined in this book will be your rungs, and you will understand how psychological and biological factors are entwined. THE ZEEBrA approach emphasizes recovery and remission from depression and will help you find the light.

1

What Is Depression?

Almost everybody experiences depression now and again: those feelings of sadness, a lack of energy, fatigue, and sometimes even hopelessness. Depression, which comes from the Latin word *deprimere*, meaning "pressing down," certainly can feel as if a heavy weight were pressing on your head, shoulders, or heart.

In difficult or frustrating situations such as the death of a loved one, loss of a job, or divorce, these sad or "down" feelings are perfectly normal reactions. But when the sad feelings are stronger, they settle in for no apparent reason, or they go on longer than a situation seems to warrant, they can indicate the presence of a depressive disorder.

This chapter introduces the various types of depression, their symptoms, and possible causes, as described in the fourth edition of the *Diagnostic and Statistical Manual of Mental Disorders (DSM-IV)*—the bible of the mental health profession—and in psychiatric literature. Look upon this chapter as Depression 101, an introduction to the disease that will help you discuss depression with your doctor and other mental health professionals. It may also help you understand why some current views of the disorder hamper treatment.

Symptoms of Depression

You know it if you feel "down." But how do you know if you're truly suffering from depression? There is no test or objective criteria that can firmly establish the presence of depression, since it isn't a disease like diabetes or rheumatoid arthritis with a common, identifiable mechanism. Depression is different things to different people: It can show up as any combination of symptoms that range from the emotional to the behavioral to the physical. In some people these symptoms are obvious, but in others they are quite vague, making an accurate diagnosis difficult.

Still, certain symptoms are likely indicators of depression. According to the *DSM-IV*, a major depressive episode is characterized by the presence of five of the following symptoms during the same two-week period, including at least one of the first two symptoms on the list:

- Persistent sadness, anxiety, or feeling of emptiness most of the day, nearly every day
- Marked decrease in interest or pleasure in almost all activities nearly every day
- Binge eating/weight gain or anorexia/weight loss
- Sleeping too much or experiencing insomnia
- Fatigue, lethargy
- Feeling restless or inordinately slowed down
- Feelings of worthlessness or inappropriate guilt
- Trouble concentrating and remembering
- Feeling suicidal

(Note that these symptoms, with the exception of suicidal feelings, are considered normal for up to two months after the loss of a loved one.)

So does it mean that you *aren't* depressed if you aren't experiencing any of the above symptoms? Not necessarily. Many less obvious symptoms may also point to depression, but they aren't on the above list. These include physical symptoms such as a persistent stomachache, emotional symptoms like irritability, and behavioral symptoms like throwing yourself into your work. (Then again, these symptoms might be indicative of something entirely apart from depression.)

Here are some of the wide-ranging symptoms that may indicate depression:

- Aches and pains, digestive problems, or other physical complaints that are unresponsive to treatment
- Alcohol or drug abuse
- Chain smoking
- Constant exhaustion
- Crying a lot
- Decreased physical activity just about every day
- Engaging in reckless, risky behaviors
- Great difficulty getting up in the morning
- Irritability, frustration
- Lack of energy or motivation
- Diminished sex drive
- Working unnecessarily long hours
- Chronic insomnia

Depression can negatively affect a person's life in numerous and profound ways. The disorder makes it hard to function effectively at work, which can result in job loss and decreased income. It can cause a withdrawal from life that, in turn, leads to the loss of relationships with family and friends. It can negatively affect physical health by contributing to or worsening other illnesses or because the sufferer simply doesn't have the energy or will to take care of himself or herself. And it can also increase the risk of disease and death: According to the National Institute of Mental Health, people with depression are four times more likely to have a heart attack than those who have no history of depression. And after suffering a heart attack, the chances of having another one and/or dying are significantly increased. Depressed people are also at a higher risk of alcohol or drug abuse.

When depressed individuals first go to their doctors seeking help, they usually complain of fatigue, sleep disturbances, or unexplained pain, rather than feeling sad or "low." Most people initially mention these problems to their general practitioners, internists, or other first-line physicians, rather than to a psychiatrist. These doctors often attempt to treat the problem before referring patients to psychiatrists, which means that prescriptions for most antidepressants and antianxiety medicines are written by nonpsychiatrists. Indeed, a 2009 study pointed out that general practitioners write 62 percent of the prescriptions for antidepressants and 65 percent of the antianxiety medicines, with psychiatrists and addiction specialists accounting for only 21 percent of the antidepressant and 13 percent of the antianxiety prescriptions.

The fact that people generally notice a "physical" problem first means that diagnosing depression can be tricky, especially if you're trying to diagnose yourself. That's why it's important to see a mental health professional if you think you may be depressed. Depression can be treated. If left untreated, it can endanger your mental, emotional, and physical health.

Kinds of Depression

The *DSM-IV* lists many kinds of depression, the most common types being major depressive disorder and dysthymic disorder. Other kinds include bipolar disorder, postpartum depression, psychotic depression, seasonal affective disorder (SAD), atypical depression, double depression, secondary depression, masked depression, and chronic treatment-resistant depression.

Major depression

Major depression is characterized by a combination of symptoms that interfere with a person's ability to eat, sleep, work, function normally, and engage in activities that were once considered enjoyable. Specifically, if you have experienced five or more of the primary indicators of depression listed previously, for at least a two-week period, and one of the symptoms is a depressed mood or an inability to take pleasure in things you used to enjoy, you are probably experiencing a major depressive episode.

> Lisa, a fifty-three-year-old professional, found it harder and harder to get up in the morning. She had recently lost her husband to cancer and was raising their two children alone while working long hours. It had been more than a year since her husband's death, yet she didn't want to see or talk to her friends, and she could hardly get herself to eat anything. All she really wanted to do was sleep. A nightly glass or two of wine was the

only routine she looked forward to. She finally sought treatment when her thoughts led to ruminations about suicide. Lisa's depression following her grief had affected every area of her life.

The death of a loved one, divorce, disability, chronic physical illness, trauma, substance abuse, childbirth, and the loss of a job are all common triggers of major depression. While some people experience just a single episode, at least half of those who experience an episode of major depression will suffer another one, sometimes without any obvious trigger. And for those who have experienced several episodes, the likelihood of recurrence can be greater than 90 percent. However, only 50 percent of those diagnosed with major depression receive any kind of treatment.

Minor depression (dysthymia)

Minor depression, also known as dysthymia or dysthymic disorder, is a chronic, mild depression that lasts for at least two years and includes at least two of the primary indicators of depression listed previously. While it is less intense than major depression and may not be disabling, minor depression is a long-term condition that is severe enough to interfere with normal functioning and significantly hamper one's ability to enjoy life. It's estimated that more than three million Americans over the age of eighteen suffer from minor depression. In the general population (i.e., among people who do not already suffer from some form of depressive disorder) the lifetime risk of developing either major or minor depression is about 20 percent.

John, a divorced forty-five-year-old, worked sixty-hour weeks as an electrician. Although he was able to meet his obligations and see his kids on the weekend, he complained that he felt "empty" and "dissatisfied" almost every day and his energy was always low. He no longer enjoyed spending time with friends or playing guitar.

Although many psychiatrists and researchers regard dysthymia as a milder and less important form of depression, new research has found that those suffering from dysthymia have many impairments in psychosocial functioning. The study analyzed survey responses from 43,093 noninstitutionalized U.S. adults, of which 328 respondents were identified as having dysthymia. Compared to the general population and 712 respondents identified as having acute major depression, those with dysthymia were more likely to use supplemental Social Security Disability Income, were more likely to receive Medicaid health insurance, and were less likely to work full time. Dysthymia is a significant health burden and greatly impairs the lives of those struggling with it.

Bipolar disorder

Formerly known as manic depression, bipolar disorder consists of at least one period of major depression and at least one period of mania, or elation. Mania is defined as a euphoric, expansive, or irritable mood that is not part of the individual's normal personality and is accompanied by at least three of the following symptoms:

- An inflated sense of self-importance
- A decreased need for sleep
- Extreme talkativeness
- Rapid flitting from one idea to the next
- Distractibility
- Overindulgence in activities that are pleasurable, resulting in negative consequences (e.g., spending money recklessly, making unwise business investments, engaging in high-risk sexual activity)

> The moods of thirty-year-old Robin could bounce from sky-high happiness to face-pressed-into-the-mattress depression. When she was in her "happy" moods, she talked nonstop, socialized endlessly, drove fast, and went on fantastic shopping sprees. But when the "low" moods hit, she barely spoke or ate and didn't leave the house. In fact, she didn't even get out of bed, sometimes for days.

Mania and depression "cycle" in bipolar disorder, as the mood swings from high to low and back again. The effect of such mood swings on personal and professional lives can be devastating, resulting in lost jobs, broken relationships, poor parenting, and financial disarray. Approximately 2.6 percent of Americans are affected by bipolar disorder, a condition that strikes both sexes equally and typically strikes by the age of twenty-six.

Postpartum depression

It's estimated that 10 to 15 percent of women who have recently given birth experience postpartum depression, which is characterized by a major depressive episode that occurs within one month of delivery. A new mother can find herself feeling "down," inadequate, guilty, anxious, or irritable for no apparent reason. She may also feel ambivalent or even negative toward her newborn child. These symptoms may last as long as a year.

When twenty-four year-old Janice held her first baby in her arms, she thought she was the most beautiful thing she had ever seen. But when the second one came along, she looked at him and thought, *So what?* Her lack of interest in this new baby, her older child, and just about everything else in her life alarmed her. She managed to give the kids what they needed, but in the case of her newborn, she could hardly stand to hold him long enough to feed him. She would put him back in his crib as soon as possible and sit staring out into the backyard until one of the kids demanded something else.

A minor form of postpartum depression, the "baby blues," usually begins one to three days after delivery and affects up to 80 percent of new mothers. This form of depression is characterized by mood swings, irritability, insomnia, crying jags, and feelings of helplessness or vulnerability. The "blues" can last several weeks.

Postpartum depression is complex and is believed to result from several factors, including the abrupt changes in hormone levels that occur after the birth of a baby. Whereas the "baby blues" typically lasts no more than a few weeks, postpartum depression can persist for many months.

Psychotic depression

Psychotic depression occurs when severe depressive illness coexists with some form of psychosis, producing hallucinations (seeing or hearing things that don't really exist), delusions (irrational thoughts and fears), or another break with reality. People who have psychotic depression usually know that their thoughts and fears aren't based in reality and try to hide them because they are ashamed, a fact that interferes with diagnosis. It's been estimated that 25 percent of people who are hospitalized for depression suffer from psychotic depression.

Thirty-seven-year-old Alex returned from a new job overseas after the sudden death of his father. After the funeral, he found himself increasingly depressed and spending most of his days in his bedroom. Over the course of a year, Alex became progressively more paranoid and had thoughts of being targeted by the Central Intelligence Agency due to his travels abroad. He was convinced he was being followed and would be killed if he were discovered.

Seasonal affective disorder

SAD is a seriously depressed mood that occurs when the seasons change, typically in the fall and winter months, although some may experience it during spring and summer. Besides exhibiting the classic signs of depression, those with SAD tend to crave sweets and starchy foods, sleep too much, lack energy, and withdraw from social situations. Many experts believe that SAD is caused by a lack of exposure to sunlight, as it occurs much more often in northern climates where the days are very short during the winter.

Janet was twenty when her family moved from Florida to Massachusetts. All was well during the summer they arrived, but by Halloween Janet was lethargic, uninterested in her schoolwork or her friends, and started craving carbohydrates. The shorter the days grew, the more depressed Janet became.

Atypical depression

Despite being called "atypical," this kind of depression is actually quite common, affecting up to 40 percent of those who are depressed. What makes it unusual is that people with this form of depression enjoy an improvement in their mood when something positive happens (known as mood reactivity), as opposed to those with "regular" major depression who remain "low" no matter what happens. Those with atypical depression also suffer from at least one of the following symptoms: excessive sleeping, overeating or weight gain, leaden paralysis (a heavy, leaden feeling in the arms or legs), and/or rejection sensitivity.

Double depression

This kind of depression occurs when a person with minor depression (dysthymia) also suffers an episode of major depression: two depressions at once.

Secondary depression

When depression appears following the arrival of a medical problem such as a stroke, Parkinson's disease, Alzheimer's disease, or acquired immunodeficiency syndrome (AIDS) or a psychiatric condition such as panic disorder or bulimia, it's known as secondary depression.

Masked depression

This kind of depression manifests as physical complaints (stomachache, insomnia, constipation, and so on) that seem to have no organic cause. It can take a long time to diagnose this kind of depression. Typically, a physician spends a great deal of time administering tests and following up on multiple symptom clues that eventually lead to no definable diagnosis.

Chronic treatment-resistant depression

When depression lasts for more than a year and does not respond to treatment with antidepressants, other medications, and/or psychotherapy, it is considered both chronic and treatment resistant.

Who's Most at Risk for Depression?

Depression is surprisingly common, affecting about 120 million people worldwide. The National Institute of Mental Health estimates that depression affects nearly 15 million American adults each year, or almost 7 percent of the U.S. population over the age of eighteen. As for age of onset, depression can surface at any age; however, the average age is thirty-two.

Both sexes can be affected by depression, although women are at least twice as likely as men to experience it, no matter what their economic status or race. But it's not just adults who suffer. As many as one in eight adolescents of both sexes and one in thirty-three children suffer from clinical depression (depression that is serious enough to require intervention). Yet, less than one-third of those suffering from depression actively seek or receive treatment.

Depression tends to run in families, and those who have a family history of depressive disorders are up to three times more likely to suffer from the illness than those in the general population. Another risk factor is depression itself. Those who have experienced an episode of major depression that was not connected to a general medical condition are at least 50 percent more likely to experience another one. And the risk rises to 90 percent after the occurrence of several such episodes.

The cost of depression is high. Over the next twenty years, depression is projected to become the number one cause of disability in high-income countries such as the United States and the number two cause of disability worldwide. In the United States alone, the yearly cost of depressive illness is estimated at $30–44 billion. But the personal cost of depression is inestimable, as the amount of pain, suffering, lost wages, and destruction of relationships simply cannot be measured. And some people wrestling with depression pay the highest price of all—the loss of life. More than 90 percent of those who commit suicide suffered from a diagnosable mental disorder, usually a depressive disorder or a substance abuse disorder.

Causes of Depression

Doctors used to believe that depression was the result of certain thoughts or triggers. But research indicates that it's far more complicated than that. Depression is rarely due to a single cause: It's more likely the result of a combination of biochemical, physical, genetic, and/or psychological factors.

Biochemical factors

Brain scans have shown that the brains of depressed people function differently from those of "normal" people in the areas regulating mood, behavior, appetite, sleep, and thinking. This may be due to the fact that those with depression typically suffer from imbalances in the levels of brain chemicals called neurotransmitters—specifically serotonin and norepinephrine, and possibly dopamine. Low levels of serotonin are linked to sleep problems, binge eating, and irritability, while too little norepinephrine can cause low mood and fatigue. In the case of dopamine, the problem may be due to either the presence of too much of the neurotransmitter for long periods of time or dopamine levels that are too low.

Why do neurotransmitter levels drop? It may be because the body is experiencing production problems. Deficiencies in amino acids or vitamin and mineral cofactors may result in decreased production of these critical chemicals affecting mood. Or, it may be that the body is breaking down the neurotransmitters too quickly. There are many possible mechanisms that can account for low levels of neurotransmitters leading to ineffective neurochemical function.

Depression and Suicide: Stats and Facts

Suicide is the eighth-leading cause of mortality in the United States, accounting for thirty-two thousand deaths each year. More than two-thirds of the reported suicides are caused by depression.

1. Although depression is diagnosed two to three times more frequently in women than men, men are more than four times more likely to die by suicide. Women, however, are up to three times more likely than men to attempt suicide.
2. The risk of suicide increases around the time of a significant anniversary, during periods of high anxiety, in conjunction with drug or alcohol abuse, and/or when depression is either untreated or treated inadequately.
3. Suicide risk also increases in those who tend to be impulsive or have a family history of mental illness, substance abuse, suicide, separation, divorce, or family violence of any kind.
4. Treatment of those at high risk for suicide is surprisingly lacking. In a large study done in Canada, nearly one-half of patients who had thought about suicide, and one-fourth of those who had attempted it reported that they had not received care or even thought that they needed it.
5. About 15 percent of depressed people whose depression is untreated end their lives by suicide.

Physical factors

In a large percentage of people with certain medical conditions or illnesses, depression is a co-occuring disorder:

3–50 percent of those with cancer
50–75 percent of those with eating disorders
20–40 percent of those who have survived a heart attack
10–20 percent of those with HIV
50 percent of those with Huntington's disease
30 percent of those with chronic pain
50 percent of those with Parkinson's disease
25–50 percent of those who have suffered strokes
60 percent of those with disabling tinnitus
27 percent of those with substance abuse problems
30–35 percent of those with Alzheimer's disease

In addition, depression is often seen in conjunction with anxiety disorders and nicotine addiction. Depression may be caused by some of these conditions, and it can also contribute to the onset of others, including eating disorders and substance abuse problems. Researchers have also found that depressed people are more likely to develop type 2 diabetes and cardiovascular disease. And with certain conditions, such as Alzheimer's disease and substance abuse, depression may be both a cause and an effect.

Various medications, whether prescription, over the counter, or recreational, may also contribute to the onset of depression, including antipsychotic drugs, antihistamines, beta-blockers, birth control pills, high blood pressure medications, anti-inflammatory medications, adrenal hormone agents, and corticosteroids.

Other physical factors that can contribute to depression include a lack of exercise, ingestion of too much refined sugar or refined carbohydrates, an imbalance in amino acids, and deficiencies in certain nutrients such as biotin, calcium, copper, vitamins B and C, folic acid, iron, magnesium, and potassium.

An overactive immune system: a major physical factor

"Sickness behavior" is a normal reaction to infection that causes fatigue, sleepiness, poor concentration, and a lack of desire to do anything productive. Interestingly, sickness behavior and depression have many symptoms in common. It shouldn't be surprising then that there is a link between an overactive immune system, due to an infection or injury, and depression.

During prolonged infection or injury, chemicals called proinflammatory cytokines, which are produced during the inflammation process, can contribute to depression by causing changes in the neurotransmitters. Cytokines can also lead to deficiencies in neurotransmitters by continually stimulating their release.

Medications That Can Cause Depression

Medications or street drugs that can bring about depression as a side effect include the following:

alcohol
amphotericin B (Fungizone)
antipsychotic drugs
beta-blockers (betaxolol, nadolol, propranolol, timolol)
bismuth nitrate
carbamazepine
cis-retinoic acid
contraceptives, oral
corticosteroids
cycloserine (Seromycin)
cyclosporine
digitalis
estrogen therapy
flunarizine
H-2 blockers (cimetidine, ranitidine)
Interferon
Levodopa
maxinodol
mercury
methyldopa
methylxanthines (caffeine, theophylline)
metoclopramide (Reglan)
metronidazole
nifedipine
organic nitrates
phenytoin
psychostimulants (fenfluraimen, methylphenidate, pemoline, phenylpropanolamine)
reserpine
sedative-hypnotics (barbiturates, benzodiazepines, methaqualone)
thallium
thiazide diuretics
vinblastine
vincristine

Recent studies have found changes in the cytokine levels of patients with major depression. Several studies have shown that high levels of pro-inflammatory cytokines and low levels of anti-inflammatory cytokines appear in people with depression. One study, involving twenty-three subjects with unipolar depression and twenty-five healthy controls, measured the cytokine levels of the patients at the time of admission into the study and after eight weeks of antidepressant treatment with sertraline (Zoloft). At the time of admission, the proinflammatory cytokines (such as IL-2, IL-12, and TNF-alpha) were significantly higher in patients with depression. The anti-inflammatory cytokines IL-4 and TGF-beta1 in the subjects with depression were found to be significantly lower. After treatment with sertraline, there was a noticeable decrease in the proinflammatory cytokine IL-12 and an increase in the anti-inflammatory cytokines IL-4 and TGF-beta1. This and several other studies support the idea that depression may in some cases be due to an overactive immune system.

The role of the immune system needs to be considered whenever depression symptoms are present. Many treatments for depression focus only on restoring neurotransmitter imbalances, yet these imbalances may result from increases in immune system activity, which trigger an inflammatory response in the brain.

Hormonal factors

Hormones are also linked to depression. Although pubescent girls are no more likely than boys of the same age to suffer from depression, as they enter adulthood, females quickly outnumber males among depression sufferers.

In women, temporary episodes of depression can occur seven to ten days before onset of the menstrual period (premenstrual syndrome or, in more serious cases, premenstrual dysphoric disorder) and during the first fourteen days after delivering a child ("baby blues" or, in more serious cases, postpartum depression). Depression can also be a symptom of perimenopause and menopause.

In men, low levels of the male hormone testosterone may be linked to depression. Low or low-normal levels of testosterone have been found in men who were not helped by standard antidepressants, and testosterone replacement has been used with success in men suffering from depression.

Genetic factors

Studies have shown that depression occurs at much higher rates in families in which either a grandparent or parent has had depression. In fact, a family history of depression can increase one's risk of depression by as much as three times, although it's just the inclination toward depression that is inherited, not the disorder itself. In addition, highly heritable personality traits such as anxiety and neuroticism tend to strongly correlate with depression.

Psychological factors

Stressful or traumatic situations, such as the death of someone close, divorce, disability, a lack of social support, chronic illness, an accident, the loss of a job, or the loss of personal dreams or goals, can trigger or contribute to depression. In addition, people who have suffered many difficult life events, had a very stressful early life, or tend to be negative thinkers may be more inclined toward depression.

Aging appears to be another trigger, with approximately 16 percent of older people suffering from depression, some for the first time in their lives. This is not too surprising, considering that older people are more likely to experience the loss of loved ones, social isolation, the end of a significant relationship, chronic illness, a decrease in income, and/or a loss of independence. They are also more likely to suffer from nutritional deficiencies, both from poor intake and poor absorption, which can increase their risk of depression.

2

Depression Can Be Cured

Depression is a disabling illness that strangles one's life and spirit and severely impairs both psychological and physical well-being. It is surprisingly common, affecting more than 15 million individuals in the United States alone, but the statistics regarding recovery are dismal. Standard treatment for depression brings about a complete recovery or nearly complete elimination of symptoms in only 33 percent of patients, and in roughly 70 percent of those, depression recurs.

Most of us do not need quoted numbers to know that depression is a widespread problem that is difficult to solve: We see the devastation in our lives and the lives of our family members and friends who are struggling with it. I have listened to patients suffering from depression for more than twenty years, and it is abundantly clear to me that our current treatments are tragically inadequate.

Susan is twenty years old and has been in therapy for the last eight years. She has tried eight different medications over the years with no sign of relief from her depression and mood swings.

Harold, a twenty-six-year-old living at home with his parents, has struggled with depression since high school. He has attempted suicide twice and has been hospitalized for severe depression four times. Although he is exceedingly bright, he has been unable to complete college.

Melanie woke up every morning questioning why she should get out of bed. She always feels irritable with her two children and her husband, and she frequently explodes with anger. "I have been in therapy for years. I have tried every medication they make and nothing works for me."

What is a Psychiatric Evaluation?

Numerous scientific articles have analyzed the reasons for our difficulties in treating depression, but rather than wade through the conclusions of lengthy research papers, let's instead consider what happens when the typical patient visits a psychiatrist. In fact, let's imagine that it's you stepping into the office. You've been referred to a psychiatrist by your physician, who has been prescribing you antidepressants for sleep problems, fatigue, anxiety, and depression.

One of the first things you notice when you step into the psychiatrist's office is that it is not a typical medical office. There are no stethoscopes, blood pressure cuffs, or other instruments that doctors use to take precise measurements of patients. Instead there are two chairs and a box of tissues. Clearly, this is not going to be a standard medical exam, despite the fact that psychiatrists are physicians who attend four years of medical school after college, followed by at least four years of specialty training in psychiatry. You start to feel a little anxious.

The doctor sits down, offers you a seat, and encourages you to describe your symptoms: "So what brings you in today?" You feel even more anxious, as you are not sure where to begin. If you're feeling depressed, these symptoms might include loss of interest in activities you used to find enjoyable, crying spells, increased irritability, fatigue, changes in your sleep patterns, and a feeling of worthlessness. The psychiatrist writes down all of these symptoms and structures the interview to get the information she needs to make a diagnosis.

You start to wonder, *What is a psychiatric diagnosis?* You may continue to wonder how a psychiatrist can make a diagnosis based only on a conversation with you rather than from objective criteria. So, you end up feeling even more anxious and confused than when you walked in the door.

The psychiatrist consults the *DSM-IV,* that big, gray book that sits behind her on the bookshelf. She is trying to come up with a list of symptoms from the things you've told her that match one of the lists of symptoms in the book. For example, the *DSM-IV* lists the following symptoms under the category of a major depressive episode:

- Suffering a depressed mood most of the day nearly every day
- Markedly diminished interest in activities
- Significant weight loss (when not dieting) or weight gain
- Sleeping more than usual or having difficulty sleeping
- Feeling fatigued nearly every day
- Feeling worthless or inappropriately guilty
- Having difficulty concentrating or making decisions
- Thinking about death or attempting suicide

Each form of depression has its own symptom list. If your personal symptom list matches a list found in the *DSM-IV,* the psychiatrist can make an official diagnosis. For example, bipolar depression has a somewhat different symptom list, consisting of major depression plus at least one period of mania (an unusual euphoric, expansive, or irritable mood, accompanied by symptoms such as an inflated sense of self-importance, extreme talkativeness, and distractibility). The symptom list for postpartum depression includes feeling inadequate, guilty, or anxious for no apparent reason following the delivery of a baby; while psychotic depression's symptom list features severe depression plus hallucinations or other forms of psychosis.

The basic symptom list compiled by the psychiatrist may look different than any *DSM-IV* list, depending on the pattern and severity of your individual symptoms. You start to realize that this is pretty complicated! You hadn't realized that there is more than one kind of depression. Yes, the doctor is trying to zero in on your exact list of symptoms so she can make an individualized diagnosis. That's a good thing. After all, everybody is different, right? After the diagnosis is made, she will talk with you about appropriate treatments.

About those DSM lists . . .

As psychiatry developed into a field of medicine, it became necessary to have clear diagnostic categories so that professionals could discuss and research the difficulties that patients suffering from mental illness endured. The goal was to create precisely defined categories, but how precise was the science behind their development?

The first edition of the *DSM*, published in 1952 by the American Psychiatric Association, described 107 mental disorders. The list of disorders to be included was voted upon by members of the association; about 10 percent of the membership was asked to approve a draft of the initial *DSM*. Somewhat fewer than half of those (or 5 percent of the total membership) did so and were overwhelmingly in favor of adopting the *DSM*. That means that 95 percent of members had no input into a document that would come to be accepted as the standard for mental health diagnosis.

Exactly what should be labeled "mental illness"? How do we decide if someone is mentally ill? The various "symptom lists" in the *DSM* are simply the subjective opinions of experts. They can't be any more than that, for there is no objective way to identify psychiatric illness, no germ, no blood test, or other test that can establish its presence. The best psychiatrists can say is that, "We know it when we see it." And apparently we see a lot of it, for the *DSM-IV*, which was published in 1994, lists 365 disorders, more than three times as many as contained in the original *DSM*. Are there really that many more psychiatric disorders these days? Or have we gone overboard and labeled every little problem a disorder? That's a matter of opinion—and opinions change. For example, early versions of the *DSM* listed homosexuality as a mental deviation; modern editions do not.

The current *DSM* separates its 365 mental disorders into nearly three hundred discrete categories. There are ten different diagnoses related to depressed mood. Are there really that many separate and distinct mental ailments? Is major depression really a completely different entity than melancholic depression? Is atypical depression really completely different from undifferentiated depression? Or are they actually the same, with different manifestations of the same underlying problem? Nobody really knows. And nobody *can* know, objectively speaking. The ballooning of diagnoses and categories compounds the challenge of diagnosing an individual patient.

Educated guessing

Your psychiatric diagnosis will be made on a doubly subjective basis. The psychiatrist will make personal (subjective) decisions as to which symptoms will be included or excluded on your symptom list. While some symptoms obviously need to be included, others aren't so obvious. For example, there is a *DSM* directive stating that a feeling or behavior can be included on a patient's symptoms list only if it causes "clinically significant distress or impairment in social, occupational, or other important areas of functioning." It is not always 100 percent clear when symptoms can be said to cause "clinically significant" impairment, which essentially means your

The *DSM* of the Future

The fifth edition of the manual is slated for publication in May 2013. The *DSM-V* may introduce new diagnoses and change current ones. Some of the proposed additions include the following disorders:

Temper dysregulation disorder with dysphoria
Binge eating disorder
Hypersexual disorder
Hoarding disorder
Restless legs syndrome
Cannabis withdrawal
Nicotine-use disorder
Alcohol-use disorder
Premenstrual dysphoric disorder

In addition, crosscutting dimensional assessment tools will be offered to track overall changes in a patient's status (e.g., measurements of substance use, sleep problems, and mood changes) and symptom severity.

Are these genuinely new disorders or new ways of looking at old ones? Who determines the criteria? Are they just "fads" that will no longer be considered psychiatric diagnoses in the future? We don't really know.

psychiatrist has to make a lot of educated guesses about your symptoms. The subjectivity is doubled when your psychiatrist compares these educated guesses with the subjectively compiled lists of symptoms in the *DSM*.

Despite this subjectivity, the *DSM* is a helpful tool. It allows mental health professionals to classify a patient's condition so they can better understand the difficulties that a patient is facing. It also provides a standard, uniform "language" to use in discussing patients. The problem is that the *DSM* has gone from being a reference book for consultation to a "bible" that most clinicians accept without reservation and on which they base their diagnostic and treatment decisions. The result is that nearly every patient's symptoms *must* somehow conform to a list.

What's missing from your psychiatric evaluation?

It's also important to consider what was *not* included in your hypothetical initial psychiatric evaluation. Psychiatrists do not always ask you about various medical illnesses and physical symptoms that you, your siblings, your parents, and your grandparents currently have or have had in the past. Rarely would a psychiatrist listen to your heart, monitor your pulse rate, examine your eyes, look at your skin, or otherwise try to determine if any of your physical symptoms might be related to your depressed mood, lack of energy, or insomnia. Your hypothetical evaluation did not include a discussion of what you typically eat or which chemicals you have been exposed to, and there was no order for laboratory work to check your nutritional status and hormone levels or measure the environmental toxins that may have accumulated in your body. Additionally, there was no attempt to discover whether allergies you may or may not be aware of could be influencing your mood.

These omissions clearly demonstrate that psychiatry does not operate on the principle that what occurs in the body affects what occurs in the mind. To those in the psychiatric profession, the brain is the brain and the body is the body; they are two separate and very distinct entities. This separation of brain and body often prevents physicians and mental health professionals from discovering the real cause of depression.

A shot in the dark

Back to your hypothetical psychiatric evaluation. Now it's time to decide on the treatment strategy, which is a much more difficult proposition than making the diagnosis. Why? Because psychiatrists prescribe medicines without understanding the causes of the disorders they seek to treat. So they are, in essence, shooting blind.

Internists, cardiologists, gastroenterologists, and other medical specialists offer patients specific medical treatments designed to resolve an underlying biological problem. In the case of a bacterial infection, for example, a physician prescribes antibiotics; for high cholesterol, he may recommend a statin drug or exercises and dietary changes to reduce it; and so on. An internist or infectious diseases specialist studies a sample of blood to determine exactly which bacteria is triggering the symptoms and then prescribes the antibiotic best suited for eliminating it.

Psychiatrists, on the other hand, have no way of knowing what may be causing the depression because there are no "depression germs" or other brain abnormalities that obviously cause mental disorder. Yes, certain genes are associated with some mental disorders, but these genes incline toward a disorder rather than predict it. Certain imbalances in brain chemistry also appear to be associated with depression, but no one has ever shown that these chemical imbalances actually *cause* depression.

Thus, psychiatrists make treatment decisions in the dark, prescribing one medicine after another, hoping that one, or some combination of more than one, will work. Most psychiatrists rely on their personal favorites. Some favor older medicines for depression, such as Zoloft and Prozac, while others lean toward newer ones, such as Cymbalta and Remeron. Either way, patients usually undergo courses of multiple psychiatric medications and are typically prescribed two or more antidepressants to take simultaneously, in addition to medication for sleep and, perhaps, anxiety. A recent study published in the *Archives of General Psychiatry* confirmed this trend, finding that a staggering 59.8 percent of visits to office-based psychiatrists resulted in two or more psychotropic medication prescriptions. About one-third of the office visits resulted in three or more prescriptions. And if the initial prescriptions didn't solve the problem, new ones were offered.

This means that your psychiatrist will try one medicine after another to see what works. Less than half will be lucky enough to find relief with the first one. More likely the first medicine won't provide sufficient relief, so you'll be given a second, third, fourth, and even fifth trial of medication. Some doctors keep adding medications without stopping ineffective ones. Polypharmacy is the sad reality in treating depression.

Jason, a forty-four-year-old lawyer, was placed on disability because of his chronic depression. Fifteen different medications and electroconvulsive therapy (ECT) could not help Jason find relief. By the time I met him, he was unable to work, and his week consisted solely of visits to therapists, specialists, and physicians. His promising career was destroyed by recurrent depression. However, after a thorough evaluation, including an rEEG and complete metabolic and nutritional testing, Jason is now on his way toward recovery. With two medications suggested by rEEG and a strict gluten-free diet after a diagnosis of celiac disease, Jason is now able to work consistently.

Missing the target

Medicines are great blessings in modern life. They help hundreds of millions of people every year. During the many years I've been in practice, I have seen psychiatric medicines restore health and function to a great many people. But our ability to treat depression with medications is not as good as we once thought. Two-thirds of patients suffering from depression who have been "effectively" treated with antidepressants continue to suffer from residual symptoms that impair their day-to-day function, with 28 percent experiencing mild impairment, 23 percent moderate impairment, 12 percent severe impairment, and 4 percent very severe impairment. This means that a large percentage of those who are "cured" by standard medicines continue to experience residual symptoms of depression that impair important aspects of their lives.

The evidence for antidepressant efficacy is not very impressive. The medical literature (based on studies from 1987 to 2004) suggest that 94 percent of antidepressant trials have positive beneficial results, but the actual number is closer to 51 percent, because approximately one-third of the negative trials submitted to the U.S. Food and Drug Administration (FDA) were never published. That means that about half of the trials failed to show any benefit exceeding that of a placebo, an inactive pill that contains no medication at all.

I've sadly seen the ineffectiveness of psychiatric treatment for depression many times in patients of all ages. The struggles with depressed mood, irritability, and fatigue persist despite repeated trials of many medications.

I talk more about the controversy over psychiatric medicines in Chapter 3. For now, it's enough to note that much of the "science" behind antidepressant effectiveness may, in fact, be myths created by pharmaceutical companies to sell drugs.

Overcoming the Shortcomings of Current Treatment

In short, the psychiatric treatment of depression is inadequate for several reasons:

- We consider depression and related ailments to be purely psychological disorders with theoretical abnormalities in brain chemicals, unaffected by what's happening in the patient's body.
- We slice depression into several different *DSM*-defined disorders, but since we can't find a brain-based reason for any of these forms, we prescribe medications on a nearly random basis.
- Not surprisingly, our success rate is poor, and even when we do consider a patient to be improved, there may be residual symptoms and frequent side effects.

Compounding these problems, we tend to blame patients for our failures. You can see our bias in the terms we use, saying a patient has "failed treatment" and is "treatment resistant." But if a patient is taking medication prescribed by his physician and doesn't recover, who has failed? I believe it's time we stop failing millions of people who come to mental health professionals seeking relief from depression.

For too long, psychiatry has been vacillating between psychotherapy and drug therapy, and now it has been hijacked by the pharmaceutical industry. Many psychiatrists seem to have forgotten the basic biochemistry they learned in medical school and that, as physicians, our goals should be to identify the causes of mental illnesses and find cures that relieve our patients' suffering.

Many of my colleagues in psychiatry have embraced a purely pharmacological model. They provide no therapy, practicing medicine by seeing patients for ten to fifteen minutes at a time to do "med checks," when they adjust doses or change medications. These med-check visits are encouraged by insurance companies, which have devised special billing codes for them.

Since many patients do not respond well to the first medicine, the med-check concept actually encourages the addition of a second or even third medicine, perhaps for sleep and anxiety. It's not at all unusual for patients to be given three to five medications to treat what was originally a single diagnosis. As side effects worsen, patients become increasingly frustrated with the medication approach, deem all medications to be "evil," and refuse any of them. Already numerous consumer groups are disseminating information on the dangers of medication. Some alternative physicians and traditional doctors have also completely rejected all medicines for depression, encouraging their patients to use vitamins and herbs instead.

Patients, then, are caught in the middle. Depression cannot be seen or heard or palpated during a physical exam. Yet, depression is life threatening and life robbing, a disabling disorder that, according to the World Health Organization, is the fourth leading cause of disease worldwide. The idea that we have such vague, unfounded ideas about how to treat this wide-ranging, debilitating disorder should be abhorrent to all medical professionals.

Adopting an Integrative Approach

We *can* do better, much better, if we take advantage of decades' worth of largely ignored research that shows that depression is not "all in your head." The mind and body are one; what happens in the body invariably affects the mind. Nutritional status, the levels and kinds of toxins present in the body, hormone levels and whether or not they are balanced, allergies, coexisting physical diseases, and other factors play important roles in the development and course of depression.

It's time for an approach to depression that is integrative, one that combines traditional medical science with nutritional and complementary therapies. To be truly successful, this approach must also be scientific, basing each and every prescription or recommendation on objectively measured abnormalities or deficiencies in the body, instead of subjectively derived lists of symptoms matched to equally subjective lists in a manual.

An integrative approach to depression based on biochemical individuality does not dismiss medications but addresses the nutritional and/or metabolic abnormalities that may be contributing to the problem.

3

Current Treatments Are Less Effective Than We Think

At the beginning of this book, I pointed out that only 33 percent of patients who seek help for depression experience complete or nearly complete elimination of symptoms via medicines and that in 70 percent of those who seem to recover, the symptoms reappear.

Standard treatment for depression isn't good or even good enough. I think the numbers speak for themselves, and the fact that so many people relapse or simply walk away from treatment in despair proves that we are failing to help many who suffer from depression. For too many patients, standard treatment is not successful.

The overwhelming majority of psychiatrists and psychiatric researchers support our current practices. And they justify their support by pointing to thousands of studies that demonstrate the effectiveness of antidepressants and other medications that are used to counteract depression.

And their support is based on evidence: There are literally stacks of studies conducted by highly esteemed researchers from Harvard, Yale, Stanford, the Mayo Clinic, and other prestigious universities, research centers, and hospitals around the world attesting to the efficacy of antidepressants and other medications in treating depression. Can all of these studies be wrong? They are not filled with errors; however, some are tainted by the fact that the researchers receive financial support from the same pharmaceutical companies that stand to earn millions (perhaps billions) of dollars if the studies come out "right." Let's take a look at these flaws in the psychiatric research.

Pharmaceutical Support Undermines Credibility

In the United States hundreds of millions of dollars are spent every year on studies testing the effectiveness of psychiatric medicines. This research is supported by the government, universities, and, most of all, the same pharmaceutical companies that manufacture these medicines. Estimates vary, but it's safe to say that pharmaceutical companies pay for the largest percentage of this research.

At first glance this seems reasonable. Why wouldn't the companies that manufacture and sell the medicines want to conduct research proving that their products are safe and effective? Indeed, shouldn't we consumers demand that they do so? The problem is that pharmaceutical companies conducting or sponsoring their own research have a major conflict of interest. On one hand they want to make the best possible medications, but on the other hand, they want to sell as many drugs as possible. Since the companies are bottom-line businesses, their desire to increase sales often wins out.

Drug studies can be extremely expensive, necessitating millions of dollars to formulate the study plan, to pay for the researchers and laboratory equipment, to recruit and possibly compensate volunteers, to hire statisticians to crunch the numbers, and so on. The government and universities usually don't want to spend that kind of money on investigating an unproven medicine, so the financial burden must be borne by the pharmaceutical companies. But the company doesn't really mind, because writing the check means it gets to control what happens during and after the study.

An Industry-wide Problem

According to a 2008 study published in *The New England Journal of Medicine*, approximately one-third of the negative antidepressant trials submitted to the FDA were never published. The authors found that the medical literature from 1987 to 2004 suggested that 94 percent of antidepressant trials had positive beneficial results (when compared to a placebo). But when taking into account the unpublished negative trials, the

Direct-to-Consumer Advertising

Billions of dollars are spent every year on direct-to-consumer advertising (DTCA), with an estimated $3.2 billion spent in 2003. But how do these advertisements influence patients and their doctors?

First and foremost, DTCA is only an issue in the United States and New Zealand, because it is illegal in the rest of the world. Proponents argue that those who may go untreated can receive valuable information that may improve their health. On the other hand, opponents argue that DTCA may lead to the unnecessary medicating of many healthy people, potentially harming them and increasing their financial burden.

These arguments aside, what we do know is that DTCA increases the use of medication. Although DTCA has no effect on specific antidepressant choices, empirical evidence has suggested that when DTCA spending is increased by 10 percent within a class of medications, there is a corollary increase in the use of that drug class by 1 percent. In the case of antidepressants, Adam Block, economist for the Joint Committee on Taxation in the U.S. Congress, determined that nondepressed individuals accounted for 94 percent of new antidepressant use due to direct-to-consumer advertising. DTCA may lead to as many as fifteen nondepressed people receiving antidepressant treatment for every one depressed person.

This general trend toward inappropriate and excessive prescribing is reflected in an FDA survey in which 73 percent of primary care physicians and 63 percent of specialists felt pressured to prescribe as a result of their patients' exposure to DTCA. This patient demand has led to changes in the way physicians are prescribing medications. In a separate study, a reported 23.5 percent of physicians believed that DTCA changed their prescribing practices.

actual number of positive antidepressant studies dropped to 51 percent. By selectively publishing positive studies, pharmaceutical companies are misleading the medical community and the public into believing that antidepressants are more effective than they actually are.

In the United States, the FDA is trying to safeguard against this practice of selective publication with the creation of a registry and database. In 1997, legislation allowing public access to information about ongoing clinical trials was passed by Congress. Under this law, drug companies must register all clinical trials they intend to use in support of their drug during the FDA approval process. The Internet-based registry www.clinicaltrials.gov was created in 2000 to provide the mandated public database. Due to problems with the database—including incomplete information—in 2007 the Food and Drug Administration Amendments Act was passed. According to the act, the registry must be updated within twelve months of study completion (twenty-four months if the drug is currently under FDA review) with information on the participants and trial results.

These changes may help solve some of the selective publication problems, but they don't address the issue of financial conflicts in drug research. As a group of researchers from Harvard Medical School's Massachusetts General Hospital pointed out, "Financial conflicts of interest are exceedingly common in biomedical research. Investigators with conflicts of interest are more likely to arrive at positive conclusions, perhaps as a result of biased study design, industry suppression of negative results, preferential funding by industry of projects that are likely to succeed, or biased interpretation of results."

A trio of Yale University School of Medicine investigators came to similar conclusions about the conflicts of interest that arise when scientific researchers and universities hired to conduct research are financially tied to pharmaceutical companies. They found, among other issues, that the universities hired to perform pharmaceutical research were often part owners of the very companies that hired them. By extension, this means that the universities are often part owners of the medicines they are testing, giving them a powerful financial interest in results that come out right.

Does this really make a difference? Aren't medical researchers genuinely interested in finding the best treatments? Of course they are. But when money enters the picture, vision can begin to cloud a bit. That may be why studies are much more likely to "prove" a drug is superior to a placebo when they are funded by the pharmaceutical industry or when the researchers have a financial interest in the study outcome. Indeed, as investigators from Harvard Medical School pointed out in a 2005 paper published in the *American Journal of Psychiatry*, studies supported by a pharmaceutical company and studies in which at least one of the researchers has a financial conflict of interest are 4.9 times more likely to report that the medicine being studied "works," compared to studies that are not financially tied to pharmaceutical companies.

Do Our Pills Really Work?

Even if psychiatric medicines, like all medicines, are oversold by the pharmaceutical companies, and even if these companies are much too cozy with psychiatrists and doctors, we still need the answer to a key question: Do the medicines work?

If you looked at the thousands of published studies on the efficacy of psychiatric medicines, you would have to conclude that the answer is yes, to some degree and for many people. But, as I pointed out earlier, a great many studies that produced negative results have been deliberately withheld from publication, so it's difficult to get an accurate picture of the true effects of a given medication. There is one thing you can be sure of: Those "buried studies" most likely indicate that the medicines being studied are not terribly effective or are not effective at all.

A small number of researchers and practicing psychiatrists have been questioning the efficacy of psychiatric medications for some time. In 2001, the British psychiatrist Joanna Moncrieff, MBBS, MSc., published a paper in which she boldly stated, "There are no signs that the rapidly escalating use of antidepressants is reducing the burden of depressive disorders." In other words, although more and more people were being diagnosed with depression and treated accordingly, the situation was not improving.

A decade and many millions of antidepressant prescriptions later, her words continue to ring true. Indeed, a study published in the *Journal of the American Medical Association* in 2010 found that standard antidepressants are no more effective than a placebo for people with the less severe forms of depression, despite the fact that antidepressant medicines are considered to be "the best established treatment for major depressive disorder."

Specifically, the researchers found that Paxil (a selective serotonin reuptake inhibitor, or SSRI, related to Prozac) and imipramine (one of the older antidepressants that has long been in use) did not reduce symptoms to a clinically relevant degree in people with mild, moderate, or severe depression. That is, these drugs may have slightly lowered the numbers on the Hamilton Depression Rating Scale (HDRS), a test used to measure the severity of a patient's depression. But the reduction was so slight that it didn't make any difference in the day-to-day functioning of the patients. The antidepressants only made a difference for those in the "very severely depressed" category; that is, those with a Hamilton score of twenty-five or higher. For everyone else, the benefits of taking antidepressants compared to a placebo "may be minimal or nonexistent."

The results of this study are shocking, especially when you consider that about 70 percent of patients begin with Hamilton scores *below* twenty-two, meaning that, for them, *any* antidepressant won't be much more effective than a placebo. Yet, almost all patients diagnosed as being depressed are given prescriptions for antidepressant medicines.

Depression Has Tripled, Despite a Flood of "Miracle" Medicines

Robert Whitaker recently published a book titled *Anatomy of an Epidemic* in which he carefully scrutinizes fifty years worth of the psychiatric literature and reveals a rather embarrassing secret: Over the long run, many patients who are *not* medicated do better than those who are. Through the 1970s, before the advent of the "second generation" psychiatric medicines such as Prozac, relatively few people suffering from depression were given prescriptions for such medications—especially those with mild or moderate symptoms. A large number of mildly or moderately depressed patients recovered over the course of several months, and most continued to be well for years before another bout of depression hit—if it struck at all. Today, however, doctors often immediately prescribe psychiatric medicines, which Whitaker argues can set the stage for chronic, recurring depression and lifelong reliance on medication.

Whitaker notes that in 1987, 1.25 million Americans were on disability because of mental disorders. Today, that number has more than tripled to 4 million. If psychiatric treatment is as good as the psychiatric establishment says it is, why has the number of these patients more than tripled over the past twenty years, a period during which numerous new medicines were introduced, some trumpeted as the next "wonder drug"? And why has the number of children on disability due to mental illness skyrocketed from about sixteen thousand to six hundred thousand.

As Whitaker points out, a careful analysis of the psychiatric literature shows that only about 15 percent of depressed people treated with medicine remain healthy over the long run; the remaining 85 percent are caught up in chronic depression. Over the past several decades, then, the bulk of patients have shifted from experiencing isolated episodes of depression, often spaced years apart, to suffering long-term emotional disability. And, depending on the medications, the emotional distress may be accompanied by cognitive decline.

The problem is largely due to our almost total reliance on short-term studies, typically lasting only six weeks, that claim to prove that antidepressant medications work. Yes, medication may help many people, but these studies almost always fail to track their patients during the years and decades that follow. Thus, we don't know what happens after the study has ended. They also typically fail to compare people who are medicated to those who are not. There is a major gap in our knowledge, for the few studies that *have* tracked long-term results and compared the medicated to the nonmedicated suggest that many people would be better off taking no medication at all.

What about the Side Effects?

The list of side effects that may be triggered by antidepressants is long and includes the following:

agitation
anxiety
blurred vision
constipation
decreased libido
dizziness
dry mouth
erectile dysfunction
fatigue
insomnia
osteoporosis
nausea
restlessness
weight gain

Some of these side effects may be easy to avoid or counteract. For example, taking the medication with food or eating smaller and more frequent meals can eliminate nausea for many people. But other side effects, including weight gain, decreased libido, and severe constipation, may be more difficult to deal with and require additional medicines or significant adjustments in lifestyle. Psychiatrists frequently add new medicines to the ones patients are already taking in an attempt to alleviate side effects, but that means patients risk experiencing new side effects, which may require even more medicines.

> Twenty-three-year-old Heather started our first meeting together by announcing, "I am not taking any medications that cause weight gain! I gained thirty pounds on the last antidepressant, and I can never do that again."
>
> Jim, a forty-eight-year-old who had been wrestling with depression for more than a decade, sighed as he said, "Sometimes I don't know what's worse, the depression or the side effects. I've completely lost my sex drive, and things are stressful enough between my wife and me."

Undoubtedly, the most worrisome side effect of antidepressant use is the increased risk of suicide. In March 2004, the FDA instructed the manufacturers of a number of antidepressants to add a warning to their labels making doctors and patients aware of the fact that these medicines had been linked to a worsening of depression and/or to an increased risk of suicide. The antidepressants implicated were as follows:

- Prozac (fluoxetine)
- Zoloft (sertraline)
- Paxil (paroxetine)
- Luvox (fluvoxamine)
- Celexa (citalopram)
- Lexapro (escitalopram)
- Wellbutrin (bupropion)
- Effexor (venlafaxine)
- Serzone (nefazodone)
- Remeron (mirtazapine)

The FDA warning noted, "anxiety, agitation, panic attacks, insomnia, irritability, hostility, impulsivity, akathisia ([severe] restlessness), hypomania, and mania have been reported in adult and pediatric patients being treated with antidepressants for major depressive disorder as well as for other indications, both psychiatric and nonpsychiatric."

In May of 2007, the FDA issued a new warning about the increased risk of suicide among young adults taking antidepressants. This warning concerned an even larger number of medications:

- Anafranil (clomipramine)
- Asendin (amoxapine)
- Aventyl (nortriptyline)
- Celexa (citalopram hydrobromide)
- Cymbalta (duloxetine)
- Desyrel (trazodone HCl)
- Elavil (amitriptyline)
- Effexor (venlafaxine HCl)
- Emsam (selegiline)
- Etrafon (perphenazine/amitriptyline)
- fluvoxamine maleate
- Lexapro (escitalopram oxalate)
- Limbitrol (chlordiazepoxide/amitriptyline)
- Ludiomil (maprotiline)
- Marplan (isocarboxazid)
- Nardil (phenelzine sulfate)
- Norpramin (desipramine HCl)
- Pamelor (nortriptyline)
- Parnate (tranylcypromine sulfate)
- Paxil (paroxetine HCl)
- Pexeva (paroxetine mesylate)
- Prozac (fluoxetine HCl)
- Remeron (mirtazapine)
- Sarafem (fluoxetine HCl)
- Seroquel (quetiapine)
- Serzone (nefazodone HCl)
- Sinequan (doxepin)
- Surmontil (trimipramine)
- Symbyax (olanzapine/fluoxetine)
- Tofranil (imipramine)
- Tofranil-PM (imipramine pamoate)
- Triavil (perphenazine/amitriptyline)
- Vivactil (protriptyline)
- Wellbutrin (bupropion HCl)
- Zoloft (sertraline HCl)
- Zyban (bupropion HCl)

Side effects that many find hard to talk about are related to the numerous sexual problems associated with antidepressants. An estimated 30–60 percent of patients treated with SSRIs experience some kind of side effect that affects their sexuality. This is most likely a conservative estimate, as many patients prefer not to discuss these issues or simply stop taking the medication. Typically, these types of sexual dysfunction include impotence, decreased libido, male ejaculatory disorder, and female orgasm disorder.

The presence of sexual side effects may be disruptive enough to cause many patients to stop treatment altogether. Patients or their physicians may also favor lowering the dosage of antidepressants to avoid these side effects. In both cases, patients struggling with depression may not receive the therapeutic dose of medicine they need, resulting in continued suffering from depression.

A New Way

I am not against medication. The problem is not the medicines themselves; it's in the way they are researched, advertised, and used. Antidepressants can play a key role in restoring health when used as part of an integrative approach that encompasses personalized medicine and nutritional biochemistry. This requires that we find just the right medicine in the right dosage for each individual patient. It requires a better understanding of the research and conflicts of interest between medicine and the pharmaceutical industry. As you will see, personalized medicine for the treatment of depression has finally become a reality.

4

Depression and Biochemical Individuality

Measurement is the basis of scientific medicine. When you visit your doctor for a routine examination, the measurements begin as soon as you step into the exam room—or perhaps while you're still in the hallway and the nurse asks you to step on the scale to check your height and weight. The doctor's physical examination includes semiobjective measurements such as asking how much it hurts when a certain area is pressed or peering into your throat to see if it looks red, plus a series of objective measurements such as an electrocardiogram (ECG), your cholesterol levels, liver and thyroid function, and more. All of these measurements help the physician to construct a "profile" of your body and to determine the level of disease or damage it has sustained.

While psychiatry is a branch of medicine, it is "the measureless medicine," the only specialty that does not use objective measurements to diagnose and treat disease and then assess the effectiveness of the treatment. We *cannot* measure the problems psychiatrists see objectively, as we truly have no idea what we're looking for. Exactly what *is* psychiatric disorder? What triggers it? What damage does it cause in the brain, if any? We don't know the answers.

We can see the results of psychiatric disorder, in the form of symptoms, but we have no idea what causes it. We cannot, for example, find and treat the "depression tumor," obliterate the "depression germ," or counteract the effects of the "depression gene." We cannot even find a marker of psychiatric distress, something that serves as a red flag, such as low iron levels in anemia or high blood sugar in diabetes. In short, objectively speaking, we don't always know what we're trying to treat or how to find it, we don't know what our treatments should accomplish, and we can't tell if they are effective.

Medical Markers

Disease markers, which are simply indications that a certain disease *may* be present, have long been used by physicians as guidelines for diagnosing and treating patients. Elevated cholesterol, for example, is a marker for heart disease, as too much cholesterol can contribute to the clogging of the arteries that feed the heart muscle. Since it is impractical to cut open the coronary arteries and inspect their linings for signs of clogging, doctors use the cholesterol test to gauge the probability that heart disease is present. If the levels are high, diet and medications that reduce cholesterol can be prescribed in hopes that this will also lower the risk of coronary heart disease. However, coronary heart disease cannot be *detected* by the cholesterol test because elevated cholesterol and heart disease are not the same thing. An elevated cholesterol reading can only act as a marker of heart disease, an indication of possible risk.

Another commonly used disease marker is the prostate-specific antigen (PSA) blood test that may indicate the presence of prostate cancer. A PSA level less than four is considered safe, but if it rises above six or seven, the doctor begins to wonder if the patient has prostate cancer. And once the PSA exceeds ten, the doctor typically becomes concerned enough to order a prostate biopsy. PSA itself is not cancer; it is a normal substance made by the body. But elevated levels "mark" the potential presence of the cancer.

In sum, the use of markers as indications of disease is well established in medicine, even when we don't fully understand the relationship between the two. The marker tells us something may be wrong and gives us a treatment goal, such as reduction of elevated cholesterol.

Treating the "Crowd," Not the Individual

I've already talked about some of the problems brought about by the inability to measure, count, quantify, and objectify the causes and cures of psychiatric disorder. Yet another problem is the inability to personalize both diagnosis and treatment. And this is a severe handicap.

Most physicians try to tailor a treatment to the individual's needs. An internist, for example, can send a blood sample to the laboratory to find out exactly which bacteria is causing a disease and then select the antibiotic best suited to combat it. An oncologist can measure and "stage" a cancerous tumor to determine how advanced and aggressive it is and then narrow down the list of potential treatments accordingly. A cardiologist can come up with a "healthy heart" diet tailored to a patient's food preferences. And a dermatologist can inspect a rash and have a pretty good idea of which medicine will treat it most effectively.

Treatment of the physical body can also be evaluated fairly accurately. The internist can get the blood retested to see if the bacteria have disappeared; the oncologist can measure the tumor to see if it has decreased in size; the cardiologist can recheck the blood levels of cholesterol; and the dermatologist can see if the rash has disappeared. If the treatment hasn't worked well, another can be tried. But when it comes to the mind, all the psychiatrist can do to evaluate treatment is ask the patient about any changes in symptoms, or perhaps give the patient a subjective "paper and pen" test like the HDRS, which asks questions about how the patient feels.

Unable to measure the "thing" that is causing a patient's distress or to determine how that distress is different from others, the psychiatrist cannot zero in on the approach that has the greatest chance of success for that individual. It's like trying to treat anemia without knowing if it's caused by iron deficiency, lead poisoning, copper deficiency, or a genetic disorder. So the psychiatrist must take a "shot in the dark" approach, starting at the top of the list of medicines recommended for that condition and working his way down, hoping one hits the mark. Yet these recommendations are based on studies involving hundreds of people, which means such medication "solutions" are, by definition, impersonal.

Not only is this approach impersonal, but it is also prone to error. Nonpersonalized psychiatric medicine is *almost guaranteed* to produce one treatment error after another until the doctor stumbles upon the right approach or the patient says "Enough!" The only way to avoid serial treatment errors is to personalize psychiatric treatment. And the only way to do that is to find a *specific* objective problem, marker, or imbalance (or some combination of these) within a patient's brain or body that can be used as a reliable guide to diagnosis and treatment.

One Person Is *Not* the Same as Another

The unspoken, underlying basis of psychiatry is "sameness." From a *DSM* point of view, all patients with a particular type of depression (e.g., major depression, dysthymia, and bipolar disorder) have more or less the same condition. For example, a forty-two-year-old mother of three who works as a corporate attorney and has been suffering from insomnia, fatigue, and binge eating is considered pretty much the same as a seventy-eight-year-old retired repairman dealing with inappropriate guilt and suicidal ideation. As far as the *DSM* is concerned, they both fall into the category of major depression and should, therefore, respond to similar medications.

Likewise, a female college freshman grappling with a marked decrease in pleasure in the activities she used to enjoy is considered nearly identical to a thirty-five-year-old father of two who suffers from anxiety, restlessness, and emptiness. They both suffer from dysthymia and therefore (according to the *DSM)* should get better after taking the same types of medicines. It's all very neat and tidy, complete with distinct *DSM* code numbers for the various types of depression (e.g., major depression is 296.3, while dysthymia is 300.4). But effective treatment within these codes is not one-size-fits-all.

According to modern psychiatric principles, the psychiatrist's job is to discover the patient's symptoms, use those symptoms to categorize the patient, and then treat him or her according to recommendations for that category. It's kind of like herding cattle into different corrals according to the colors of their hides. If most patients with major depression who were treated with one or more of the recommended medications recovered, all would be well. We could say that even though we don't understand the underlying mechanisms of the disorder, let alone why the medications work, at least our patients are getting better. We could say that most of our patients fully recover, many enjoy partial recovery, while only a few are not helped at all.

But that's not the case. Many people suffering from depression are not helped, even after trying multiple medicines. And among those who enjoy initial relief, the relapse rate is staggering.

Clearly, our current approach is limited. In addition, a great deal of research suggests that the underlying basis of psychiatry is incorrect. Patients suffering from the same disorder are *not* identical and cannot be grouped strictly according to symptom-based disorder categories. On the contrary, symptoms can be misleading indicators of what's gone wrong with the brain or body. That's because each of us is a distinct individual with a unique biochemical and physical profile, which means that disorder states also manifest in unique ways.

Are the Mind and Brain Separate?

Psychiatry has essentially ignored the physical reasons for depression and most other psychiatric disorders. Instead, a depressed mood becomes intangible, an indescribable "ghost" that somehow hijacks one's thinking as a result of mental conflict or stress. These ghosts may accumulate over the years, as in long-term emotional abuse that lasts throughout childhood, or they may show up all at once, as seen in a frontline soldier who develops posttraumatic stress disorder.

Oddly enough, despite insisting that psychiatric disorders have little to do with the physical brain, psychiatrists treat their patients with medicines specifically designed to increase levels of the brain chemicals serotonin or dopamine, or otherwise influence the physical brain.

The physiology of the human body includes the brain. If physiological abnormalities exist in the body, then it's logical to assume that these abnormalities affect the brain. The brain, weighing roughly three pounds, requires about 20 percent of the energy produced by the body. If nutritional deficiencies or some other physiological problem decreases the body's energy production, the brain's incredibly high need for nutrients and energy is not met and the brain no longer functions optimally, potentially leading to psychiatric problems. To make matters more complex, each of us is unique with a "biochemical signature" as distinctive as our fingerprints. This means that every aspect of the brain and body must be thoroughly investigated when searching for the cause of psychiatric distress and the most effective treatment.

An Early Possibility Ignored

Perhaps the earliest suggestion that those with the same disorder are not necessarily the same came from a relatively small series of electroencephalograms (EEGs) taken from patients suffering from different psychiatric disorders. An EEG is a reading of the brain's electrical activity, similar to the ECG performed by physicians checking the status of the heart.

Not long after the first use of EEGs on humans in the 1920s, researchers wondered if it would be possible to find a "depressive brainwave pattern," a "schizophrenic brainwave pattern," a "female hysteria brainwave pattern," and so on. To their dismay, they could not find any such patterns. The EEGs of depressed patients did not have distinctly different patterns from those of people with other disorders. Neither did those of schizophrenia patients, hysteria patients, or others. Indeed, sometimes the EEGs of various patients with depression looked quite dissimilar, or the EEG of a depressed patient might look quite a bit like that of a patient who had schizophrenia. This lack of correlation between a specific disorder and a specific EEG pattern caused early researchers to conclude that there was no connection between electrical activity in the brain and psychiatric disorder. Thus, the EEG was pretty much abandoned by the psychiatric community as a diagnostic tool.

But, suppose they had come to a different conclusion. Suppose they had said, "Hmmm, there's no EEG correlation among people with depression, but there is a lot of variation in EEG patterns. Does this mean that the brain activity of people with depression is *not* always the same? And if so, could it be that depression, as we define it, is *not* a single disorder with a single cause and a single set of treatments?"

Is it wise to insist that a given psychiatric disorder is the same thing in all of those who suffer from it, when we admit that we have no idea what causes or cures it? Asking this question and engaging in research to find the answer could have taken psychiatry down an entirely new path: one that emphasized the *differences* between those with depression, for example, rather than the superficial symptomatic sameness. Instead, psychiatry embarked on a decades-long quest to categorize patients strictly according to their subjective symptoms.

Psychiatric Symptoms and Brain Function

Well into the twentieth century, all psychiatric disorders were believed to be mental illnesses that arose from internal conflicts triggered by childhood emotional trauma, unresolved sexual issues, being female, or family conflicts. While it was understood that stroke, Parkinson's disease, and certain other conditions were caused by physical damage to the brain, problems such as depression, anxiety, obsessive behavior, and so on, were

Can One Disease Have Different Causes and Cures?

Is it really possible that a psychiatric disorder such as depression can be made up of different entities, each with separate causes and treatments?

We don't know enough about the biochemistry of depression to definitively answer that question. But we can say with certainty that sometimes what we think of as a single disorder is actually a conglomeration of many.

Cancer, for example, is the uncontrolled and dangerous reproduction of cells within the body, whether it arises in the brain, breast, basal ganglia, or elsewhere. However, breast cancer behaves very differently from leukemia (cancer of the white blood cells), which destroys the immune system, or melanoma (skin cancer), which begins on the surface of the skin and works its way into the body. Sometimes, even a single form of cancer can take different shapes. Prostate cancer, for example, may be fast moving and aggressive or slow growing and relatively "safe."

Yet the discipline of psychiatry is based on the assumption that each kind of psychiatric disorder is the same thing or, at least, all of those with specific forms of a psychiatric disorder have the same illness.

categorized purely as mental illness because no one could find any corresponding brain damage or abnormality.

In the latter part of the century, however, high-tech brain-imaging devices such as magnetic resonance imaging (MRI) allowed researchers to take a closer look at the brain from many different angles. The brain can now be viewed as a whole, and connections between various brain areas can be mapped. This has made it possible to see how a problem in one part can affect the whole, even if that problem, by itself, does not seem terribly significant. Researchers can also identify anomalies in specific areas of the brain that appear to be linked to individual psychiatric disorders. These new glimpses into the brain do not reveal any bacteria or "wounds" that cause illness, but they do suggest that certain changes in the brain are associated with specific disorders.

Scans have shown, for example, that a small structure known as Brodmann area 25 (BA25), which is situated deep within the front portion of the brain, tends to be hyperactive in depressed people. Furthermore, its activity level becomes more normalized as the depressive symptoms are relieved. Interestingly, it doesn't seem to matter whether the hyperactivity is eased by medication or psychotherapy, as long as it comes back to normal.

It makes sense that BA25 would be involved in depression, for it is directly linked to the amygdala, which processes feelings such as anxiety and fear, and the hypothalamus, which plays an important role in the stress response. In addition, BA25 contains a generous supply of specialized transporter molecules that help determine how easily brain cells in the area are able to access the brain chemical known as serotonin. Several psychiatric medications, including Prozac, Zoloft, and Paxil, are aimed at improving serotonin levels in the brain.

The genetic coding for these serotonin transporter molecules comes in two variations dubbed "long" and "short," with the long version spurring production of more transporter molecules. Brain scan studies on healthy volunteers have shown that those with the short gene have smaller BA25s than those with the long gene. In addition, BA25 in these people does not act in concert with the amygdala and other brain areas as it should.

Is the sped-up activity in BA25 the cause of depression or a result? Perhaps both cause and result? We don't yet know.

Other areas of the brain have also been linked by imaging studies to specific disorders. For example, overactive and overly unified nerve cell firing in the basal ganglia and frontal cortex are both prevalent in people suffering from obsessive-compulsive disorder (OCD). Faulty performance of the ventromedial prefrontal cortex is found among those with posttraumatic stress disorder. And severely depressed people sometimes have an abnormally small hippocampus, a tiny part of the brain situated deep within the medial temporal lobe that creates new nerve cells.

We don't know what all this means or how to correct the errant brain areas. We can imagine, however, how difficult it is for a person to maintain "normal" moods when a part of the brain is out of sync or not interacting properly with the other parts. Think of an orchestra in which the flute section plays faster than the other sections, or the violin section plays the piece in C major while all the others are playing in C minor.

One thing is for certain: There *is* a connection between the physiology of the body and the chemistry in the brain.

5

Genetics, Epigenetics and You

In our search to determine the unique cluster of factors contributing to an individual's depression, we first ask, Is depression genetic?

Certain studies of identical twins, adoptees, and others seem to indicate that the answer is yes, to some extent. For the twin studies, researchers looked for depressed people who were part of a set of identical twins and then checked to see if the other twin was also depressed. In the adoption studies, rates of depression among biological families, their children who were put up for adoption, and the adopting families were compared in an attempt to separate genetic influences from those that were social or environmental. Of these studies, many found that genes can cause a predisposition toward developing depression, with the genetic influence accounting for as much as 37 percent in certain forms of the disorder.

This may seem like an alarmingly large number, but bear in mind that numbers like this represent averages and may be irrelevant in an individual case. For example, if the number were 50 percent, it could mean that for some people the odds of developing depression are as high as 100 percent, for others exactly 50 percent, and still others as low as 0 percent. These percentages are based on studies involving hundreds or even

A Quick Review of Genetics

Genes are the "blueprints" inside of cells that determine the form and function of each cell in the body and therefore make you who you are. They are passed on from generation to generation, but in each new birth they are combined in a totally unique way, with half the genes received from the mother and half from the father.

Each gene consists of a section of DNA, which is composed of two strands that are coiled around each other. There are some twenty-five thousand genes in the human genome (the name for the entire collection of genes). Not all genes are active at any given time. When the body needs access to the information stored in a particular gene, the appropriate section of DNA uncoils and exposes the gene so that it can be "read" and acted upon. Afterward, the gene recoils itself and the genetic information remains hidden and quiet until it is needed again.

Every single cell in the body contains and is controlled by genes, even though any one particular cell has no use for a lot of the information in the genome. A liver cell, for example, doesn't need to "read" the genes that tell the heart how to beat, while a hair cell can safely ignore genetic instructions for making a baby.

According to genetic theory, the genes are very stable. Heritable genetic changes (mutations) occur very slowly, over hundreds of thousands or millions of years. These mutations, which are designed to make an organism more successful at survival, are passed from generation to generation and spread very gradually throughout the larger population. Changes that occur during a person's life, however, such as becoming obese or developing asthma, cannot be passed on to succeeding generations because they do not alter a person's DNA. Thus, according to our understanding of genetics, a man might suffer from depression after struggling through an emotionally difficult childhood and develop cancer in midlife as a result of exposure to industrial chemicals, but neither the depression nor the cancer will be passed on to his children because the diseases did not alter his DNA.

thousands of people, which means that they may not describe a specific person's situation at all.

I prefer to think of genes as "suggestions" that incline a person toward or away from a certain illness. In some people, the suggestion is strong and it doesn't take much to trigger a full-blown problem. In others, however, the suggestion is barely whispered and the problem may never manifest at all.

Fat Mice and Skinny Mice, Genetics and Epigenetics

Suppose it were possible for changes that occur in a person's lifetime to be passed on to the next generation or the next several generations?

In 2006, researchers from Duke University performed a very simple experiment that radically altered our understanding of genetics. They examined a group of mice that carry a gene (the agouti gene) that turns them into obese "eating machines" with a propensity for developing diabetes and cancer. And their coats are yellow, instead of the usual brown. When agouti mice breed, most of their offspring receive the agouti gene and resemble their parents in size, color, appetite, and lifespan (which is uncommonly short).

The Duke researchers allowed the agouti mice to mate with each other and then altered the diets given to those that became pregnant. In addition to standard mice food, they were given a diet high in genistein, an isoflavone found in soy foods.

Defying all genetic expectations, the majority of the offspring were slender and brown coated, with normal appetites and, therefore, no increased risk of suffering from cancer or diabetes, even though *they still had the agouti gene.* It was as if the agouti gene and its effects had been erased from their bodies, yet nothing in the genetic code had been changed. On a genetic level they were still pure agouti, but on a functional "real world" level, they were not. And it all happened because of what they ate in gestation.

In another experiment, the same researchers found they could increase the propensity of agouti mice babies to be yellow-coated, obese, voracious eaters by exposing their pregnant mothers to the chemical BPA (bisphenol A), a substance found in many of our everyday household items, including baby bottles, plastics, and food-can linings—again, without changing their genes at all.

These experiments demonstrate the incredible power of *epigenetics*, the study of how a gene whose DNA sequence remains unaltered manages to change how it expresses itself in future generations.

Epigenetics: A Collection of "Overrides"

At any given time, a large percentage of the genes in the genome are inactive, wrapped up in the DNA coil and ignored for minutes, days, weeks, years, and even decades. The body decides which ones it needs to "switch on" at any given moment, instructing the DNA to "activate" and "inactivate" genes as necessary.

But sometimes the genes are switched on or off by outside forces that the body does not control or cannot counteract, overriding the body's normal instructions, which is what happened when the agouti mice were fed genistein or exposed to BPA. The collection of "overrides" is known as the epigenome, a compilation of all the ways in which the genes have been turned on or off.

Epigenetic changes occur in a couple of different ways. In one method, a tiny molecule called a methyl group (which consists of one carbon atom and three hydrogen atoms) attaches itself to a specific spot on a gene. It then acts like an override switch, forcing the gene to remain either unwrapped and "switched on" or coiled up and "switched off," no matter which signals are sent by the body. The gene is not changed, altered, or mutilated in any way. It's simply locked in either the "on" or "off" position for a time, which could be years, decades, or even a lifetime.

At first, the epigenetic changes to the genome may be minor, with just a few genes held in the "on" or "off" position. But as the years pass, more and more of these changes occur and eventually the "genetic instruction book" is significantly rewritten, with a "revised edition" that is quite a bit different from the original. This can be seen most clearly by comparing the epigenomes of identical twins. Young twins typically have very similar sets of epigenomic changes, while the changes seen in older twins can be different—sometimes vastly different.

What Starts the Epigenetic Process?

It is difficult to pin down all of the epigenetic factors that may affect human beings because it is unethical to expose people deliberately to something that may be harmful or to deprive them of something that is necessary for good health. Thus, much of the evidence comes from animal experiments. They have shown that a number of factors have

Shining a Light on Epigenetics

Imagine that you had strings of multicolored lights strung around the outside of your house that were red, blue, green, orange, and white. You control each lightbulb individually via your computer, which you've programmed in a certain way. You want only red, white, and blue lights to shine on the Fourth of July; green and red ones in December; orange ones on Halloween; blue and white ones during the coldest part of winter; and so on.

One Fourth of July you notice that the orange lights are on while the red, white, and blue ones are off. The orange ones remain on through the summer, then refuse to come on for Halloween. During the Christmas season, the blue bulbs come on while the red and green ones stay dark, ruining the seasonal look. Only red ones come on during the coldest part of winter.

You check your computer program and find that everything looks fine; the computer code has not been changed. Theoretically, the lights should be working. Then you check the light strands and discover something unusual. There are tiny devices on many of the lights, forcing them to remain in the on or off position no matter what instructions might be issued by your computer.

Year after year, those tiny devices remain there, overriding instructions to turn on certain lights at certain times. But when you inspect the light strands each year you notice that while many of the tiny devices remain in place, others have disappeared, so you never know what to expect from your lights. This is much like what happens to your genes as a result of epigenetic changes.

"epigenetic potential," including diseases, substances found in food, physical and emotional stress, drugs, and various chemicals.

Emotional stress and epigenetics

Several animal experiments have focused on the effects of stress suffered early in life on epigenetics and behavior later in life. In one such study, emotional stress was created in newborn mice by removing them from their mothers for three hours each day during the first ten days of their lives. Doing so triggered epigenetic changes that lasted at least a year, which is a long time in the life of a typical mouse, and reduced the ability of these mice to deal with stress and to remember things.

Another study looked at epigenetic differences in the brains of two groups of newborn mice. In the "good-mothering" group, the newborns received more frequent licking and grooming from their mothers during the first seven days of life, while in the "bad-mothering" group they received less frequent affection. As time passed, it became evident that the baby mice in the "good-mothering" group were less anxious and better able to recover from stress then those in the "bad-mothering" group.

Some might say that this is not a surprise: Good mothers who licked their infants a lot were probably better adjusted mice to begin with and passed on their "well-adjusted" genes to their offspring, while bad mothers who neglected their maternal duties probably passed on their "unhappy genes." In other words, this phenomenon could be more genetic than epigenetic.

To test this argument, researchers performed another study in which they deliberately switched the newborn mice, placing the offspring of the "good mothers" with the "bad mothers," and those of the "bad mothers" with "good mothers." The results were intriguing. When the young mice grew up, they exhibited the stress-handling abilities of their foster mothers, not their biological mothers. In other words, nurture was more important than nature; environment trumped genetics.

The same thing happened with infant monkeys. When the offspring of abusive and nonabusive mothers were switched, the ones raised by the nonabusive mothers exhibited similarly good mothering skills when they grew to adulthood even though they were the biological offspring of "bad mothers."

These and other studies have made it clear that the care received during infancy can trigger changes in a number of different genes that regulate mood and behavior. Similar changes can be seen in humans, although we must wait until an individual dies before we can identify epigenetic changes in specific mood and/or behavior genes.

In a 2008 study, researchers studied the brain tissue of twelve people who had committed suicide and had been abused as children, twelve others who committed suicide but had not been abused, and twelve mentally healthy people who had died for reasons other than suicide. The epigenetic markings on a gene that plays a role in the ability to handle stress were different in the abused suicide victims compared to the nonabused suicide victims, indicating that changes occurring during a person's life (or perhaps during the lives of a person's parents) could override their genetic programming.

Nutrition and epigenetics

The agouti mice study referred to earlier shows that exposure to toxins and good nutrition can influence epigenetics. As you recall, adding nutrients such as genistein (an isoflavone found in soy foods) to the diets of the pregnant mice caused the epigenetic "switching off" of the agouti gene. This happened because genistein is rich in the methyl groups that caused the epigenetic change. Studies with large population groups have revealed other potential nutrition-epigenetic links.

For example, Dutch adolescents and young adults who suffered at the end of World War II, when there was a significant drop in food availability (the "Hunger Winter" of 1944–1945), were later found to be significantly less likely to develop colorectal cancer in adulthood. This drop in cancer risk was matched by methylation changes to their DNA. And laboratory studies investigating the ways in which overconsumption of alcohol in pregnant mice can cause fetal alcohol spectrum disorders has linked alcohol consumption to "aberrant changes in DNA methylation patterns with associated changes in gene expression" that may be responsible for the lifelong damage suffered by the offspring.

Nutrigenomics

Researchers are studying links between nutrition and genetics in an effort to discover exactly how the thousands of substances in food can influence the epigenome and how that knowledge can be used to make personalized dietary recommendations. Essentially, these researchers are figuring out how to use nutrition to "switch on" or "switch off" specific genes, much the same way the Duke University researchers did with the agouti mice.

Nutrigenomics does not involve developing genetically modified foods; instead, the focus is on learning how to "switch off," for example, the breast cancer susceptibility genes (*BRCA1* and *BRCA2*) that increase the risk of developing breast cancer or how to "switch on" genes that strengthen the immune system when disease has already struck. In essence, food and substances in food would be used as medicines that act on our genes. The science is in its infancy, but the promise is tremendous. I believe that within the next decade, we'll be able to prescribe foods or substances taken from foods to people suffering from a variety of ailments. This will be truly personalized medicine at its best, for we'll be able to pinpoint and alter an individual's genetic expressions naturally.

How Do Epigenetic Changes Play Out?

Everyone is born with a genome, a unique assemblage of genes derived from both parents, as well as an epigenome, a set of "switches" that have locked some of those genes into the "on" or "off" position.

The fact that the epigenome is inherited may seem odd, for every high-school biology student learns that any changes to the genome occurring during a person's lifetime (whether due to mutations, exposure to radiation, epigenetics, or other factors) are not passed on during reproduction and that infants are born with a clean genetic slate. However, we've learned in the past several years that this is not true. Research has made it clear that some epigenetic switches are faithfully copied when sex cells divide, as well as when sperm and egg combine, ensuring that the newly created genome is already influenced by an epigenome. More epigenetic changes may occur in the womb, as the fetus is exposed to differing levels and types of nutrients, chemicals such as BPA, alcohol, stress hormones generated by the mother's body, and many other factors.

You can see the inherited epigenome in action in fruit flies, some of which carry a mutant copy of the Krüppel gene. If these fruit flies are exposed to the antibiotic geldanamycin, some of them will develop odd growths on their eyes. This will continue for the next thirteen generations, even though the offspring were never exposed to the medicine and have no changes to their genes.

Whether epigenetic changes are good or bad depends on what the specific alteration does. In the case of the agouti mice, inheriting the epigenetic "switch" that turns off the "overeating and obesity gene" is very helpful. Researchers from Rutgers University discovered that epigallocatechin-3-gallate (EGCG), one of the active ingredients in green tea, prevented epigenetic changes to certain cancer-fighting genes. This allowed the cancer-fighting genes to remain active and prevented cancer from growing and spreading. But epigenetics can also increase the risk of disease. For example, the bacteria called *Helicobacter pylori* (more commonly referred to as *H. pylori),* which is implicated in ulcers, can trigger epigenetic changes in the digestive tract that may lead to cancer. Abnormal epigenetic markers have also been identified in a number of different cancers, including those of the breast, prostate, cervix, and stomach.

There's something else that the epigenome does: It makes each person absolutely unique. Even identical twins who begin life with indistinguishable genomes/epigenomes accumulate different epigenomic changes as they progress through life, especially if they have different life experiences, consume different diets, or otherwise lead divergent lifestyles.

We can now see how the epigenome is created and how it influences an individual's life, as well as the lives of offspring, sometimes for multiple generations. Unfortunately, we have not yet been able to identify a certain epigenomic change that leads to depression, and we cannot zero in on a medicine, diet, or other approach that will reverse that change.

What we *can* do is set the stage for a helpful rather than a harmful epigenome by consuming a nutritious diet, reducing stress, and otherwise giving the body the tools it needs to build good health. At the same time, we can avoid dangerous habits and behaviors that might set up a deleterious change in the epigenome—a change that may be passed on to the next generation and beyond.

Unique Person, Unique Disease

This chapter raises more questions than it can answer, but two points are absolutely clear: The brain is inextricably linked to the body and everyone is unique, which means that no two cases of psychiatric disorder are identical. These facts have become the foundation for a new way of viewing and treating depression. Now that we understand every patient's uniqueness, we can and must provide personalized medical treatment in psychiatry that will help prevent the endless trial-and-error polypharmacy that is so common in the treatment of depression.

Our genes provide the blueprints for who we may become; they do not, however, determine who we are. Mood disorders can be understood, and recovery is based on biochemical individuality. Knowing this simple fact provides optimism and hope.

6

Individualizing Medicine with THE ZEEBrA Approach

The theories as to what causes depression are not based on strong science, and our treatments are not working nearly as well as they should: Psychiatry is in crisis. Only about 70 percent of depressed patients show substantial clinical improvements when they take their medicines as prescribed, and of these people, two-thirds continue to have residual symptoms that interfere with their ability to function. In 26 percent of those the dysfunction is mild; in 23 percent, it's moderate; in 12 percent, severe; and in 4 percent, very severe. That means 39 percent of people who experience improvement from medications are still left with *moderate to very severe residual symptoms of depression*. Add this to the 30 percent of those not helped by treatment, and we have an appalling number of depressed patients we are failing to help.

There's simply no denying it: The usual and customary treatment mode (typically based solely on a subjective psychiatric examination and the construction of a symptom list) often leads to a wild goose chase as the psychiatrist blindly searches for a medicine that might work. "Body" factors such as nutrition, toxins, hormones, allergies, biochemical risks, and medical disorders are typically ignored.

No amount of tweaking this approach will work, for the basic underlying concepts are flawed. We need an entirely new way of looking at patients. We must stop treating them according to lists of subjective symptoms and we must stop acting as if one person is interchangeable with the next. Instead, we must start seeing patients as the highly individualized, integrated entities that they are and then diagnose and treat them accordingly.

The Way It Could Be

I began this book by asking you to imagine that you had been sent to a psychiatrist by your family practitioner because you were suffering from sleep difficulties, a lack of energy, agitation, "the blues," and other symptoms. As you recall, during the imaginary psychiatric examination you were asked only about how you felt, and your answers became the sole basis of your diagnosis of depression and the subsequent medications you received.

Imagine that this psychiatrist asks you, in detail, about your diet, the medicines and supplements you take, the health of your relatives, and what you do every day, trying to identify exposure to any situations or substances that may be implicated in depression.

Next, this psychiatrist requests laboratory tests to look for physical problems that might cause or exacerbate depression, such as the following:

- Toxic metal buildup
- Hormonal imbalances
- Vitamin deficiencies
- Amino acid and fatty acid imbalances
- Low or high levels of minerals
- Parasites
- Celiac disease and other food sensitivities
- Imbalanced levels of digestive enzymes
- Dysbiosis ("bad" bacteria, yeast, or other flora in your intestines)

As a result of his findings, the psychiatrist ushers you into a nearby room, where a technician places a little "hat" that looks something like a spiderweb on your head to take an EEG of your brainwave patterns. These patterns are then compared to the readings from thousands of other people (leading to an rEEG), depressed and nondepressed, to determine which medications would most likely be helpful to a person with your particular brainwave pattern. (I explain this test in detail in Chapter 14.)

When all these tests are completed, the psychiatrist does not give you a prescription, as he wants to see the results before making a treatment decision. After all, your depression may be rooted in a food sensitivity, nutrient imbalance, or some other biological factor that can be corrected without the use of psychiatric medicines.

When the results have come in and the psychiatrist sees you for a second visit, he may recommend a medicine in addition to nutritional support. But the medicine will be carefully selected and targeted, and therefore will be much more likely to work. It won't be a "try it and see if it works" prescription based on studies of hundreds of people who are nothing like you; it will be individualized, targeted treatment based on specific imbalances. In other words, it will be specifically for you.

Integrative Psychiatry

The approach I just described is called integrative psychiatry, a way of looking at each person as a unified whole with unique biochemistry and nutritional needs that, when balanced, allow for optimal health and vitality. The practice of integrative psychiatry is based on five basic tenets:

1. Focus on individual's unique personality, environment, and metabolism
2. Care for the whole patient, not just the disease
3. Understand the interconnections of the human body and mind
4. Restore health instead of simply reducing symptoms
5. Increase the body's nutrient reserves to promote long-term health

By focusing on the individual as a whole, integrative psychiatry can often produce improvement and encourage healing where traditional, symptom-based treatments have failed.

Jill, a thirty-three-year-old single mother struggling with depression and bulimia, had requested a consultation with me. After having tried many medications, she was seeking a natural treatment for her depression. Many of the medications she had tried left her with side effects that either decreased her sex drive or impaired her ability to care for her handicapped son. She needed relief immediately; her symptoms of depression and bulimia were interfering with every aspect of her life. After my consultation, I recommended different medications for Jill based on her rEEG. Although Jill's preference would have been to take no medication, these new drugs drastically improved her symptoms.

Mary was forty-two when I first met her. By that time she had struggled with alcohol abuse and depression for many years. She was not alone in her struggles, as her siblings and father had a history of depression and substance abuse. Working with Mary, I ordered a complete metabolic and nutritional evaluation. Based on the results I determined that Mary had a B_{12} deficiency and high levels of casomorphin (a morphine-like chemical generated from the improper digestion of casein in dairy). After eliminating dairy and all casein from Mary's diet and providing her with B_{12} injections, Mary's depression lifted.

Harry was fifty years old when he considered "a different approach" to treating his depression. In his five years struggling with fatigue and depression, Harry had been treated with antidepressants, antipsychotics, and antianxiety medications without significant relief. After taking a complete history and testing, Harry was found to have low testosterone, zinc deficiency, and sleep apnea. When these were corrected, Harry's symptoms improved. Now Harry has no symptoms of depression.

The fact that each of these patients required a different treatment to return to optimal health is not surprising. One person may need nutritional support and some medicine, another lots of exercise and psychological guidance but no medicine, and yet another may need medication with relatively little change in diet and lifestyle. That's the difficulty and the beauty of integrative psychiatry. It can be more difficult to sort through all the possibilities to develop a treatment plan, but when your psychiatrist does, it is much more likely to be effective.

THE ZEEBrA Approach

To ensure that every aspect of a person—mind, body, and spirit—is investigated and restored to balance, I've devised a simple mnemonic: THE ZEEBrA.

T is for Take care of yourself.
H is for Hormones.
E is for Exclude.
Z is for Zinc (and other minerals).
E is for Essential fatty acids and cholesterol.
E is for Exercise and energy.
B is for B vitamins (and other vitamins).
r is for referenced-EEG.
A is for Amino acids and proteins.

It may not be immediately obvious how this list of items relates to depression, but each item is very important. Here is a brief explanation; I delve into each component further in Chapters 7 through 15.

T — Take care of yourself

Psychiatrists have assumed, without proof, that depression results from chemical imbalances in the brain. Treatment has been primarily prescribing medicines that may restore proper balance. But even if we had medicines that could do so consistently, shouldn't we be investigating the possible causes of the imbalance?

Since brain and body are connected, any upset in the body can cause or contribute to disturbances in the brain. Most people agree that stress is linked to some cases of depression. But how about excessive sugar in the diet? The brain is fueled almost entirely by glucose, the form of sugar found in the blood, and low levels of glucose can cause irritability, anxiety, and other mood disturbances, including depression. It sounds counterintuitive, but eating too much sugar can cause glucose levels to fall dramatically.

> Heather started the day with a sugar-laden coffee drink, had a doughnut midmorning, kept a cache of candy and cookies in her desk at work, and ended the evening with a big bowl of ice cream. Her mood crashed right about the same time as her blood sugar, about half an hour after she'd eaten something sweet. I suggested she start the day with a protein-rich breakfast and snack on whole grains coupled with a small serving of protein (e.g. cheese, cottage cheese) to keep her blood sugar levels more stable. Her high-sugar bedtime snack was also eliminated. As a result, Heather's depressed moods improved—without the use of medication.

In addition to excess sugar, sleeping problems may play a role in the development and continuation of depression, particularly obstructive sleep apnea, which causes one to literally stop breathing intermittently while sleeping. Obstructive sleep apnea is not only linked to depression, but it may also interfere with the actions of certain antidepressants. To make matters worse, certain medications used for depression make the sleep apnea worse, and this, in turn, can heighten the depression. How many people with obstructive sleep apnea or other sleep disorders are caught in a vicious cycle of depression that their doctors cannot break because they don't know about it?

Poor digestion can also be a factor in depression. Most psychiatrists are aware of the fact that depression can interfere with appetite, but few fully understand the relationship between good digestion and good mental health. Proper digestion involves the effective breakdown of food and absorption of nutrients. Key to this process are probiotics, otherwise known as the friendly bacteria in the gut. Probiotics have been shown to improve nutritional status as well as overall mood and symptoms of anxiety.

Chapter 7 discusses diet, sleep, and stress and examines their link to depression along with ways to ensure that problems in these areas are detected and resolved.

H — Hormones

The idea that hormones are linked to depression in women is firmly grounded in science and popular culture. You can see the effects of hormones at an early age when pubescent girls, who before puberty were no more likely than boys of the same age to suffer from depression, quickly become significantly more likely to be depressed. In later years, they may suffer from depression associated with premenstrual dysphoric disorder, postpartum depression, and menopause.

Although it's not as well known, hormones have also been linked to depression in men. Indeed, the male hormone testosterone used to be prescribed for men suffering from depression, but that practice was stopped decades ago with the advent of modern antidepressants. But, hormone treatment for depression may be making a comeback. In 2003, a small study conducted at Harvard Medical School's McLean Hospital found that about half the men studied who were not helped by standard antidepressants had low or low-normal levels of testosterone.

Chapter 8 discusses the link between hormones and depression, showing why it's important for those suffering from depression to have hormone levels checked and possibly corrected. Adjusting hormones can often relieve and permanently eliminate long-standing depression in many individuals.

E — Exclude

The integrative medical approach involves testing for and excluding problems associated with digestion that can exacerbate depressed moods. Celiac disease is a case of the body actually attacking itself. It stems from a haywire immune system launching a full-scale attack on harmless substances in the body and, in the process, damaging the small intestines and other parts of the body. A substance called gluten, found in wheat, barley and rye, sets off the errant immune response, which leads to constipation, diarrhea, abdominal bloating, lack of appetite, vomiting, bloody stools, and other symptoms. These other symptoms include depression, as well as nutrient deficiencies that may develop because of the intestinal problems and lack of appetite. If certain nutrients are depleted, the depression may worsen.

Celiac disease, elevated neuropeptides from improper digestion of wheat and dairy foods, food allergies, and other problems with the digestive system, including Crohn's disease and ulcerative colitis, must be ruled out in a physician's examination. Chapter 9 examines these intestinal contributors to depression.

Z — Zinc and other trace minerals

In addition to keeping the immune system strong and the memory sharp, zinc plays an important role in the production and use of neurotransmitters—those brain chemicals that help modulate mood. This is why low levels of zinc have been linked to major depression, and why supplemental zinc has an antidepressant effect in many people.

Zinc also enhances the effects of antidepressant medications in certain people. For example, a 2009 study published in the *Journal of Affective Disorders* reported on sixty people, ages eighteen to fifty-five, who were suffering from major depression. They were all treated with imipramine, a standard antidepressant. In addition, half were randomly assigned to receive 25 milligrams per day (mg/day) of zinc, while the other half received a placebo. When the study subjects were retested after twelve weeks, researchers found that zinc supplementation significantly reduced depression scores in people who had not been helped by antidepressants in the past. This study suggests a major role for zinc in depression, especially among those who fail to get relief from antidepressants alone. Every depressed patient should be tested for zinc deficiency and treated if found to be deficient.

Another mineral that is important to mood is magnesium. Of all the minerals needed for human health, magnesium is the one most likely to be deficient. A magnesium deficiency can trigger a host of problems with mental and physical health, including depression, insomnia, irritability, nervousness and anxiety, apathy, and migraine headaches.

Case studies have shown that giving patients 125–300 mg of magnesium per meal and at bedtime can lead to rapid recovery from major depression. In my own practice, magnesium supplementation has been invaluable in relieving the insomnia and anxiety often associated with depression.

A great deal of research has clearly shown that a lack of zinc, magnesium, and other minerals can cause or worsen depression and that many people suffering from various forms of depression are deficient in these minerals.

Chapter 10 looks at the problem of mineral deficiency among depressed people, explains why these nutrients are vital for mental health, and describes how they can be used either to reduce depressive symptoms or "supercharge" standard therapy.

E — Essential fatty acids and cholesterol

An imbalance in the right kind of fat can also be involved in depression. The brain is a fatty organ that cannot function without the presence of copious amounts of essential fatty acids (EFAs), as well as cholesterol and other members of the lipid family. Indeed, 60 percent of the brain's dry weight is fat, and at least 25 percent of its white matter consists of phospholipids derived from EFAs.

EFAs support the manufacture, release, reuptake, binding, and later the disposal of neurotransmitters, and a great deal of research has shown that they play a key role in depression.

For example,

- in one study, treatment with 6.6 grams per day (g/day) of the EFAs known as eicosapentaenoic acid (EPA) and docosahexaenoic acid (DHA) for eight weeks led to significantly improved Hamilton scores;
- a study of children between the ages of six and twelve showed that EPA and DHA supplementation significantly improved symptoms of major depressive disorder;
- adolescent research revealed the existence of an inverse relationship between EPA levels in adipose (fat) tissue and depression—the lower the EPA, the greater the risk of depression;
- other research found that low levels of DHA in the blood and skewed ratios of omega-6 to omega-3 fatty acids were predictive of future suicide risk.

Cholesterol is also essential for good mental health. Lower levels of cholesterol in the blood are associated with a heightened risk of developing major depressive disorder and being hospitalized, as well as an increased risk of death from suicide. A recent study published in the *Journal of Psychiatric Research* found that depressed men with low total cholesterol levels (less than 165 milligrams per deciliter [mg/dL]) were *seven times more likely to die prematurely* from unnatural causes such as suicide and accidents.

The link between cholesterol and depression involves the neurotransmitter serotonin:

1. Low cholesterol decreases the number of serotonin receptors in the brain.
2. Decreasing the number of serotonin receptors may lead to decreases in serotonin levels.
3. Low serotonin is associated with an increased level of aggressive impulses.

Simply checking the levels of EFAs, cholesterol, and other fats in all depressed patients may help identify many who will benefit greatly from simple dietary changes or supplements.

Chapter 11 looks at the relationship between depression and EFAs, cholesterol, and other fats; explains why so many Americans are deficient in key fats; and shows how to ward off depression through the intake of adequate amounts of these substances.

E — Exercise and energy

When you're depressed, the last thing you want to do is huff and puff your way through a jog or bounce up and down in an aerobics class. Even engaging in your favorite sport with your friends is unappealing. Yet, exercise combats depression on multiple levels by triggering the release of endorphins and other brain chemicals that help lift the mood, slowing the release of certain immune system substances that can deepen depression and improving sleep.

A great deal of research has shown that exercise is an effective anti-depressant in cases of mild to moderate depression. Psychiatrists tend to underestimate the benefits of exercise and rarely prescribe it. British physicians, on the other hand, can actually prescribe exercise as a treatment for depression, with the National Health Service subsidizing some or all of the cost. Patients, however, find it difficult to overcome their feelings of hopelessness and lack of energy to begin moving again.

Chapter 12 explores the relationship between exercise, energy, and depression and offers a "prescription" for enhancing energy and starting an exercise program.

B — B vitamins and other vitamins

Many of the B vitamins are critical for both mood and energy regulation:

- B_1 (thiamine)
- B_3 (niacin)
- B_6 (pyridoxine)
- B_9 (folate)
- B_{12} (cobalamin)
- Inositol

Of these B vitamins, research has strongly linked folic acid and vitamin B_{12} to depression. For example, low levels of folate in the blood have been linked to poor treatment outcomes in patients with major depressive disorder who are taking Prozac, while higher levels of B_{12} in the blood are significantly associated with recovery.

Many Americans are not consuming enough B vitamins, and even if they do, they unknowingly deplete their supplies by eating refined sugar and carbohydrates, which rob the body of these precious vitamins.

Ample supplies of other vitamins, including vitamin C and vitamin D, are also needed for good mental health. An increasing amount of research is investigating the link between depression and vitamin D, which influences the growth and regulation of every cell in the body. A study of one thousand senior citizens found that those with major depression or dysthymia were more likely to have significantly lower levels of vitamin D than other senior citizens in the study. An intriguing study with healthy volunteers found that giving people vitamin D in the winter, when levels tend to be lower because of a lack of sunlight, increased their "happy feelings" and decreased their "sad feelings." An estimated 41–57 percent of the U.S. population is deficient in vitamin D, with dark-skinned individuals particularly at risk because their skin requires more sunlight to manufacture the vitamin.

Chapter 13 is devoted to the B vitamins and other vitamins that play a role in depression. I discuss how they influence mood, what happens when they are in short supply, ways to measure vitamin levels in the body, and how to increase these levels, if necessary.

r — referenced-EEG

The EEG is a device that measures electrical activity in the brain much like the ECG monitors the electrical activity of the heart. While a cardiologist can use an ECG to find evidence of heart disease, the EEG does not show a "depression brainwave pattern," a "schizophrenia brainwave pattern," or some other objective indicator of psychiatric disorder. Because of this, psychiatry lost interest in the EEG as a diagnostic tool decades ago.

The same is true today: There is no way to diagnose depression or other mental disorders by looking at EEGs. The EEGs of depressed people do not look alike and do not share some common deviation.

But while there is no correlation among the EEGs of people with depression, there is a relationship between certain variations in EEG patterns and responses to certain medications. While the EEG cannot be used to diagnose psychiatric disorder, it can be used to guide treatment. By comparing a patient's EEG with those of thousands of others patients, it's possible to predict which medicine(s) that patient is most likely to respond to. This eliminates the torturous guesswork and lengthy experiments with one medicine after another that too many patients are forced to endure.

Comparing a patient's EEG to those of thousands of others contained in a database to help select medications results in an rEEG . It's the first objective, physiologically based measure that guides psychiatrists in making prescribing decisions.

Chapter 14 explains how the rEEG is performed and why it makes the process of selecting medicines and gauging their effectiveness so much more precise and effective than ever before.

A — Amino acids and proteins

A lack of protein is not usually considered a cause of depression, but a shortfall in the amino acids that make up protein can contribute to emotional distress. Various amino acids are necessary for the synthesis of all major neurotransmitters, which, in turn, affect every facet of one's emotional health, including thoughts, feelings, and behaviors.

We tend to think that because we eat plenty of protein, we should have all the amino acids we need. However, the increase in carbohydrate consumption has led to a steady decline in the percentage of protein in the diet. In addition, the burgeoning use of antacids interferes with the body's production of the hydrochloric acid (HCl) and pepsin necessary to digest protein. We tend to worry these days that we eat too much protein; for some people, however, the real issue is that they are either not eating or absorbing the amino acids necessary for good physical and mental health.

Chapter 15 investigates the protein-depression link and explains how to tell if protein intake is inadequate, what happens as a result, and what to do about it. It also explains the best time of day to consume protein and why.

Does THE ZEEBrA Approach Work?

THE ZEEBrA is an integrative approach that is based on common sense. Yet, it may seem dramatically different to many psychiatrists. The brain and body are viewed as a whole, as we take into consideration the effects of nutrition, disease, and other bodily influences on mental health. And with the rEEG, there is finally an objective means of determining which medicine(s) is most likely to work for a given individual. At last, an objective, integrated, and truly balanced approach to finding relief from depression.

7

T – Take Care of Yourself

First and most fundamental: THE ZEEBrA approach encourages you to take care of your body.

It may seem odd to begin an "antidepression program" by saying that you have to take care of your physical body. Because of the strong relationship between physical and mental health, certain physical diseases and health habits can set the stage for depression. The fact that so many lifestyle choices and diseases can contribute to depression underscores the need to take good care of the body as well as the mind.

In some cases, the link between physical disease and mental disorder is obvious. A brain tumor, for example, can cause personality changes, while severe dehydration can trigger confusion. In many other cases, the links are subtle and, therefore, often overlooked.

It's impossible to cover in this book all the physical diseases, habits, and factors that cause or worsen depression. This chapter focuses on simple yet major physical factors, some of which you can address on your own, without the aid of a clinician. They include diet, digestion, sleep, sugars, and stress.

Diet and Depression

Diet has long been linked to physical ailments such as diabetes and cardiovascular disease. And low levels of individual dietary elements, including the B vitamins, omega-3 fatty acids, and zinc, have been associated with a greater risk of suffering from depression. But it's not just individual nutrients that matter: The entire diet can influence mood.

A 2010 study published in the *American Journal of Psychiatry* compared habitual diet to mental disorders in 1,046 women ranging in age from twenty to ninety-three. Specifically, the researchers looked at the effects of a "healthy" diet made up of vegetables, fruit, meat, fish, and whole grains, to that of an "unhealthy" diet characterized by refined grains, fried foods, sugary products, and beer. They found that the unhealthy diet was associated with a higher prevalence of depressive and anxiety disorders. Another study, also published in 2010, looked at the effects of diet on 7,114 adolescents. The results were no surprise; the participants who ate "poor" diets consisting of more unhealthy and processed foods were more likely to suffer from self-reported depression, compared to those eating "good" diets that more closely adhered to government dietary recommendations.

It's impossible to devise a single diet that gives everyone the best chance of enjoying excellent psychiatric health, given that everyone is biochemically unique. However, I can say with certainty that the Standard American Diet, filled with fried, refined, sugary, junk foods is best avoided. On the other hand, a diet rich in fresh organic vegetables and fruits, along with whole grains and moderate amounts of fish, meat, and poultry, is much more likely to encourage good mental, as well as physical, health.

Digestion and Depression

Digestion might seem like a simple process: Chew the food well enough, mix it with stomach acid and a few enzymes, and that's all there is to it. That's the general idea, but it's a much more complicated process that depends on hundreds of events taking place at just the right time and in the right "strength." This is an area where I see a lot of problems, and a lot of room for rapid and significant improvement, among my patients.

Digestion begins with the sight, smell, or even thought of food, as the brains sends "get ready" signals to the digestive system. While food is being chewed, it mixes with enzymes in the saliva that begin to break down fat and starch. Once swallowed, food travels down the esophagus and into the stomach, where it is bathed in hydrochloric acid (HCl), an acid so powerful that a single drop can burn a hole through a piece of wood. But hydrochloric acid does more than dissolve food into constituent parts: It is also required, among other things, for the absorption of vitamin B_{12} and minerals and for the production of an enzyme called pepsin, which is necessary for the digestion of protein. For these and other reasons, hydrochloric acid is absolutely vital for digestion.

We often inappropriately blame excess hydrochloric acid for the painful symptoms of gastroesophageal reflux disease (GERD), commonly called heartburn or acid reflux, and take pills such as Prilosec, Nexium, Maalox, and Tums to cut back on acid levels. These pills can indeed reduce heartburn symptoms, but they do so at the expense of good digestion. (Ironically, what physicians typically assume to be heartburn caused by excess acid may be triggered by *low* acid levels.)

After being processed in the stomach, the food moves into the small intestine. Here it is doused with sodium bicarbonate to neutralize the hydrochloric acid, and fat, protein, and carbohydrates are broken down into even smaller constituent parts before being absorbed across the intestinal wall. Most of the absorption of vitamins and minerals also takes place here.

Digestive enzymes

Digestive enzymes begin breaking down food as soon as it enters the mouth, continuing their work in the stomach and small intestines until the food has been broken down into microscopically small pieces that move into the intestinal wall and are absorbed into the body. There are numerous enzymes that work at specific "stations" in the body, and each must do a good job or the process fails. The body uses zinc, protein, vitamin C, and other nutrients to manufacture these enzymes, which means that good nutrition leads to good digestion, and good digestion helps ensure that all the necessary nutrients are absorbed.

The reverse is also true: Bad nutrition can lead to bad digestion, and bad digestion worsens the problem by causing bad nutrition. Once someone is caught in the negative feedback loop, it's very hard to break-out. More likely, the downward spiral of poor digestion equals poor nutrition equals worse digestion equals worse nutrition continues, gradually growing worse with the passing of time. This becomes worse with age, as the production of stomach acid declines naturally.

For many patients with digestive problems, supplemental digestive enzymes are available and can be very helpful. They can, among other things,

- rapidly improve digestion, which automatically improves absorption and nutritional status;
- reduce or eliminate gas, bloating, and certain other symptoms of poor digestion;
- support the development of healthy intestinal bacteria;
- protect against inflammation in the gut.

There are a number of digestive enzymes, including bromelain from pineapple, papain from papaya, and trypsin from animal sources. A good, broad-spectrum supplement contains a variety of enzymes designed to digest specific parts of food. Thus, it should include enzymes such as amylase to digest carbohydrates and sugars; cellulose for vegetable and vegetable fibers; lipase for fats; and protease for proteins and the peptides that make up protein molecules.

The dosage depends on the person, and individual requirements vary widely depending on diet, lifestyle, and biochemical individuality. I recommend working with a health professional who understands digestive enzymes and is familiar with the various brands and products and then starting with the dosage on the product label, adjusting up or down until the optimal dose is discovered. (The optimal dose may change over time as one's nutrition, health, and lifestyle changes.) The dosage may also vary depending on the size and type of meal being eaten.

Because everyone is different, some people respond rapidly, noticing improvements in digestion and fewer gastrointestinal symptoms almost immediately, while others may not see any improvements for days or weeks. It's important to stick with the initial dose for a few weeks before adjusting it and to work with a health professional who truly understands nutritional medicine.

Even if someone is eating a perfect diet, if he or she lacks the acid and enzymes necessary to digest and absorb it, the nutrients in the diet may literally go to waste. That's why digestive enzymes can be so helpful, even in those consuming healthful diets.

Probiotics

Plentiful supplies of digestive enzymes and powerful stomach acid are not the only things required for good digestion: An astonishing number and variety of bacteria are also necessary.

We tend to think of all bacteria as being harmful, but the right bacteria situated in the intestines perform a number of chores, including assisting in the breakdown of food, synthesizing nutrients, and guarding against infection and illness. These helpful bacteria are called probiotics, and they should vastly outnumber the unfriendly bacteria (pathogens) that can trigger inflammation, allergies, and disease. Unfortunately, a number of factors can harm the probiotics, allowing the unhealthy bacteria to reproduce and spread, damaging the gut, interfering with nutrient absorption, and triggering depression, fatigue, constipation, diarrhea, and other gastrointestinal symptoms. Following are some things that can harm the friendly bacteria:

- Antibiotics
- Birth control pills
- Nutrient deficiency (lack of B vitamins, EFAs, zinc)
- Infections
- Stress
- Radiation
- Excessive use of alcohol

Some studies have shown that as the levels of beneficial bacteria fall, the levels of inflammation and inflammatory substances rise, and excessive amounts of one of these inflammatory substances, a group of chemicals called cytokines, may increase one's risk of developing depression. Other studies have indicated that taking probiotics can improve the mood.

In one such study, 132 healthy volunteers were randomly assigned to drink either a yogurt drink containing probiotics or a placebo drink, daily for three weeks. Their moods were measured at the beginning of the study and ten and twenty days after the three-week "drinking" period was completed. At the end of the study period, those who had initially rated their mood as poor, and drank the probiotic-containing yogurt, reported an improvement in mood. In a recent double-blind, placebo-controlled study, patients with chronic fatigue syndrome who took probiotic supplements enjoyed a reduction in their anxiety.

The mood-enhancing results seen with probiotics may be partially due to the fact that as probiotics are restored to healthful levels, inflammation drops, and the amount of the amino acid tryptophan, a precursor to the neurotransmitter serotonin, rises.

Probiotics can be obtained from foods such as yogurt, kefir, and other fermented milk products, as well as sauerkraut, miso, kimchi, and other fermented foods. Eating these foods can be very helpful, but since many of the helpful bacteria in food are destroyed by stomach acid, supplementation may be required. Indeed, I have found that using supplements containing billions of probiotic bacteria is necessary to restore intestinal health in many people. Generally, I begin by recommending probiotic supplements containing at least 10–15 billion cfu (colony forming units) and containing two key probiotic strains called *L. acidophilus* and *B. bifidum*. A good supplement has an enteric coating designed to protect the capsule, plus the probiotics within, from hydrochloric acid as it journeys through the stomach. The date of manufacture should be checked to make sure the product is fresh, and storage conditions should be noted (some brands need to be refrigerated).

Even if someone is eating a healthful diet, he or she may lack the helpful bacteria necessary to digest and absorb it. That's why many otherwise healthy people can benefit from probiotic supplementation.

Sleep and Depression

Difficulty sleeping is a common symptom of depression, as is, in a smaller number of depressed people, oversleeping. But the sleep-depression equation doesn't only move in one direction, from depression to poor sleep. Poor sleeping can be both a contributing factor to, and a result of, depression.

"I am so depressed," Tanya told me during our initial encounter. This thirty-two-year-old woman had tried multiple antidepressants over the past three years with continued depression and fatigue. She was having difficulty caring for her two children and was less productive at work. As I listened to Tanya, what was most striking was her three-year struggle with chronic insomnia. On an average night she slept a combined five hours, spending most of the night tossing and turning and watching late-night infomercials. Rather than prescribe an antidepressant, I focused my treatment on nutritional supplements and medication to enhance her sleep. Sleeping eight hours per night and waking fully rested was all Tanya needed. She stopped her sleep medications after four weeks, and within three months she felt like herself again. Although she had come to my office because of her depression, she was never prescribed an antidepressant.

Both the body and the brain need sleep in order to refresh and restore optimal functioning. A lack of sleep, or disturbed sleep, can lead to increased irritability and tension, which can set the stage for depression, or make existing depression worse. Not getting enough sleep can also encourage people to engage in poor dietary habits such as eating highly refined, carbohydrate-rich foods, which can also exacerbate depression.

Many people are not sleeping nearly enough, and the problem is growing worse. In 2001, only 38 percent of Americans were getting the recommended minimum of eight hours of sleep per night. But in 2009, that figure had fallen to an alarming 28 percent. In 2001, 13 percent of Americans were sleeping less than six hours per night. By 2009, the number of people surviving on that inadequate sleep regimen had risen to 20 percent. All told, 40 million Americans suffer from chronic, long-term sleep disorders, with an additional 20 million experiencing occasional sleeping problems. Sleeping problems can be caused by a number of factors, including physical disease, poor sleeping habits, and even nutritional imbalances (a fact which surprises most patients and psychiatrists alike).

Sleep difficulty may be caused by a disease

A major contributor to sleeping difficulties is sleep apnea, a disorder that causes a person to stop breathing at night, up to a minute or even longer each episode, tens or even hundreds of times during a night. The problem may be caused by collapse of the soft tissue at the back of the throat during sleep, failure of the brain to maintain normal breathing, or a combination of the two. If left untreated, sleep apnea can cause or contribute to cardiovascular disease, sexual difficulties, weight gain, and other ailments, including depression.

People with sleep apnea are five times more likely to become depressed than those without the disease, and 20 percent of those who are depressed also suffer from sleep apnea. Studies show that simply treating sleep apnea can relieve depression in some people, so it's important that people with depression be checked to make sure they don't have the disorder. Or, if they do have the disorder, to ensure it is being treated properly. Symptoms of sleep apnea include the following:

- Waking up feeling unrefreshed in the morning
- Feeling tired during the day
- Memory problems
- Tossing and turning while sleeping
- Choking or gasping while sleeping
- Snoring loudly
- Headaches in the morning or at night
- Excessive nighttime urination
- Swelling of the legs
- Chest pain or sweating during sleep

Many people think that sleep apnea only strikes the obese. That's incorrect, for normal-weight and thin people can also suffer. I remember a slim and fit forty-three-year-old man with complaints of depression who was found to have a severe case of sleep apnea that required the use of a continuous positive airway pressure (CPAP) machine and mask through the night to keep oxygen flowing through his lungs. The CPAP helped him sleep and resolved his symptoms of depression.

A host of factors can exacerbate sleep problems, including stress, caffeine, alcohol, many prescription and over-the-counter medicines, hormonal imbalances, allergies, asthma, hyperthyroidism, chronic pain, and many nutritional deficiencies, the most common of which are magnesium and zinc.

Restless legs syndrome is another disorder that can make it difficult to sleep. The syndrome causes a powerful, sometimes irresistible, urge to move the legs, which is often worse at night or when one is lying down. Restless legs syndrome can make it difficult to fall asleep and stay asleep.

Improving sleep with good sleep hygiene

Medications can help many people overcome sleep problems, but I like to start, whenever possible, with more natural methods such as improving sleep habits, referred to as sleep hygiene.

Many people can solve their sleep difficulties by adopting the following bedtime rituals:

- Go to bed and get up at a regular time every day
- Avoid caffeine after lunch
- Make sure your bed, pillows, and bedding are comfortable and supportive
- Set the thermostat so that your bedroom is slightly cool throughout the night.
- Use blackout curtains, get rid of TVs or radios with lights, and otherwise make your bedroom as dark as possible
- Only use the bed for sleep and sex
- Don't use the bed for work, watching television, or anything else that causes your brain to associate the bed with other activities
- Develop a prebed ritual, which might include reading for a while, bathing, deep-breathing exercises, yoga, or other relaxation techniques
- Avoid the computer, electronic games, texting, and similar activities before bedtime
- It's also important not to try too hard. If after implementing these rules you don't fall asleep within twenty or thirty minutes, get out of bed, go to another room, and read until you're sleepy

Improving sleep with natural remedies

Ideally, you should try to sleep without taking a pill every night. But if improving sleep habits doesn't solve the problem, you may want to try natural remedies, under the direction of a health professional trained in integrative medicine, such as melatonin, magnesium, valerian, inositol, 5-hydroxytryptophan (5-HTP), and gamma-aminobutyric acid (GABA). It's important to keep in mind that natural remedies are not regulated the way pharmaceuticals are so not all brands are made using high-quality ingredients and exacting manufacturing standards.

Melatonin for sleep. Melatonin, a hormone produced by a part of the brain known as the pineal gland, works with the body's built-in "clock" to regulate sleep and wake cycles. Under ideal circumstances, the clock signals the body to produce more melatonin during the evening, keeping the levels high through the night, and then to reduce melatonin as morning approaches. As melatonin levels rise, you become sleepier; and as they fall, you become more awake and alert. It's also interesting to note that the body needs the mineral zinc to manufacture melatonin. Zinc plays a key role in staving off depression (see Chapter 10 for a more detailed discussion).

The sleep produced by melatonin supplements is remarkably normal, especially compared to the "drugged" sleep experienced by some people taking sleeping pills. One example that comes to mind involves a fifty-six-year-old female patient who had struggled with sleep problems for nine years. I prescribed 1 mg of melatonin, and she was quickly back to sleeping "normally again," as she described it.

I have found that taking 1–3 mg of melatonin helps many people go to sleep within thirty minutes. The hormone is cleared from the body fairly quickly, so it doesn't linger and make one feel tired or sluggish throughout the day. Although it has been used by millions of people, in numerous countries for many years, and is considered safe when used as prescribed, it can cause side effects such as drowsiness, stomach upset, headaches, and even depression, so it should be used with caution and only if needed.

Magnesium for sleep. Although it's perhaps better known for working with calcium to cause the body's smooth muscles to contract and relax at the appropriate times, the mineral magnesium is also important for sleep. Considered to be an "antistress" mineral, magnesium supplements can reduce the levels of cortisol in the body and prevent nighttime muscle cramps, both of which can help improve sleep.

Magnesium is also one of the first minerals to disappear from food when it is processed, and one of the first to leave the body when a person is stressed. Between the tremendous amounts of processed foods we eat and the stress of modern life, as well as the fact that magnesium supplies are depleted by alcohol, caffeine, and certain medications, it's no wonder that many people do not have optimal levels of magnesium in their bodies. A deficiency in magnesium ties directly into depression as symptoms include irritability, nervousness, anxiety, apathy, emotional lability, insomnia, and depression.

Case studies of individual patients have shown that taking 125–300 mg of magnesium (either magnesium glycinate or magnesium taurate) per meal and at bedtime helps relieve the symptoms of major depression.

I have found that 200–300 mg of magnesium glycinate or citrate before bed helps those who have trouble falling asleep as well as those who fall right to sleep but wake up three hours later and cannot fall back to sleep. It may take a few weeks for magnesium to help. The only major side effect of magnesium supplementation is loose stools. As with every aspect of THE ZEEBrA approach, individual variability is the norm, and you need to find the right dose that works for you.

Valerian for sleep. Many herbs have been promoted as sleep aids, but the only one I've consistently found to be useful is valerian, which has been called the "herbal Valium" because it is helpful in reducing anxiety while improving sleep. Valerian was used in a four-week study involving thirty people with sleep disorders. Some of the research subjects were placed on a four-week regimen of valerian, and the remaining were given a placebo. Neither the patients nor the researchers knew which patients were given the herb as opposed to the placebo, a procedure termed a double-blind study. The study concluded that valerian reduced the amount of time needed to go to sleep in people suffering from sleep disorders. Another study showed that valerian improved sleep even in people who had been taking Valium, Librium, Klonopin, and other benzodiazepine medicines.

I've found that 300–500 mg of valerian before bed can help people enjoy better sleep. Valerian does not work immediately and needs to be taken for a few weeks for optimal results. The herb's potential side effects include headache, restlessness, sleeplessness, and irregular heartbeats. Anyone taking valerian should be vigilant for these side effects.

Inositol and 5-HTP for sleep. Manufactured by the body as well as by intestinal bacteria, the vitamin inositol has many duties, including helping to transmit nerve signals and preventing the buildup of fats in the liver and other organs. I have treated many patients who have had improvements in chronic sleep difficulties using inositol.

Research has supported the use of inositol in depression and OCD. I have found that patients who ruminate with obsessive thinking in the evening find relief with 1 teaspoon (about 2.8 g) of inositol around 8 p.m. and then 1 teaspoon before bed. This tends to decrease the obsessive thinking, enabling them to more easily "turn off" the thoughts that interfere with sleep.

Another natural remedy for insomnia that I recommend to my patients is 5-HTP, which is a precursor to the neurotransmitter serotonin and is then chemically changed to make melatonin. Among other duties, 5-HTP helps to increase serotonin levels as many of the popular antidepressants strive to do. Several studies have suggested that taking 5-HTP can help reduce anxiety, and I've found that it can also help improve sleep quality. I recommend 50–200 mg of 5-HTP thirty to sixty minutes before bedtime. *You should not take 5-HTP if you are currently taking a prescription antidepressant.* (Inositol and 5-HTP are discussed further in Chapter 13.)

GABA for sleep. GABAis also a useful sleep aid for many patients. GABA, a neurotransmitter, helps brain cells calm down and become less excited. By reducing brain cell excitability, GABA is known for its ability to act as a natural tranquilizer, reducing stress and anxiety while increasing alertness. People with low levels of GABA often experience anxiety, depression, irritability, headache, and hypertension.

I typically recommend mixing 500–750 mg of GABA with a cup of water and drinking half of the mixture thirty minutes before bed. If you wake up in the middle of the night, take the other half. It is important to take a small test dose of GABA before trying the higher dose, as a few patients become agitated on GABA. First, try 100–250 mg of GABA and if you feel relaxed or have no reaction, which is most common, increase the dosage to 500–750 mg at night before bed.

A brief note on supplements

Supplements are sold without prescription in vitamin stores, supermarkets, and drugstores, as well as on the Internet. The fact that they seem to be available everywhere may give a false sense that they are absolutely safe. However, they do have side effects, can be harmful if used in excess, and may interact with other supplements, medicines, and health conditions. Remember, it's important to use them under the direction of a health professional who is experienced and trained in integrative medicine.

Improving sleep with medications

Pharmaceutical researchers have created a number of medicines to aid sleep, including the familiar benzodiazepines (Valium, Lunesta, Sonata, Ambien, and Klonipin), as well as many lesser-known ones. These medicines can be helpful, but they tend to be overused, often produce a "sleep that doesn't feel like real sleep," as one of my patients put it, and may become less effective over time. In addition, many patients become psychologically and physiologically dependent on them.

For these reasons, I look upon sleeping pills as temporary measures to help people while they improve their sleep hygiene, investigate natural remedies, and follow THE ZEEBrA approach.

Sleeping pills are not long-term solutions. According to a 2007 study financed by the National Institutes of Health, the general conclusion was that sleeping pills do not greatly improve sleep. In the study, participants received either a placebo or a prescription sleeping pill such as Ambien, Lunesta, and Sonata. The study concluded that on average the prescription sleep medication increased total sleep time by just under twelve minutes for newer medication (such as Ambien and Lunesta) and by roughly thirty-two minutes for older medication (such as Halcion and Restoril) as compared to a placebo. When asked how well they slept, participants reported, on average, that they slept an additional thirty-two minutes with newer sleep medications and an additional fifty-two minutes with older medication. The drugs, it seems, do a better job of increasing how long you think you've slept. Sleeping pills are mildly effective, but for the most part they are not solutions to long-term sleeping problems.

Sugar and Depression

The second major physical factor that can contribute to depression is sugar consumption. We know intuitively that what we eat affects our energy levels and mood. We often eat to feel better—scarfing a chocolate brownie, perhaps, after a rough day at work—and it works. We do feel better, for a little while. Knowing that food can improve the mood for the better, it's not surprising to learn that it can also do the reverse. One of the biggest food offenders is sugar.

The brain runs almost exclusively on glucose, the form of sugar found in the blood. When blood glucose levels run low, the mood can be affected in major ways. Signs of insufficient glucose to the brain include weakness, irritability, anxiety, headaches, fainting and, yes, depression. Low blood glucose results from eating too little (as in dieting, fasting), not eating often enough (as in skipping meals), or, ironically, eating too much sugar. The problem can be particularly acute when a person eats a high-sugar food like a candy bar by itself, without foods that contain protein or fiber. It's easier for the body to break down sugar than to break down complex carbohydrates (e.g., whole grains, fruits, or vegetables). Thus, the glucose derived from that candy bar hits the bloodstream a lot faster and in larger amounts than the glucose from, say, a piece of rye bread. And when it hits, blood glucose levels soar, spurring a surge of insulin throughout the bloodstream.

Insulin and sugar cravings

Insulin is a hormone that helps ferry glucose either into hungry cells where it's used for fuel or into fat cells where it's stored for future usage. But a problem occurs when insulin "overdoes it" and clears too much glucose from the bloodstream, causing blood sugar to drop to abnormally low levels, along with a corresponding decline in mood. Depressed, irritable, fatigued, weak and—guess what?—craving sugar, those subjected to this state of affairs usually want to gobble up more sugar, but that just starts a vicious cycle that keeps the problem in play indefinitely. Eating more sugar spurs the release of more insulin, which clears away more blood glucose and sets the stage for further bouts of low blood sugar and poor moods.

Mood disturbances caused by low blood glucose can be particularly problematic for those who have insulin resistance, a condition in which glucose has difficulty entering the hungry cells, even when blood sugar levels are normal to high. You can think of insulin as the "key" that "unlocks" the hungry cells and allows glucose to enter and "feed" them. In certain circumstances, most notably obesity, lack of exercise, aging, genetic factors, or hormonal changes, the insulin "key" no longer "unlocks" the cells properly, so less glucose can enter, and it takes longer for the cells to get their fill. In severe cases, the cells begin to starve while blood sugar levels go sky high, otherwise known as full-fledged diabetes.

When the cells resist the effects of insulin, blood levels of both insulin and glucose rise, negatively affecting kidney function and increasing blood fats, including triglycerides and cholesterol. As the hungry cells become more insistent in their demand for fuel, sugar cravings can become irresistible. Exhausted, depressed, shaky, and hungry, a person with low blood sugar may feel like she could eat a horse, especially if it were sugarcoated.

To avoid the mood-destroying effects of low blood sugar, it's important to include foods containing protein and complex carbohydrates with every meal or snack, or whenever the blood sugar starts to slip. Because these foods contain fiber and protein, the digestion process takes longer than it does with simple sugars, so glucose is released more slowly and evenly into the bloodstream.

Remember that fruits and, to a lesser extent, vegetables also contain natural sugars that can drive up blood glucose levels, so they too should be eaten along with some complex carbohydrate or a small amount of protein (e.g., cottage cheese).

How sugar packs on the pounds

When glucose skyrockets and insulin soars, the deposition of fat isn't far behind. That's because the body needs to do *something* with all of that extra blood sugar. The solution? Insulin converts it into fat, which is then stored in the hips, thighs, and derriere in women and around the waist in men. Making matters worse, insulin can overdo it to cause a blood-sugar crash. The crash activates the adrenal glands, which work to push the blood sugar back up by releasing adrenaline. The adrenaline, in turn, triggers the release of another hormone, cortisol, which causes intense cravings for sugar. Cortisol also has a particular affinity for depositing fat in the abdominal area. Cortisol tends to make cells even more resistant to insulin, thereby increasing the likelihood of additional blood-sugar crashes and fat deposition in the future.

Getting a handle on your sugar intake

Since sugar can play many roles in bringing on and/or maintaining depression, it's important for anyone at risk to cut back on sugar intake as much as possible. In a recently published book entitled *Beat Sugar Addiction Now!*, author Jacob Teitelbaum, MD, promotes a step-by-step approach for breaking sugar cravings and limiting sugar intake. Obviously all forms of sugar can't be avoided all the time, but the amount of sugar in the diet can be limited just by following a few simple rules.

Tips for cutting back on sugar

Following are some easy ways to cut back on sugar intake without feeling deprived:

- Use less sugar in cooking. Try cutting out one-quarter of the sugar in a recipe and see if it still tastes good. If it does, cut back a little more the next time and repeat until you find out how much sugar you can eliminate without ruining the finished product. Many recipes contain plenty of unnecessary sugar.
- Try xylitol, a safe and natural sweetener that comes from birch-tree bark and corn husks. Xylitol is a sugar alternative that does not raise insulin or blood-sugar levels. I urge you to use pure xylitol crystals, as they are free of fillers and other additives. I caution against the use of other sugar alternatives, such as artificial sweeteners.
- Throw away the sugar bowl so you won't add sugar to your foods at the table.
- Try using small amounts of cinnamon, cardamom, ginger, nutmeg, and other spices for a "sweet" flavor without adding sugar, or to replace some of the sugar in certain recipes.
- Eat plain popcorn rather than candy or cookies for snacks.
- If you like jelly and jam, try the low-sugar versions.
- If you really need to eat cookies, stay away from the worst offenders: chocolate chip, chocolate covered, or sandwich-style. Try plain graham crackers, ginger snaps, or vanilla wafers instead.
- Eat fresh fruit instead of canned, whenever possible.
- If you do eat canned fruit, make sure it's packed in fruit juice or water instead of syrup.
- Cut back on sugar-laden desserts, prepared sweet baked goods, ice cream, and other sweets.
- Instead of frosted layer cake, try plain angel food cake with fresh fruit.

Sugar-containing foods and drinks

Most of the sugar in our diets doesn't come from the sugar bowl or even desserts. It's hidden in a wide array of foods, including things such as ketchup, salad dressing, and barbeque sauce. Be aware of the sugar content of foods and limit your intake, particularly in the morning.

In addition, refined foods such as white bread, white rice, instant potatoes, or cornflakes can act like sugar in the system because the body quickly breaks them down into glucose. Therefore, it's wise to treat these foods as if they were straight sugar and eat them only in conjunction with high-protein, high-fiber foods that slow the release of glucose into the bloodstream.

The many faces of sugar

Although sugar is sometimes listed as such on food labels, most of the time it isn't listed simply as "sugar." Sugar hides in processed foods under a number of different names, including the following:

- Brown sugar
- Concentrated fruit juice
- Corn syrup
- Dextrose
- Fructose
- Glucose
- High fructose corn syrup
- Honey
- Lactose
- Maltodextrin
- Maltose
- Molasses
- Raw sugar
- Sucrose

If one of these sugar additives is listed in the first four ingredients on the label (which means it's one of the main ingredients), be assured that this is a high-sugar food. Look for a healthier, low-sugar alternative.

You can undoubtedly think of many other ways to lower your sugar intake; these suggestions are just a start. The important thing is to become aware of the massive amounts of sugar that are currently in many of our foods, and find pleasant, doable ways to scale back your intake. You can do much to improve good mood just by eating less refined sugar.

Stress and Depression

Another factor implicated in depression is stress. Stress is a perfectly normal response to the difficulties life throws our way. It's normal. In fact, millions of years ago the body developed a set response to stress that prepares us to either fight or flee in order to protect ourselves from a stressor. This stress response involves a rapid reordering of body processes: Blood is shunted to the muscles, the blood-clotting mechanism is "put on alert" in case we're injured, fat and glucose are released into the bloodstream to "feed" the muscles, the pupils dilate, and other changes occur that are designed to turn us instantly into a fighting and/or running machine.

In days past, the stressor was often a large and hungry animal, or perhaps an enemy soldier, intent on killing or capturing us. In such situations, a massive, all-out physical response to allow us to fight or run like heck made sense, for the stakes were high and the price of failure was great. It didn't matter that repeatedly triggering the side effect damaged the immune system and otherwise harmed the body over time, for surviving the immediate threat was much more important.

Today, however, stress is rarely a matter of life or death. Yes, there are times we have to jump out of the way of an oncoming car, or we may be physically attacked, but most modern stress comes in the form of chronic psychological or social conflicts. Unfortunately, our bodies haven't adapted to modern society by developing a softer stress response more appropriate to twenty-first-century life—and less damaging to the body. Thus, millions of people are unknowingly harming their bodies and setting the stage for emotional distress by repeatedly triggering the stress response.

The best solution is to learn how to control the response to ensure that it is not turned on every time you get upset. The best way to prevent a full-blown fight-or-flight response is to simply say "no"; tell yourself that there is no one to fight and nowhere to run, and it's not worth the damage to your mind and body to trigger the stress response.

There are many ways we can learn to develop control over our emotions and the fight-or-flight response, including practicing relaxation techniques, psychotherapy, meditating, and "burning off" anger and energy by exercising. (I talk more about this in Chapter 19.)

I am not alone in advocating for stress reduction in our busy, complicated lives. In her book, *The SuperStress Solution*, Roberta Lee, MD, vice chair of the Department of Integrative Medicine at Beth Israel Medical Center, describes a four-week approach to building stress resistance and resilience. Lee emphasizes nutrition, sleep, and exercise as fundamentals to combat stress and to restore physical and mental balance.

There's not enough room in this chapter—or indeed the entire book—to discuss all that we need to do to ensure a healthy body. But if you make sure you're getting eight hours of good, quality sleep every night, adopt a health-enhancing diet, and keep your stress to a minimum, you've gone a long way toward developing the good physical health that supports good emotional health.

8

H – Hormones

Chapter 7 covers physical contributors to depression that you can control by making lifestyle changes: sleep problems, poor diet, and stress. The second element in THE ZEEBrA approach is H for hormone. Hormone disturbances are an often missed and hidden factor contributing to depression.

Fatigue, dry skin, high cholesterol, constipation, irregular periods, and acne: Any of these, and many more physical problems, may be the overlooked clue that explains why someone is depressed and why standard antidepressant treatment fails, no matter how many medicines are prescribed.

The link between these seemingly unrelated problems and depression is hormones, those substances produced by the body to regulate certain cells and organs. Some hormones, such as testosterone and estrogen, are well known, while others toil in obscurity. But whether popular or not, many hormones can affect mood. Psychiatrists often overlook the link between depression and certain hormones, despite published studies indicating that everybody being evaluated or treated for depression should have their hormone levels checked.

If a particular hormone level is low, the treatment options are to replace it with either a synthetic (manufactured), natural (animal-based), or bioidentical (exact match) hormone. Because some hormones such as melatonin and DHEA are considered safe, they can be sold over the counter. Other hormones, such as testosterone and estrogen, require a physician's prescription. Hormone replacement therapies are controversial and understudied. You will want to learn about each option and weigh in on your treatment plan, if necessary. Hormone replacement therapy is not necessarily the solution for everyone.

In the meantime, it's important to understand how disturbances in the levels of a few key hormones can set the stage for depression.

The Thyroid and Depression

The thyroid is a small gland, shaped something like a butterfly, that wraps around the voice box and windpipe (larynx and trachea). It has several duties, including controlling the heart and respiratory rates, but it doesn't do these things on its own. Instead, the thyroid sends out hormones, or chemical messengers, that tell other parts of the body what to do. In fact, every cell in the body depends on adequate levels of thyroid hormones.

I like to think of the thyroid as the manager of a large factory, constantly barking out orders—telling this department to speed up and that one to slow down, ordering that a certain machine be left on longer than planned and another one be turned off a little sooner than expected. This manager has to be aware of everything that is happening in the factory, to understand how to keep everything humming along, and to be able to give commands at a moment's notice. Should it falter, even a little, things start to go wrong.

The thyroid communicates with the rest of the body via hormones such as thyroxine (T_4) and triiodothyronine (T_3). The chief communication problems that can arise are either too little hormone production, called hypothyroidism, or too much, called hyperthyroidism. Thyroid hormones are responsible for regulating body metabolism and are critical for the production of cellular energy.

Hypothyroidism and hyperthyroidism don't trigger a specific disease that is obviously linked to thyroid problems, the way that the measles virus causes measles or the way damage to certain parts of the liver

Symptoms of Low Thyroid Levels (Hypothyroidism)

Depression	Acne
Anxiety	Eczema
Memory and concentration problems	Hair loss
Low libido	Recurrent infections
Constipation	Irregular menstrual periods
Elevated cholesterol	Severe premenstrual syndrome
Gum disease	Ovarian cysts
Obesity	Endometriosis
Hypoglycemia (low blood sugar)	Fluid retention
Muscle aches and pains	Fatigue
Dry skin	Intolerance to cold
	Diminished sweat production

triggers type 1 diabetes. Instead, hypo- and hyperthyroidism trigger a variety of symptoms that often seem unrelated to the thyroid and to each other. Therefore it may take some time for the real problem to be diagnosed. In the case of hypothyroidism, as much as 50 percent of sufferers are never diagnosed at all. And many of those who are diagnosed are not provided with adequate treatment. This is a shame, for even a modest imbalance of thyroid hormones can set the stage for depression.

Low thyroid and depression

Doctors have known for years that the symptoms of low thyroid include depression and fatigue, which often clear up if the thyroid problem is properly treated.

> Janet, a forty-three-year-old teacher, insisted that she be checked out for "something" medical. For two years she had tried many antidepressants without relief from her depression. Coinciding with her persistent depression was slow-but-steady weight gain (including "puffiness" in the face) and acne. As she suspected, her thyroid was running in low gear and not producing enough hormone, and as she had hoped, her symptoms began disappearing soon after she started taking thyroid hormone.

A proponent of the thyroid-depression connection is Dr. Mark Starr, author of *Hypothyroidism Type 2: The Epidemic*. In his comprehensive book he describes the relationship between low thyroid function and many chronic health conditions, including depression.

Most doctors and psychiatrists are aware of the thyroid-depression link, yet the thyroid levels of most depressed patients go unchecked. Many patients referred to me for evaluation and treatment of depression have not had their thyroid levels checked, and far too many patients who make their way to my office were told that they do not have thyroid disease because of a single blood test.

Faulty testing equals faulty diagnosis

Even when doctors and psychiatrists do check the thyroid, they are generally misled by the rather unreliable thyroid test most of them use.

A doctor who suspects a thyroid problem does not check the levels of thyroid hormone directly, measuring the amount of T_3 and T_4 in the bloodstream. Instead, an indirect measurement is made. The standard thyroid test is the TSH, or thyroid-stimulating hormone test. TSH is a hormone, released by a part of the brain called the pituitary gland, which tells the thyroid gland that the body needs more thyroid hormones. TSH acts like a message to the factory manager, requesting either "More production!" or "Less production!"

The TSH test measures the amount of TSH circulating in the blood. In a sense, the test asks the question: To what extent does the pituitary think the body needs more thyroid hormone? If the TSH level is high, doctors reason, it must mean there are lots of requests for more thyroid hormone, and this, in turn, must mean that the thyroid is not pumping out enough hormone. Thus, the person with a high TSH is suffering from low thyroid production, or hypothyroidism.

On the other hand, if the TSH level is too low, according to medical theory, it must mean that the cells and organs aren't requesting much thyroid hormone—not even routine amounts—and this, in turn, "proves" that the thyroid is hyperactive, pouring out too much hormone.

And if the TSH "request for hormone" level is considered just right (in the optimal range of 0.4–4.5 milli-international units per liter [mIU/L]) everything must be okay. In short, a high TSH request means the thyroid is putting out too little hormone; a low TSH request means the thyroid is pumping out too much; and a moderate TSH request means the thyroid gland is working well.

This makes perfect sense, until you realize it's built on the never-tested assumption that the body always requests the right amount of thyroid hormone. But suppose the pituitary gland gets it wrong and requests too little or too much thyroid hormone? Every physician understands that human physiology can easily get out of tune and do too much or too little of something: Why don't we ever question whether the pituitary's request for more or less thyroid hormone is off-kilter? Why automatically assume that the request is exactly right and that the thyroid gland is not malfunctioning?

In addition to the possibility that the pituitary may make the wrong request, there's also the prospect that the thyroid can be sending out enough thyroid hormone, but for some reason the body isn't able to use it properly. This is similar to what happens with type 2 diabetes: The pancreas secretes adequate amounts of insulin to control blood sugar, but the body's cells aren't able to respond properly to that insulin. More and more insulin must be released over and above the "proper" amount, until the cells, flooded with insulin, finally respond. Could it be that the thyroid is producing what seems like an ample amount of hormone, but the body can't use it properly and keeps requesting more? If that's the case, the pituitary gland looks at the amount of thyroid hormone in the blood, decides that all is well, and does not request an increase, even though the cells are screaming for more.

There's another problem: How much TSH is normal and healthy? Remember, either too much or too little TSH suggests the thyroid is not functioning properly. But what's "just right"? Although the TSH test has been popular since the 1960s, no one has yet scientifically demonstrated what the healthy TSH level or range should be. The truth is, we're just guessing.

Many integrative medicine physicians actually consider a TSH level of more than 2.5 mIU/L (remember, the upper limit of the optimal range is 4.5 mIU/L) to be an accurate reflection of sluggish thyroid function. I've seen many patients with "normal" TSH levels who were clearly suffering from hypothyroidism, or lack of thyroid hormone. I remember well forty-three-year-old Jane who came to see me because of a "mild depression that started slowly a year or so ago," as she put it.

Jane had already been to her family practitioner, who tested her TSH and found it was normal. As I spoke with Jane I learned that she was suffering from depression, fatigue, elevated cholesterol, constipation, acne, and dry skin. Her depression and fatigue were indistinguishable to her. These problems can all arise if there isn't enough thyroid hormone in the body.

I also noted that Jane reported that she was always cold. So I ordered tests of her T_3 and T_4, finding that they were indeed on the low side. I referred Jane to an integrative medicine physician who treated her with replacement hormones. This treatment resolved Jane's depression and solved her skin and constipation problems, saving her the frustration of going on one antidepressant after another without relief.

With these three built-in complicating factors—the assumptions that the TSH "request level" is always correct, that the body can use all the thyroid hormone properly, and that we actually know how much is enough—it's possible that many people's thyroid problems are misdiagnosed on the basis of the TSH test. And it's likely that many people suffering from depression who might respond to thyroid hormone replacement are not offered this treatment.

Correcting thyroid levels to relieve depression

The concept of treating low thyroid hormone levels by introducing more thyroid hormone is not new. Studies investigating the use of thyroid hormone to treat depression began in the late 1960s. In one of these early studies, depressed patients were given the antidepressant medicine imipramine along with either T_3 or a placebo. Those taking the antidepressant plus T_3 in this double-blind study enjoyed a faster and more substantial recovery than those taking the antidepressant plus placebo, indicating that replacing missing thyroid hormone helped relieve depression. A 1996 meta-analysis, or summary analysis, which used statistical means to combine the results of eight different studies, found that T_3 effectively increased the improvements seen with antidepressants given for treatment-resistant depression. Other studies have supported these findings.

It always fascinates me that psychiatrists have been using T_3 as a hormone strategy for treating depression, yet most other physicians use only T_4.

I believe that everyone who is depressed, or is being evaluated for depression, should be checked for a thyroid deficiency. Testing should go beyond simply the TSH test, which is insufficient and can be misleading. Patients should find a physician who is knowledgeable about a comprehensive integrative approach that includes evaluating all symptoms of thyroid deficiency, measuring the basal metabolic temperature, and testing the levels of T_3 and T_4 in the blood. If there's an indication of hypothyroidism, I recommend thyroid replacement therapy with T_3 and T_4. I have consistently seen results with the addition of natural desiccated thyroid replacement therapy that includes T_3 and T_4.

Special note on the thyroid and iodine

The thyroid uses iodine to create thyroid hormones, which means that an iodine deficiency can result in thyroid deficiency.

In areas where diets are low in iodine, people are more likely to suffer from goiter, which is a tremendously swollen thyroid gland that makes the neck bulge out like a little tire sitting on the shoulders. People whose diets are low in iodine are also more likely to suffer from the stunted mental and physical growth called cretinism, which arises when a pregnant woman deficient in iodine gives birth to a child with a congenital deficiency of thyroid hormones.

Iodine deficiency used to be a major problem in the northwestern United States, in Appalachia, and in the Great Lakes region, which were once known collectively as the "goiter belt." Since the addition of iodine to salt, the problem was thought to have largely disappeared in the United States. However, the problem persists, and may lead to subclinical hypothyroidism, a "minor" version of the disease that's hard to detect because blood test results are still within the normal range.

Other nutrients, including tyrosine, zinc, and iron, are necessary for the thyroid gland and its hormones to function properly. If the Standard American Diet continues to stay away from naturally grown, nutritious foods and to eat processed, refined foods devoid of trace minerals, thyroid problems are likely to increase. Some researchers describe an epidemic of thyroid disease in this country. This is not just because of nutritional deficiencies but also because of toxins rampant in our environment.

Environmental toxins interfere with thyroid function

Scientists and medical professionals are increasingly aware of the dangers posed by exposure to environmental toxins. These toxins seep into our bodies through the water, food, and air supply often in such benign-looking objects as a plastic water bottle, a baby's teething ring, or air fresheners. Despite the innocent appeal of that water bottle, mounting evidence has shown that prolonged, chronic exposure to these toxins can wreak havoc on our endocrine and nervous systems.

The thyroid, part of the endocrine system, is particularly vulnerable to environmental toxin exposure. Some specific environmental toxins, including polychlorinated biphenyls, dioxins, phthalates, polybrominated diphenyl ethers (PBDEs), and other halogenated organochlorines, have been shown to affect thyroid function. These chemicals interfere with the production, transportation, and metabolism of thyroid hormones. These chemicals disrupt our bodies through a vast number of mechanisms, but commonly many of these chemicals use their structural similarity to thyroid hormone to interfere with its normal function. Their similar appearance to thyroid hormone allows them to bind to thyroid receptors and to effectively change the way the thyroid normally functions.

The best way to avoid toxin damage to the thyroid is to limit exposure to environmental toxins by:

- using natural cleaning products when available;
- limiting exposure to pesticides, insect repellants, air fresheners, or any other aerosol chemical product;
- eating organic foods;
- using glass, ceramic, or metal containers for food storage.

I can't emphasize enough how important it is to check for thyroid deficiency. A few blood tests, a comprehensive history, and a physical examination more than outweigh the money and time lost on wasted trials with antidepressants that can't work because they're not resolving the real problem: an inadequate supply of thyroid hormone.

DHEA and Depression

Dehydroepiandrosterone (DHEA) is a hormone produced by the adrenal glands. It has several functions on its own and is also used by the body to manufacture testosterone and estrogen. The body's production of DHEA rises to its highest level in a person's midtwenties and slowly declines as the years pass.

DHEA is the most abundant steroid hormone used by the body. Like all steroid hormones, DHEA is made from the often-maligned cholesterol molecule. Without adequate cholesterol you cannot maintain adequate levels of DHEA or other steroid hormones. (Low cholesterol is addressed further in Chapter 11.) When under stress, the adrenal glands increase the production of hormones, including DHEA. After DHEA is secreted into the bloodstream it changes chemically in the liver into DHEA-sulfate (DHEA-S). DHEA-S is the form that is measured and monitored in the blood.

DHEA has been used as an antiaging supplement, with its proponents arguing that putting more DHEA into the body increases the production of sex hormones, strengthens the immune system, and otherwise helps keep us young. This is still a controversial concept.

A different line of research has looked into the use of DHEA as a treatment for depression. In a 1999 study published in *Biological Psychiatry*, researchers tested the effects of DHEA in fifteen people who had developed midlife depression. The results were impressive, with 60 percent of those receiving DHEA responding to treatment, compared to only 20 percent of those who got the placebo responding. (It's expected that 20 percent or more of people in any depression study will respond to a placebo. Thus, a new treatment is typically compared to a placebo to make sure it's really effective and significantly more effective than a placebo.) A similar study, published in the *Archives of General Psychiatry* in 2005, also found that DHEA was an "effective treatment for midlife-onset of major and minor depression."

The results of these and other studies make sense when you consider that DHEA levels are lower in adults suffering from major depression than they are in their nondepressed peers.

Although DHEA is not a magic bullet for depression, and should only be taken under the supervision of a physician skilled in its use, it can be a helpful treatment for patients with low levels of DHEA-S.

Psychiatry is constantly caught in the search for a magic pill. Even though some research has shed a little light on the relationship between DHEA and depression, there is clearly little acknowledgment of the core concept of THE ZEEBrA approach and biochemical individuality. DHEA is a perfect example of the search for physiological imbalances leading to individualized treatments for patients suffering from depression. If a simple blood test reflects low levels of DHEA-S, then careful supplementation is indicated. If blood levels are optimal, then supplementation is not likely to be beneficial. I recommend a relatively low dose: 5–10 mg for women and 10–25 mg for men. These doses raise DHEA levels. I have also repeatedly seen improvement in mood as well as allergies, elevated cholesterol, headaches, and fibromyalgia symptoms with DHEA supplementation.

Sex Hormones and Depression

An article published in the *Archives of General Psychiatry* in 2008 described how low levels of testosterone can cause depression in older men. Health professionals had long known about the complicated relationship between female sex hormones and mood, but this new study was one of the few major research studies to link male hormones to depression.

Testosterone

Australian researchers looked at 3,987 men ranging in age from seventy-one to eighty-nine, assessing their moods and levels of free testosterone. (Some of the testosterone in the bloodstream is bound to other substances, while the rest is unbound, or "free." It's the free testosterone that's biologically active.) The men were placed in five different groups according to their free testosterone levels. The researchers found that those in the lowest testosterone group were almost twice as likely to be depressed as those in the group with the highest testosterone levels.

In 2003, researchers from Harvard Medical School's McLean Hospital tested the effects of testosterone in middle-aged men (ages thirty to sixty-five), who had both depression that did not respond to standard antidepressant treatment and low or borderline low testosterone levels. The twenty-three men in the study kept taking their prescribed antidepressant medicines, but half were also given a testosterone gel to rub directly onto the skin, while the other half were given a placebo gel. The results were impressive. Those using the testosterone gel had significantly greater improvements in their depression scores measured by standard depression scales than those using the placebo gel.

This was a small study, but it suggested that testosterone may relieve depression (either by itself or in combination with standard antidepressant medicines) when used in men who have low testosterone levels. And as the researchers pointed out, there is a "large and probably under-recognized population of depressed men with low testosterone levels."

These and other studies do not mean that testosterone is a magic antidepressant. Instead, they suggest that

- low testosterone levels are linked to depression;
- in some men, depression cannot be relieved until testosterone is raised to a normal level;
- antidepressants cannot raise testosterone to a normal level, which helps explain why they do not help some men.

Therefore, it is critical to check the testosterone levels of depressed male patients at any age. If they are low or borderline low, I try to understand the physiological factors that may be playing a role. I've been surprised numerous times at the low levels I've seen in many patients, including some men in their thirties and forties.

Rather than prescribing testosterone immediately, I have had success with natural means to raise the level of hormone by having patients

- monitor zinc levels which are important for testosterone synthesis;
- exercise regularly to strengthen muscles, which help the body keep testosterone levels up;
- reduce stress to reduce cortisol, a stress-induced hormone that can encourage the breakdown of muscles and thus reduce testosterone levels;
- cut back or avoid soy and other foods containing large amounts of phytoestrogens, which can "counteract" testosterone;
- eat plenty of the omega-3 fatty acids known as EPA and DHA found in salmon and other cold-water fish. The body can use essential fats to produce testosterone and other hormones;
- monitor cholesterol and DHEA levels, which are required for the synthesis of testosterone;
- try tribulus supplementation, an herb that enhances testosterone synthesis.

If natural means of raising testosterone are not sufficient, then I would refer patients for hormone therapy. Hormone therapy should be done under the supervision of an endocrinologist, a physician who specializes in the endocrine glands that produce hormones. The endocrinologist can rule out a pituitary gland tumor or another disease that may be interfering with testosterone production and monitor the effects of the additional testosterone. This is important, for some of the side effects of testosterone use can be harmful, including headaches, gum pain and swelling, breast growth, changes in the size and shape of the testicles, nausea, depression, and dizziness.

Estrogen and progesterone

There's no doubt that the female hormones estrogen and progesterone influence mood: Many women can sense the changes as they move through their menstrual cycle and again as they approach and go through menopause. Hormonal influences on mood in women are much more complex than they are in men, and there is no simple formula such as "more estrogen = less depression in certain women." Instead, the key is to balance the hormone levels, a tricky process that should only be done under the supervision of an endocrinologist.

There is considerable controversy around hormone replacement therapy for women. Conventional hormone replacement therapy with synthetic hormones was the standard of care until studies conducted by the Women's Health Initiative, a fifteen-year research program involving forty medical centers and more than one hundred sixty-thousand women across the country, received national attention. The Women's Health Initiative was created to address health concerns in postmenopausal women. Most notable was its study of estrogen plus progestin hormone therapy in postmenopausal women. The study was abruptly ended three years prematurely as the clinicians involved in the study concluded that the risks of the therapy outweighed the benefits. On the combination hormone therapy, women experienced increased risks of invasive breast cancer, coronary heart disease, stroke, and pulmonary embolism when compared to women taking only placebo pills.

Due to these concerns, I have consistently found natural hormones preferable to synthetic. Although there are few research studies supporting the benefits of natural hormones, the potential side effects of synthetic hormones far outweigh the benefits. Like all nutritional or natural therapies, further research on natural and bioidentical hormone therapy is unlikely as this type of treatment is not patentable and therefore, will not generate large profits for pharmaceutical companies. Make sure you work with a trusted practitioner experienced in the use of natural or bioidentical hormones before considering any tpye of hormone replacement therapy.

In Summary

Hormones such as DHEA, estrogen, progesterone, testosterone, and thyroid have widespread and powerful influences in the body. Our traditional means of testing and treating hormone imbalances are not always accurate or useful. Studies have shown that the judicious use of hormones can help relieve depression in certain people, which is why I urge physicians to check hormone levels in every patient with depression. (See Resources for help finding physicians trained in the use of natural or bioidentical hormone therapies.)

9

E – Exclude

In some cases, finding relief from depression involves not just adding medications, exercise, sleep, or supplements but removing substances from the diet. In the ZEEBrA approach, *exclude* refers to eliminating certain foods that lead to digestive disorders, which can cause or exacerbate depression. Altering the diet isn't very high-tech or glamorous in the growing numbers of patients with celiac disease or food intolerances and food allergies but improvement in depression can be dramatic. When the underlying connection between diet and depression is ignored, there is little hope for relief with antidepressants.

Depression is a multifaceted disorder, and a thorough assessment should include digestive issues. If they are present, they must be resolved before treatment for depression will be effective. Common digestive disorders contributing to depression include celiac disease, difficulties with incompletely digested proteins such as casomorphin and gliadorphin, and food allergies and intolerances.

Celiac Disease and Depression

Once considered a relatively uncommon problem afflicting young children, celiac disease is now recognized as a serious ailment that can strike at any age. It afflicts about 1 in 130 Americans, or about 2.25 million people. It begins as a "bad reaction" to a certain component of wheat and develops into a self-destructive assault on our digestive system, but the effects of celiac disease are not limited to the gastrointestinal system. The health consequences of celiac disease may affect every organ system, including the brain. In a depressed person with celiac disease, depression can only be resolved when the celiac disease is treated.

In celiac disease, the body mistakenly decides that a protein called gluten, found in wheat, rye, and barley, is a dangerous toxin. Responding just as it would to harmful bacteria, virus, or other invader, the immune system sets out to destroy the gluten. That by itself is not too bad, for humans can live quite well without any gluten at all. Unfortunately, in the battle to destroy gluten, the immune system heavily damages the surrounding area, the small intestine. Like the buildings and fields where a real-life war takes place, the small intestine can be so badly damaged that it cannot do its job of absorbing nutrients. Unable to properly break down food into component parts that can be absorbed into the bloodstream, the small intestine lets vitamins A, B_6, B_{12}, D, E, and K, as well as folic acid, and minerals such as iron, zinc, magnesium, and calcium, pass right through the bowels and out of the body. Essential fats, as well as tryptophan and other essential amino acids, are also poorly absorbed.

The intestinal damage can cause first-wave symptoms that arise soon after eating, including abdominal cramps and distention, pain, gas, and vomiting. Second-wave symptoms include diarrhea and constipation. These first- and second-wave symptoms can be so disagreeable in some people that they try to eat as little as possible, potentially leading to serious malnutrition and weight loss.

A college student suffered from abdominal distention, pain, and constipation so severe that she was literally afraid to eat. Her family physician and the psychiatrist to whom she was referred diagnosed anorexia. But no matter how much she protested that "eating makes me physically hurt," they kept referring her to mental health professionals for eating-disorder treatment. When she was sent to me for a second opinion I determined that she had celiac disease with multiple nutritional deficiencies related to this disease. With the elimination of gluten from her diet she was able to return to college and restore weight.

Patients with celiac disease can develop a bewildering variety of third-wave problems that may not heal. Although these problems may appear to be entirely unrelated, they are all linked to the intestinal damage that makes it difficult to absorb various nutrients. No matter how much food the person eats, he is always malnourished, lacking certain essential nutrients. Depending on which ones are missing, the results can include problems such as the following:

- Anemia
- Anorexia
- Arthritis
- Dermatitis herpetiformis (blistered, itchy skin rash)
- Edema (swelling caused fluid retention)
- Fatigue
- Infertility
- Joint pain and inflammation
- Migraine headaches
- Missed menstrual periods
- Numbness and tingling of the hands and feet
- Osteoporosis
- Seizures and other neurological problems
- Stunted growth
- Tooth decay and discoloration

If the absorption of zinc, tryptophan, the B vitamins, or certain other nutrients necessary for mental health is hindered, the result may be depression and/or anxiety. These nutrients are necessary to create essential chemicals in the brain such as serotonin, a deficiency of which has been linked to depression. The relationship between celiac disease and depression is common in children: One study found that adolescents with celiac disease had a 31 percent risk of developing a major depressive episode, compared to a 7 percent risk in healthy children.

The difficulty with diagnosis

Researchers have long been aware of a connection between celiac disease and depression. Research articles and studies on the two have been published in the scientific literature for years. Reports of depression among celiac disease patients appeared in the 1980s, and in 1982 Swedish researchers reported that "depressive psychopathology is a feature of adult celiac disease and may be a consequence of malabsorption." A 1998 study reported that about one-third of those with celiac disease also suffer from depression. More recently, a 2007 study compared 13,776 people suffering from celiac disease to 66,815 controls who did not. This study found that celiac disease was "positively associated" with subsequent depression, with approximately 40 percent of those with celiac disease developing depression.

Different studies report slightly different statistical conclusions regarding the numbers of celiac disease patients who are also depressed, but the point is clear: There is an association between depression and celiac disease and it is critical to assess for and treat celiac disease among depressed patients. The celiac-depression link is not often discussed or well known among psychiatrists and mental health professionals.

The symptoms triggered by celiac disease vary widely from patient to patient. Variations may depend on how strongly the immune system reacts to gluten, how much intestinal damage has occurred, which part of the intestines have been harmed, the overall quality of the diet, any coexisting physical or psychiatric disorders, as well as any treatment the patient has received. Neither antidepressants nor other medicines can halt or cure celiac disease. Often medications may exacerbate other nutrient absorption problems, making the situation worse.

Take the case of Larry, a twenty-five-year-old physical therapist who began our first meeting together by announcing that he had been diagnosed with attention-deficit/hyperactivity disorder (ADHD), anxiety, and bipolar disorder. Over the past five years he had taken more than ten different medications without any relief from his symptoms. When I saw Larry he was taking several medications, including Adderall, a stimulant, three times a day for attention problems; Xanax, a tranquilizer to treat the anxiety from the Adderall; and Seroquel, an antipsychotic to help him sleep.

During my first meeting with Larry I noticed he was deficient in iron. A twenty-five-year-old male who routinely eats meat should not be deficient in iron. Further blood testing and later a biopsy confirmed celiac disease. It took almost two years, but Larry is no longer taking any psychiatric medications and no longer has three psychiatric diagnoses. Larry's symptoms of irritability, anxiety, and insomnia had been managed with medications, but nobody sought the true cause. If we find the cause, which in this case was celiac disease, then we can better direct our treatment and in some cases find a cure.

It is easy to confuse celiac disease with anorexia, a disease that makes its victims—typically girls and women—believe that they are horribly fat and refuse to eat, even as they literally waste away. Both diseases attack nearly every organ and organ system of the body, causing overlapping symptoms such as the following:

- Abdominal pain
- Anemia
- Arthritis
- Behavioral changes
- Bowel gas
- Constipation
- Depression
- Diarrhea
- Fatigue
- Irritability
- Joint pain
- Memory loss
- Mood swings
- Osteoporosis
- Reproductive issues (infertility and miscarriages)
- Skin lesions
- Weakness
- Weight loss

It's also possible to have celiac disease without any gastrointestinal symptoms at all; no bloating, pain, gas, diarrhea, or other obvious indicators that something is wrong in the intestines. This makes the diagnosis even more difficult, even when the patient carefully lists each and every symptom for the doctor. As soon as a physician hears "migraines," "tingling of the hand," "difficulty conceiving," "arthritis," "skin rash," or any number of other symptoms, he or she likely refers the patient to a specialist. This is helpful for most people, but can be harmful for those with celiac disease because it may send them down the wrong track, with the neurologist searching for a brain or nervous system explanation for migraines or tingling, the fertility specialist looking for a sex-organ-based reason for infertility, and so on. Each specialist prescribes the latest treatments for problems related to their specialty, but these only temporarily relieve symptoms, or don't work at all, because the underlying problem is not being addressed—an intolerance to gluten.

Making the diagnosis

Diagnosing celiac disease is difficult, which is why the disease is often misdiagnosed as anorexia nervosa, chronic fatigue syndrome, diverticulitis, IBS (irritable bowel syndrome), Crohn's disease, or simply iron-deficiency anemia. Perhaps it's most important for a doctor to be aware of the diverse and often confusing symptoms of celiac disease. Otherwise, he might send a patient to several different specialists and the celiac disease is "chopped up" into several different disease categories, each of which is considered an entity unto itself instead of part of a whole.

Once celiac disease is suspected, a doctor can look for elevated levels of antibodies such as anti-gliadin, anti-endomysial, and anti-tissue transglutaminase. These are specialized proteins the immune system manufactures to "tag" gluten as the enemy so that it might be easily identified by the fighting cells of the body's internal defense system. A simple blood test reveals the presence of antibodies to gluten, which suggests the possibility of celiac disease. However, the only way to make a definitive diagnosis is to perform an endoscopy (insertion of a narrow, flexible tube into the intestines) and snip out a small piece of the intestinal lining for examination in the laboratory. Performing this can confirm the diagnosis of celiac disease and reveal the extent of damage to the intestines.

Managing the disease

There is no treatment for celiac disease—no medicine, vitamin, surgery, or procedure that can eliminate the disease and the damage it has already caused. Over time, the intestinal damage heals, if the body is able to restore adequate nutritional support.

Although celiac disease cannot be treated, it can be managed. And the way to do that is to stop eating all foods containing gluten, including wheat, rye, and barley, and anything made from them. Eliminating these items would be challenging enough for many people, but the task is more complex than that because gluten, used as a thickening and stabilizing agent, shows up in many foods. Obvious ones include the following:

- Baking mixes
- Beer
- Bread
- Cakes and pies
- Pretzels
- Cereal
- Cookies/crackers
- Pastries

- Doughnuts
- Muffins
- Pasta

A number of not-so-obvious foods that contain gluten include the following:

- Ice cream
- Ketchup
- Soy sauce
- Licorice
- Sauces (thickened with flour)
- Salad dressings
- Chutneys and pickles
- Instant cocoa
- Processed meats
- Meat substitutes (e.g., vegetarian burgers, nuggets, etc.)
- Spices (with anti-caking agents)

Other foods, such as oats, must be avoided because they may accidentally be contaminated with gluten if they are processed in the same factory as gluten foods. Even some lipsticks and lip glosses contain gluten.

Vegetables, fruits, and meat are gluten free, so they can be eaten without restriction. A number of grains and starch sources are acceptable, including rice, potatoes, corn, and tapioca. Gram flour made from chickpeas is also free of gluten; but gram flour should not be confused with graham flour (as in graham crackers), which is made from wheat.

As people are learning how to eat gluten free, it's a good idea to assume that all processed and packaged foods contain gluten until proven otherwise. Sometimes the label specifically mentions gluten, while other times the gluten comes in forms such as glucose syrup, malt flavoring, vegetable protein, vegetable starch, and modified food starch. Gluten in food is often not on the label, which only includes the ingredients, not gluten that may be used in the manufacturing process. It's in the manufacturing process that gluten from one food may work its way into another food.

I advise patients to look for foods that are specifically labeled as being gluten free. Ideally, this means the food contains no gluten, none was added during processing, the food was processed and packaged in gluten-free facilities that do not handle any foods containing gluten or with added gluten, and the packages are carefully sealed to ensure that no gluten gets in during shipping or storage.

There are, however, problems with the current labeling regulations that allow some gluten to remain in certain foods and allow manufacturers to determine how safe their foods are. So, even a product labeled "gluten-free" may contain some gluten.

If you have celiac disease, eliminating gluten is the only way to stop ongoing damage to your intestines and to give your body the opportunity to heal.

Supplements for celiac disease

Unless a person is diagnosed with celiac disease very early on, there's a good chance that he or she has nutritional deficiencies. That's why I recommend nutritional supplements to replace nutrients the body needs. This includes taking at least a multivitamin with iron, EFAs, and digestive enzymes. Testing commonly reveals individual needs for further supplementation, including iron, folate, magnesium, and amino acids (see Chapter 16).

In addition, 1–3 g of omega-3 fatty acids such as EPA and DHA can help reduce intestinal inflammation and assist healing.

You can do it!

I've seen people do remarkably well once their celiac disease was diagnosed and they began a gluten-free diet. The physical symptoms that accompany eating often vanish, and many other problems resolve or begin to improve. The fatigue that is often coupled with celiac-related depression typically vanishes, as well.

Just as I encourage every patient with depression to be tested for celiac disease, I also encourage physicians to evaluate depressed patients for the presence of two peptides, casomorphin and gliadorphin.

Casomorphin and Gliadorphin and Depression

Before the body can absorb food, it must break it down into tiny snippets that are digestible and recognized by the immune system as being safe. The breakdown process begins as food is chewed and continues as enzymes in the stomach attack the food. In order for these enzymes to work, there must be plenty of stomach acid available to activate the enzymes.

After the partially digested food moves from the stomach to the small intestine, the acid is neutralized, and different enzymes continue to cleave the food into smaller and smaller pieces, releasing amino acids, vitamins, fatty acids, and other components of the food so they can pass through the intestinal wall and into the blood vessels embedded in the intestinal wall. By the time protein from food reaches the bloodstream, it has been broken down into peptides, which are particles composed of only ten to twenty amino acids that the body can reconfigure and recombine to create larger molecules, neurotransmitters, hormones, and more.

Although it may seem simple, the digestion-absorption process is complex and absolutely dependent on the presence of just the right amount of stomach acid, numerous enzymes, and other factors. Should there be a problem with any of them, the process is impaired. If, for example, there isn't enough stomach acid to activate the stomach enzymes, or if the acid isn't strong enough, food may pass from the stomach to the small intestines partially undigested. If the intestinal wall has been damaged, even properly digested nutrients may not be absorbed.

In some cases, problems arise due to the incomplete digestion of proteins that still manage to pass into the body. This is what happens when people are unable to completely digest the protein called casein, which is found in milk, cheese, and other milk products, and gluten, which comes from wheat, rye, barley, and certain other grains. Casein is disassembled into a substance called casomorphin, and gluten is broken down into gliadorphin. Casomorphin and gliadorphin are products of incomplete breakdown, that have been "processed" enough to slip into the body, but once inside, they can behave in unfortunate ways.

Both casomorphin and gliadorphin are morphine analogs. This means they are chemically similar to morphine and may trigger morphinelike effects in the body. We don't fully understand how these two substances function in the body, but it has been theorized that they cross the blood-brain barrier and interact with parts of the brain that control behavior and feelings.

Casomorphin and gliadorphin were first found in higher concentrations in the urine of patients with autism. Other research has linked the incomplete digestion of these proteins and related neuropeptides to a variety of ailments, including ADHD, childhood psychosis, dyslexia, Down syndrome, celiac disease, postpartum psychosis, Rett's disease, and severe depression. The appearance of excess peptides in people with a range of psychiatric disorders has led some researchers to speculate that these peptides are unique carriers of information in the brain that may exacerbate many psychiatric disorders.

Levels of casomorphin and gliadorphin rise because of a deficiency or inadequate functioning of an enzyme called *DPP* IV (dipeptidyl peptidase IV), which is responsible for snipping the casomorphin and gliadorphin proteins into small pieces. If there isn't enough *DPP* IV present, casomorphin and gliadorphin are left intact and are absorbed into the body. A number of factors can cause *DPP* IV activity levels to fall, including a deficiency of zinc and other nutrients, certain antibiotics, interferon, gelatin, yeast from the *Candida* genus, and the presence of excessive amounts of mercury, heavy metals, and pesticides in the body.

Researchers have measured the levels of *DPP* IV activity in the blood of depressed and nondepressed patients, finding that there is significantly less activity in those with major depression and treatment-resistant depression, compared to healthy controls. Researchers theorize that a drop in *DPP* IV occurs during the severe phase of a depressive episode in susceptible people, making *DPP* IV deficiency both a cause and a result of depression.

More research is needed to fully understand the link between casomorphin and depression, but it's likely that a large number of depressed patients are suffering from the incomplete digestion of casein and gluten. On the scale of human evolution, casein and gluten are relatively new proteins in the human diet. Milk, cheese, and other milk products only became common several hundred years ago, while wheat, barley, and rye became widespread in the diet some ten thousand years ago, with the spread of grain-based agriculture. Ten thousand years is not a lot of time for the human body to adapt and develop mechanisms to prevent the absorption of casomorphin and gliadorphin.

Fortunately, most of us have little difficulty with gluten or casein. But an unknown number of people have difficulty completely breaking down the proteins, and the resulting casomorphin and gliadorphin may lead to psychiatric symptoms.

Kathy had struggled with OCD and depression most of her life. Her OCD started in childhood with obsessive worrying about germs, hurricanes, and the size of her head. As she got older her OCD continued but interfered less with her life than her overwhelming depression. Depression limited her ability to succeed in school and at work and eventually

Kathy ended up on disability. After urine testing revealed elevated levels of casomorphin, Kathy dedicated her life to changing her diet, eliminating casein, taking nutritional supplements, and finding a new hope for the possibilities of psychotherapy.

According to Kathy, "All of a sudden I had some understanding as to why I was feeling so out of control and depressed. No one ever looked for what was causing my problems." Kathy continues therapy, but has started working part-time, renewed connections with her friends, and is hopeful about the future. Her symptoms of OCD and depression have gone from "a nine on a scale of one to ten, to a three."

Our understanding of casomorphin and gliadorphin is still evolving, but if there's any chance that they may be causing or contributing to someone's depression, it's worth checking with a simple urine test. If either of these substances is causing a problem, the most effective treatment is simple: Stop eating the offending foods. In addition, supplemental *DPP* IV enzymes can be taken to increase *DPP* IV levels. This facilitates digestion of any casomorphin or gliadorphin that is inadvertently eaten.

Food Allergies and Depression

Food allergies must also be investigated and ruled out as a factor in depression. Food allergies are a difficult subject to deal with, for there is confusion regarding exactly what a food allergy is, whether people are truly allergic to one or more foods, and to what extent.

Many people do suffer from severe allergic reactions to foods, especially eggs, shrimp, and other shellfish. Their immune systems mistake harmless food for a dangerous enemy and launch a full-blown attack on the "invader," resulting in damage to the body during the battle. The result can be abdominal pain, diarrhea, nausea, itching, eczema, difficulty breathing, nasal congestion, dizziness, and swelling of the lips, face, throat, and tongue. In some cases the allergic reaction may be so severe that it causes anaphylactic shock, resulting in a significant drop in blood pressure, rapid heart rate, dizziness, airway constriction, and loss of consciousness. If medical treatment is not administered quickly, an anaphylactic reaction can be life threatening.

These immediate hypersensitivity reactions are called IgE-mediated food allergies because Immunoglobulin E is overactive. Most people with these types of food allergies know they have them because the reactions are usually severe. Another type of food allergy causes more nonspecific symptoms that can occur from twenty-four to seventy-two hours after ingestion of the offending food. These reactions are called delayed hypersensitivity reactions and are referred to as IgG-mediated food allergies because Immunoglobulin G is primarily overactive. These reactions may include fatigue, depression, anxiety, stomach problems, and headaches. Many patients found to have IgG-delayed hypersensitivity reactions struggle with chronic unexplained health problems, including depression.

People who struggle with food allergies or food intolerances tend to suffer from more depression than their healthy peers. It is unclear which psychological changes are secondary to nutritional deficiencies and/or inflammation. In many cases, the depression improves when the food allergies are treated.

Although there is insufficient research, years of clinical experience have convinced me that food allergies are contributing factors to many psychiatric illnesses, including ADHD, anxiety, and particularly depression. The medical profession has minimized and dismissed this association for many years. A simple blood test can help determine food sensitivities. Although testing is not always 100 percent reliable, it does serve as a guide. Elimination diets, in which limited diets are used to determine sensitivity to offending foods as new foods are introduced one at a time, are another way of determining if you are sensitive to particular foods.

Other Gastrointestinal Problems and Depression

Besides celiac disease, other gastrointestinal problems are also associated with depression. People suffering from either ulcerative colitis or Crohn's disease, both forms of inflammatory bowel disease (IBD), have been found to suffer from higher rates of depression than the general public. A study published in the medical journal *Gut* found that about one-third of patients seeking treatment for IBD also suffered from depression and anxiety. A 2006 Canadian study found that patients with IBD or other bowel disorders suffered from depression rates that are triple those of the general population. It's clear that many patients who suffer from ulcerative colitis or Crohn's disease also concurrently suffer from depression.

Some of those who suffer from ulcerative colitis or Crohn's may also present with psychiatric symptoms such as depression and anxiety without any of the normal physiological symptoms of abdominal pain, diarrhea, and weight loss. Depression or anxiety present before or, in some cases, without any physical symptoms can lead to a delay in diagnosis and treatment of the underlying gastrointestinal problems.

Depression also plays a role in the course of Crohn's disease. Individuals with Crohn's disease experience symptoms in bouts rather than continuously. Some studies have found that individuals with higher depression scores suffered more flare-ups of symptoms than those with lower depression scores.

It's important to consider all gastrointestinal disorders affecting nutrient absorption, including ulcerative colitis and Crohn's disease, when treating depression.

A Final Word

Celiac disease, difficulties with incompletely digested proteins such as casomorphin and gliadorphin, food allergies or intolerances, and inflammatory conditions of the gastrointestinal tract are often overlooked contributors to depression. Even in cases where "food problems" are a major cause of the depression, or even the sole cause, they may be overlooked. But by eliminating celiac disease, elevated casomorphin and gliadorphin levels, food allergies, and forms of IBD from the list of possible causes of depression, conventional treatments, including therapy and medication, will be more effective.

10

Z – Zinc and Other Minerals

The idea that a daily nutritional supplement containing zinc and other minerals could relieve or even prevent depression is shocking to most psychiatrists. That reaction is equally shocking, for there is a great deal of research published in well-regarded scientific journals indicating the importance of zinc and other minerals for mental health. But psychiatry has largely ignored these findings in favor of medications with limited efficacy and frequent side effects.

In this chapter, I review the research supporting the use of zinc and other minerals for the treatment of depression. The key message is this: Minerals are important to healthy brain function and mood, as they play crucial roles in the synthesis and function of neurotransmitters that regulate mood. Minerals are the "raw materials" of a healthy and happy outlook.

Zinc and Depression

Zinc is one of the most important minerals for mental health, a sort of metabolic spark plug that is ubiquitous in the body and that participates in some two hundred different enzyme reactions. It has a variety of duties, including the following:

- Aiding in the manufacture of DNA and proteins
- Assisting the immune system as it fights off viruses and bacteria
- Helping wounds heal
- Regulating neurotransmission in the brain
- Making it possible to taste and smell
- Making sex and reproduction possible
- Aiding in the synthesis of all enzymes required to digest fats, carbohydrates, and protein

Zinc is found in a number of foods, including oysters, poultry, red meat, beans, whole grains, and nuts. The recommended daily intake of zinc ranges from 2 to 12 mg, depending on age and the presence or absence of pregnancy or lactation.

Those at greatest risk of zinc deficiency are vegetarians, because they don't eat the red meat and poultry that are the best sources of zinc; alcoholics and patients with eating disorders, because they absorb less of the mineral; and those who have ulcerative colitis, Crohn's disease, or other conditions that interfere with zinc absorption. A number of medicines can deplete the body's zinc supplies, including aspirin; benazepril (Lotensin), which is used to treat elevated blood pressure; cholestyramine (Questran), which is used to reduce cholesterol; and ofloxacin (Floxin), which is used to treat pneumonia, bronchitis, and other infections.

A lack of zinc can lead to delayed growth in children and infants, hair loss, diarrhea, loss of appetite, weight loss, difficulty tasting food, acne, fatigue, elevated cholesterol, increased infections, memory impairment, impotence, and other problems. Zinc deficiency has also been linked to anorexia nervosa, impaired cognitive function, and other behavioral disturbances.

Numerous studies have also linked low blood levels of zinc to depression. A case study published in 1983 described a patient with low zinc and copper levels whose depression was not helped by medications. In 1990, British researchers measured blood levels of zinc in fourteen patients admitted to an acute psychiatric unit for moderately severe to severe depression. These levels were compared to those of healthy controls, matched in age and sex. In the depressed people, the average zinc level was lower than in the healthy people.

A few years later, in 1994, a paper published in the *Journal of Affective Disorders* reported that blood levels of zinc are correlated with the severity of depression: the lower the zinc, the greater the depression. For this study, zinc levels were measured in forty-eight volunteers suffering from depression and compared to the levels in thirty-two healthy people. Zinc levels were highest in the healthy controls, lower in those suffering from minor depression, and lowest in those with major depression.

Another study performed by a team of researchers from Belgium, the United States, and Italy confirmed that zinc levels are lower in people suffering from major depression. This study also found that levels are particularly low in people with treatment-resistant depression, raising the possibility that measuring zinc levels before commencing treatment may help identify those who are least likely to respond to standard medicine and who need the most individualized care.

Low zinc levels have also been found in females with postpartum depression. A 2008 study examined sixty-six women on the third and thirtieth days following childbirth, checking both their zinc levels and the depth of their depression. Upon analyzing the results, the researchers found a link between the severity of depressive symptoms and decreased zinc in the blood.

A 2009 study examined zinc levels in female university students. After screening a random selection of young women, the researchers selected twenty-three who were suffering from moderate or severe depression and compared them to twenty-three healthy students. Participants filled out food questionnaires and had blood samples taken to determine how much zinc they consumed and the amount of zinc in their blood. The results were clear-cut and dramatic: Both the daily intakes of zinc, as well as the zinc level in the bloodstream, were about one-third lower in the depressed women than in the healthy women. More than 20 percent of the depressed women had blood levels low enough to be considered zinc deficient, whereas none of the healthy women did.

What is the zinc-depression link?

How could a mineral influence mood to such a profound extent? We don't know the exact mechanism(s), but several theories have been advanced. An obvious one is that zinc levels are low in depressed people simply because depression reduces both appetite and interest in eating. Thus, depressed people are likely to eat less and forgo healthful foods, resulting in lower zinc levels. According to this argument, low zinc is a *result* of depression, not a cause. However, studies with depressed patients have not found any link between decreased appetite and zinc levels. So while depression may reduce the appetite, it is most likely not the cause of significantly lowered zinc levels.

Other explanations have been proposed, offering biochemistry as the link between zinc and depression. One theory holds that the body's inflammatory response system is activated when depression strikes (this is briefly discussed in Chapter 2). According to this theory, the body treats depression like a physical enemy that can be destroyed in the same way viruses or bacteria are destroyed. The inflammatory response triggers many biochemical changes, including lowering the amount of a protein called albumin, which transports zinc through the bloodstream. The shortfall of zinc in the blood, then, may be due to fewer "zinc buses" available to move it around. So while there may be sufficient zinc in the body, it can't get to the places it needs to go.

Another possibility is that the liver might be snatching up all the zinc it can in order to manufacture more substances necessary for the inflammatory response. It's as if the body is saying, "Right now, it's more important to use zinc to create the substances that fight off invaders, so it's okay to let the mood suffer."

These and other ideas have all been supported by studies with animals and humans, but we have not yet identified the precise link(s) between zinc and depression. The science of the zinc-depression link is complex and involves numerous biochemical pathways that may take years to untangle.

Can zinc relieve depression?

We can effectively use zinc for depression, even though we don't know precisely how it works. This is true of a surprising number of medicines. Exactly how they effectively treat an illness is often a mystery. Indeed, aspirin was synthesized in the 1890s and soon became one of the most popular medicines in the world, but it wasn't until the 1970s that medical scientists realized it worked by interfering with the production of inflammation-producing substances called prostaglandins.

Animal studies reinforce the idea that zinc has antidepressant properties, and that it works well in combination with certain standard antidepressants. Consider the following:

1. Lab animals given citalopram (Celexa) had significant increases in their blood levels of zinc.
2. When given Celexa or imipramine, lab animals showed increased zinc levels in the hippocampus and decreased levels in other parts of the brain.
3. Administering multiple courses of ECT, a treatment for advanced cases of depression, triggered changes in the hippocampus that suggest an increase in the activity of zinc in that area of the brain.
4. Supplemental zinc has an antidepressant effect in lab animals subjected to stress.
5. Low doses of Celexa (citalopram) and imipramine are ineffective as antidepressants in lab animals stressed by being forced to swim for long periods of time. But these medicines become effective antidepressants when low doses of zinc are added.
6. Chronic treatment with antidepressants and ECT causes zinc concentrations to increase in the brains of rats.
7. In laboratory animals, a zinc-deficient diet triggers the development of depression-like symptoms, including anorexia and anxiety. Giving these zinc-deficient animals fluoxetine (Prozac) reduces their despair.

The results of these and other animal studies suggest that zinc levels are intricately linked to depression and that the mineral has antidepressant effects. Of course, while theory and animal studies are a great beginning, the real test is in what happens to people. Although human studies on the effect of zinc on depression are relatively new, there is accumulating evidence that zinc augments the potency of standard antidepressant medicines in humans.

This was demonstrated in a study of fourteen people suffering from major depression who were randomly assigned to take either 25 mg of zinc daily or a placebo, along with their standard medicines (SSRIs and tricyclic antidepressants). The study was double-blind, which means that neither doctors nor patients knew who was receiving the zinc until the end of the study. The HDRS and Beck Depression Inventory were used to measure the depth of the patients' depression. Depression was assessed at the beginning of the study and two, six, and twelve weeks after treatment began.

The results were intriguing: At the end of the study, the patients taking zinc had significantly less severe symptoms of depression according to the Hamilton and Beck scores. Depression severity scores fell faster in the placebo-plus-antidepressant group, but by week six they were significantly lower in the zinc-plus-antidepressant group and remained lower for the rest of the study. Although this was a small study, the significant and robust findings reinforce the argument that zinc strengthens the effects of standard antidepressant medicines.

The researchers who conducted this study followed up with the first large-scale clinical trial of "added zinc therapy" in 2009. For this second study, sixty adults ranging in age from eighteen to fifty-five who were suffering from major depression were randomly assigned to receive either imipramine plus 25 mg of zinc daily or imipramine plus a placebo for twelve weeks. This was also a double-blind study, with the mood assessed via various depression scales. Overall, adding zinc to the standard medicine improved both the speed and strength of the medicine. What was even more interesting was that the volunteers who were most affected were those who had been treatment resistant and who had not been helped by the standard medicines alone. This suggests that for many of those who are not helped by standard medicines, zinc may be the missing ingredient in their treatment regimen, either in combination with antidepressant medication or on its own.

Zinc may also be helpful in individuals who are not diagnosed as having major depression yet suffer from low moods. This idea was investigated by a team of Japanese researchers who enlisted thirty premenopausal women in a double-blind study comparing the efficacy of zinc to a vitamin pill. The volunteers were randomly assigned to take either 7 mg of zinc or a multivitamin pill daily for ten weeks. Their blood was checked before and after the study, and their mood was monitored using standard depression and mood scales. At the end of the ten-week study period, the

Zinc Taste Test

There is no single, widely accepted blood test for zinc status. Instead, doctors measure zinc levels in the blood, blood cells, and even the hair in an attempt to determine exactly how much zinc a patient has available for use.

I have found that the single best method for assessing zinc status is the zinc taste test, which is based on the fact that the sense of taste depends on adequate levels of zinc in the body.

Please note that it is safe for anyone to try the zinc taste test as the solution used in the test has a very dilute concentration of zinc.

For the test, a liquid zinc sulphate supplement is kept at room temperature for two hours. The patient does not eat, drink, or smoke for an hour before the test, to make sure there are no competing flavors in the mouth. Then, the patient takes a small drink of the zinc solution (1 tsp), swirls it around in his or her mouth for ten seconds, then either spits it out or swallows it. The patient records the taste according to the categories listed below:

Responses

Category 1: Has no taste or tastes like water.

Category 2: Has no taste at first, but after a few seconds has a dry, mineral, bicarbonate, "furry," or sweet taste.

Category 3: Has a definite but not strongly unpleasant taste at first, which tends to intensify over time.

Category 4: Has an immediate unpleasant, strong, or metallic taste. The taste may linger for one-half hour or more.

Interpreting the results

A category 1 or 2 response indicates a zinc deficiency that will likely benefit from zinc supplementation.

A category 3 or 4 response suggests zinc status is adequate. Supplementation of zinc should be integrated as part of a preventative nutritional strategy.

women taking zinc enjoyed a significant decrease in their depression-dejection and anger-hostility scores, compared to the vitamin group. In addition, blood levels of zinc rose in the zinc group, but not in the vitamin group. The researchers concluded that zinc supplements may be an effective treatment for depression and anger.

Scientific evidence clearly suggests that zinc is essential for good mental health. Unfortunately, zinc research will continue slowly, at best, for no major pharmaceutical company will spend tens of millions of dollars studying a mineral it cannot patent and sell as a proprietary product. However, psychiatrists and patients interested in natural treatments for depression should understand how to assess and treat zinc deficiency.

If the results of the zinc taste test are in category 1 or 2, I generally recommend that my patients take 2–3 teaspoons of the liquid zinc taste test solution (zinc sulfate monohydrate) three times per day. Eventually, as zinc levels are restored, patients notice a stronger taste and should stop taking it as a zinc supplement once the taste is too strong. The variability in how long it takes can range from weeks to months.

If the results of the zinc taste test are in category 3 or 4, a multivitamin that contains at least 15 mg of zinc should be adequate.

Although it is safe to supplement with zinc at home, I believe that it is best as part of a comprehensive nutritional and medical treatment plan. Not all depressed people are zinc deficient and not all respond to zinc supplementation.

When twenty-eight-year-old Gabi came to my office, she was on three antidepressants with a fourteen-year history of depression. She believed that the medications "kept [her] going" but did not improve her mood.

During our first meeting I noticed many of the signs and symptoms of zinc deficiency in Gabi. She thought the zinc taste test solution tasted like water. She also had adult acne and white spots on her fingernails. Routine blood work showed that she had low levels of alkaline phosphatase. This enzyme, primarily produced in the liver, requires zinc for optimal function. Due to its zinc-dependent function, alkaline phosphatase can be used as a "functional" measure of zinc deficiency. As zinc is repleted, alkaline phosphatase levels increase.

As Gabi started taking liquid zinc, she noticed improvement in her mood and participated in the other protocols described in this book. It was almost a month before Gabi started to notice a strong metallic taste during the zinc taste test, which indicated adequate zinc status. Over the course of a year Gabi was taken off her antidepressant medication, and she no longer struggles with the darkness of depression.

Anyone who continues to have symptoms of depression should be assessed for zinc deficiency. And unless the zinc levels are on the high end of the normal range, patients should be given zinc supplementation and encouraged to eat ample amounts of zinc-containing foods.

Copper and Depression

With zinc, the problem is too little; with copper it may be too much *or* too little.

Copper is a micronutrient, which means the human body needs it in relatively tiny amounts. Concentrated in the heart, liver, brain, and kidney, copper has a variety of functions, including assisting in the growth or maintenance of the red blood cells, bones, nerves, and brain. It also aids in the manufacture of the prostaglandins necessary for regulation of the heartbeat and blood pressure; plays a part in the extraction of energy from fats, protein, and carbohydrates; and helps the body combat free radicals. Copper is found in liver and other organ meats, shellfish, whole-grain cereals and breads, dark green leafy vegetables, peas, poultry, nuts, and beans.

A lack of copper can lead to anemia, elevated blood pressure, diarrhea, difficulty breathing, lowered immune function, ECG abnormalities, and other problems. A deficiency may be caused by a poor diet, digestive or intestinal disorders that interfere with nutrient absorption, chronic diarrhea, and even excessive amounts of zinc, since copper and zinc compete for absorption in the intestines. A number of medications can interfere with copper absorption, including delavirdine (Rescriptor), which is used to treat HIV infection; ethambutol (Myambutol), used to treat tuberculosis; and penicillamine, used to treat rheumatoid arthritis. The elderly, vegetarians, athletes, workers engaged in difficult physical work, pregnant women, and premature infants are most likely to suffer from copper deficiency. Healthy adults eating a varied diet are not likely to develop a deficiency.

Elevated copper and depression

Excessive copper can be a problem, for the mineral is an important component of enzymes involved in depression (monoamine oxidase, dopamine-beta-hydroxylase, and tyrosine hydroxylase). These enzymes stimulate and regulate the production of dopamine, one of the most important neurotransmitters in the brain.

We've known for many years that depressed patients may exhibit elevated blood levels of copper. For example, a 1991 study compared copper levels in the blood of thirty-five depressed people to those of thirty-five healthy controls. Copper levels were significantly higher in the depressed group (122 micrograms per deciliter[μg/dL]) than they were in the nondepressed group (107 μg/dL), and they dropped significantly when the patients had recovered from their depression (104 μg/dL).

Ongoing research continues to expand our knowledge of the copper-depression link. For example, a 2007 study compared copper levels in seventy-eight women suffering from postpartum depression to nondepressed controls, as well as to women who had suffered from a form of depression other than postpartum depression. Copper levels were significantly elevated in the women suffering from postpartum depression (131 μg/dL) compared to women who had once suffered from other forms of depression (111 μg/dL) and to the nondepressed controls (106 μg/dL).

A recent study, published in 2010 in the *Journal of Affective Disorders*, reported that copper levels were higher in thirteen people with depression as compared to thirteen healthy people.

We don't know why copper levels rise in depressed people. We do know that copper is necessary for the conversion of the neurotransmitter dopamine into norepinephrine, so it may be that excess copper upsets the normal balance of brain chemicals. Other theories include the possibility that excess copper interferes with the production of cellular energy, or the transmission of signals through the nervous system. It may also be that both elevated copper and depression are the results of another phenomenon, perhaps an inflammation reaction in the body or a zinc deficiency.

Many years may pass before all the biochemical pathways linking excess copper to depression are identified and fully understood. In the meantime, elevated copper levels in depressed patients should be recognized and treated. Frequently, the treatment may simply be adding zinc supplements and, if possible, finding the source of the excess copper.

Some studies have shown that elevated copper levels in depressed people return to normal (or near normal) with standard antidepressants, further suggesting that normalizing copper levels is a potential treatment for depression in some patients.

Low copper and depression

There is also the problem of not having enough copper. Although there is not as much research into the problem of low copper as high

Check the Copper!

Every patient's copper level should be checked.

If it is high, eliminate sources of accidental ingestion or absorption. Possible ways that you may ingest or absorb too much copper include the following:

- Absorbing copper from dental fixtures
- Drinking water from copper pipes
- Eating food cooked in copper cookware
- Being exposed to copper at work (plumbers, machinists, welders, and others who work with copper)
- Using certain birth control pills or a copper IUD

On the other hand, if the copper level is low, supplementation may be necessary. The problem may be dietary, especially if you are on a restricted diet or some sort of crash weight-loss diet. Celiac disease, short bowel syndrome, or any other diseases that interfere with copper absorption can lead to low levels. The elderly are also at increased risk of deficiency. However, the most common cause of low copper is patients who take excessively high doses of zinc supplements, more than 100 mg/day, without professional monitoring. Excessive zinc consumption can decrease copper levels and actually cause depression. The delicate balance between zinc and copper reinforces the need for patients to have mineral levels and supplementation monitored by a health professional.

copper levels, over the years I have found low copper levels to be a significant problem. I've been surprised by the number of times I have identified low copper levels in depressed patients but pleased to see those patients' moods improve when copper levels are restored to normal ranges. The link between low copper and depression is likely dopamine: Copper is required for the synthesis of dopamine, so a lack of copper may lead to low levels of the mood-modulating neurotransmitter.

I remember well a young woman named Megan who was referred to me by her family practitioner for the treatment of depression. As we talked about her diet, I learned that this twenty-seven-year-old accountant ate a balanced and healthful diet, filled with fresh vegetables, fruits, and whole grains, plus modest amounts of fish and red meat. Her nutrient levels should have been ideal, but testing of her serum copper and red blood copper showed that her copper levels were below the normal range. Fortunately, she responded well to supplemental copper, 4 mg/day. Her copper levels rose and her depression lifted.

Magnesium and Depression

From Chapter 7 you may recall that magnesium aids in sleep, but the versatile mineral plays many other roles in the body, including a role in depression. Magnesium is an essential nutrient found in relatively large amounts throughout the body. About 54 percent of the body's magnesium resides in the bones, with an additional 27 percent in the muscles and 19 percent in the heart and liver. Relatively little magnesium is found in the blood (only about 1 percent) but stable blood levels of magnesium are crucial, and the body regulates them tightly. The mineral takes part in more than three hundred biochemical reactions, contributing to good health in many ways, including the following:

- Maintaining a healthy immune system
- Keeping the bones strong
- Regulating blood pressure
- Manufacturing proteins
- Ensuring that the nerves work properly
- Keeping the heart beating steadily

A magnesium deficiency can cause irregular heartbeat, nausea, lack of appetite, seizures, fatigue, muscle weakness, poor coordination, and other problems, including personality changes. It may also exacerbate psychological problems such as depression and apathy, irritability, nervousness, anxiety, excessive emotional reactions and frequent mood changes, decreased memory and concentration, migraines, fatigue, and ADHD. Those at risk of magnesium deficiency include people with Crohn's disease or other ailments that interfere with nutrient absorption, alcoholics, diabetics with poorly controlled disease, and senior citizens. Certain medicines can interfere with the body's ability to absorb and/or utilize magnesium, including diuretics such as furosemide (Lasix) and bumetanide (Bumex), as well as antibiotics such as gentamicin.

Magnesium is found in dark green leafy vegetables, nuts, whole-grain breads, beans, and peas. It is one of the first minerals to be stripped from foods as they are processed. Refined grains have only a fraction of the magnesium found in whole grains. It is also one of the first minerals to be depleted from the body during stress, which means that everyone suffering from chronic stress—even if it's low-level stress—is at risk of deficiency.

Many Americans are deficient in magnesium. According to the studies, "substantial numbers of U.S. adults fail to consume adequate magnesium in their diets." More precisely, about two-thirds of Americans consume less than the recommended dietary allowance (RDA) of magnesium (420 mg for men, 320 mg for women). This is not surprising, as the processed foods that make up so much of the modern diet are relatively low in magnesium. In addition, magnesium and other minerals are often removed from water used for drinking and cooking. Consumption of dietary magnesium has decreased over the past century to a shocking degree with estimates of the daily magnesium consumed decreasing from roughly 500 mg/day in the early 1900s to less than 300 mg/day today.

A dietary shortage of magnesium should be of great concern to those with mood problems, as a lack of magnesium can trigger depression. This has been demonstrated by deliberately depleting magnesium stores in mice, which then show an increase in anxiety and depression-like behaviors. In humans, the risk of developing depression increases when magnesium intake is low. In addition, patients with treatment-resistant suicidal depression or those who have attempted suicide often have low magnesium levels in their cerebrospinal fluid (CSF). However, blood levels of magnesium that are too high can also be found in depressed patients. This sounds confusing, until you remember that the body strives to keep the blood magnesium level within a very narrow range. When magnesium stores or activity gets out of sync, as appears to happen in depression, the body may overcompensate and raise the blood levels too high. So, elevated blood magnesium may also serve as a marker of depression.

Exactly how these changes in magnesium levels in the brain, CSF, or elsewhere set the stage for depression is unknown. One theory is that magnesium deficiency allows an excess of calcium to flow into certain areas of the nervous system, damaging the nerves and causing symptoms similar to those of depression. A lack of magnesium may also reduce brain levels of the neurotransmitter serotonin.

Knowing that depressed people tend to consume less magnesium, and there is less magnesium in the CSF of depressed patients, it's fair to ask whether giving supplemental magnesium can relieve depression, but this question has not been studied in depth. The idea is not new: As far back as 1921, a published study described how treatment with magnesium was successful in 220 out of 250 people suffering from what was then called "agitated depression."

In 2008, a randomized, clinical trial compared magnesium to the standard medication imipramine. For this study, twenty-three senior citizens suffering from type 2 diabetes, depression, and low blood levels of magnesium were randomly allocated to receive either 450 mg of elemental magnesium or 50 mg of imipramine daily for twelve weeks. At the end of the study period, depression ratings were equally improved in both groups, indicating that magnesium is an effective treatment in depressed people who are also magnesium deficient.

This study opens the door to the type of individualized treatment that I advocate: All patients should be tested for magnesium deficiency. Their dietary and supplemental intake of the mineral should be analyzed and any factors that may deplete the body of magnesium (such as stress) should be investigated. If the dietary magnesium intake is low or only marginally adequate, or if the blood levels are not safely within the normal range, the patient should be urged to eat a magnesium-rich diet and to take magnesium supplements.

In addition, factors that may be depleting the body of magnesium should be addressed. For example, in the case of stress-induced magnesium loss, the individual could try meditation or take stress-management classes. Magnesium-depleting medications should be switched to those that do not interfere with the mineral, and so on. Such a plan must be devised on an individual basis, as every patient is unique. Simply recommending the averages calculated from large groups of people may lead to inadequate treatment.

Four common symptoms of magnesium deficiency that help guide supplementation in patients with depression are as follows:

- Insomnia
- Constipation
- Anxiety
- Muscle spasms

In the presence of any of these symptoms, I recommend 300–600 mg/day of magnesium (in the form of either magnesium glycinate or magnesium citrate). The dose of magnesium can be adjusted based on improvement of the symptoms. Chronic constipation may disappear in as little as a few weeks.

Lithium and Depression

Still another mineral related to depression is lithium. Most people know lithium as a medicine used to prevent and treat the manic phase of bipolar disorder. What many don't realize is that lithium isn't a medicine manufactured in the laboratory. It is a natural metallic element listed in the periodic table of elements along with hydrogen, nitrogen, sodium, potassium, and others. Lithium can be found in every organ and tissue, and the U.S. Department of Agriculture has determined that it is an ultra-trace element that appears essential for human health. Research indicates that lithium helps stabilize the mood, regulate neurotransmitter signaling, protect brain cells from early death, and perform other duties. The typical American adult ingests between 650 and 3,100 micrograms (µg) of lithium each day, primarily from grains, vegetables, and drinking water.

Like many other elements, lithium influences human biochemistry. As early as the 1870s, it was used to treat mania at New York's Bellevue Hospital Medical College. Although it proved to be successful as a medicine, it was eventually set aside and ignored by the mental health community until 1949, when an Australian psychiatrist rediscovered it as a helpful treatment for mania, and it was approved for that purpose in the United States in 1970.

Research into lithium's potential antidepressant effects began as far back as the 1960s. In 1981, a paper published in the *British Journal of Psychiatry* reported that adding lithium to the standard antidepressants of eight volunteers who were treatment resistant and had not been helped by standard medications produced "remarkable relief of their depression within 48 hours." Through 2010, more than forty studies showed the value of lithium augmentation in treating depression, ten of which were double blind and placebo controlled (the "gold standard" of research studies).

A meta-analysis of the ten double-blind studies, which used statistical methods to combine these results and produce a larger, more robust look at the subject, found that adding lithium to standard antidepressant medications produced significantly better effects than those with the medicines alone. Lithium plus standard medication had a response rate of 41.2 percent, compared to a 14.4 percent response rate for placebo plus standard medicine.

Research also indicates that lithium may be helpful in treating aggressive behavior. Violent criminals have been found to have lower levels of lithium in their hair (an indication of reduced lithium throughout the body), and an investigation into the drinking water in twenty-seven Texas counties found that the incidence of rape, suicide, and homicide was significantly higher in counties with water containing little or no lithium, compared to counties with water containing larger amounts (70–170 micrograms per liter [μg/L]).

Lithium has also clearly been shown to be helpful in reducing the incidence of suicide and suicide attempts in people with mood disorders. A meta-analysis published in the *Journal of Clinical Psychiatry* in 2007 "statistically married" eight separate studies involving 329 people suffering from major depressive disorder and found that lithium reduced the risk of suicide or suicide attempts by 88 percent. These findings expanded upon a 2005 meta-analysis published in the *American Journal of Psychiatry*, which found that "Lithium is effective in the prevention of suicide, deliberate self-harm, and death from all causes in patients with mood disorders." A 2010 study compared the levels of lithium in tap water to the suicide rate in eighteen different municipalities in Japan, finding a significant negative association between the two. In other words, more lithium in the water was associated with less suicide and less lithium with more suicide.

We don't know how lithium lifts and stabilizes the mood. It influences the actions of numerous enzymes, hormones, vitamins, and other substances in the body, so it may act in multiple ways to influence mood. One possibility is that it increases the activity of natural enzyme monoamine oxidase ; another is that it helps the body metabolize the mood-influencing vitamins B_{12} and folate.

New research has shown that lithium may stabilize mood through countering the effects of inflammation in the brain. The study involved feeding rats either a diet containing lithium chloride or a diet free of lithium for six weeks. At the end of six weeks, inflammation-inducing bacteria were introduced into their brains, which were then analyzed. The researchers found that lithium reduced levels of the inflammatory compound arachidonic acid and increased levels of the anti-inflammatory compound 17-hydroxy-docosahexaenoic acid (17-OH-DHA). Excess or unwanted inflammation can damage sensitive brain cells, which can contribute to depression. Lithium may exert its beneficial effects by lowering damage-inducing inflammation.

Lithium as a prescription medicine is used in doses ranging from 600 to 1,800 mg/day. At these doses side effects are common and some are permanent, including kidney damage and thyroid damage. These side effects limit the use of lithium at prescription strength.

In my practice, I use lithium in doses found naturally in food and in supplements from health-food stores. I have had great success stabilizing mood in patients with lithium in the form of lithium orotate at doses between 5 and 20 mg. The doses are so low that I have rarely seen any side effects, and blood tests are not required to monitor levels. Lithium orotate has been particularly helpful in patients who have a family history of alcoholism, bipolar disorder, or depression.

David's experience illustrates the danger of high levels of lithium. David is a forty-nine-year-old patient with bipolar disorder who has been treated with lithium for many years. After he developed kidney damage he was unable to continue taking lithium, and no other medication helped. David remained depressed for two years before coming to see me. David got his life back on 10 mg of lithium orotate, and fortunately the damage to his kidneys stabilized and has not progressed.

Although the psychiatric community tends to view lithium strictly as a medicine, I prefer to view it as nature's mood stabilizer, necessary for most people only in the small amounts that can be acquired from food and water.

Chromium and Depression

Chromium is another trace element linked to depression. Humans require small amounts of chromium for good health, although we can't fully explain everything it does in the body. The mineral is found in a wide variety of foods, but most foods contain relatively small amounts, making it difficult to meet the adequate daily dietary intake of 50–200 μg/day. In addition, body stores of the mineral can be depleted by infection, acute or chronic exercise, physical trauma, diets containing large amounts of simple sugars, and other forms of stress.

Chromium is often recommended to help balance insulin metabolism and cholesterol levels. It has been shown to stabilize blood sugar and energy levels, and it can eliminate sugar cravings by increasing the ability of insulin to transport sugar into cells. Chromium also helps lower body-fat levels, total cholesterol, triglycerides, and low-density lipoprotein (LDL), or "bad" cholesterol), while raising high-density lipoprotein (HDL), or "good" cholesterol.

As for chromium and depression, a 2000 paper published in the *International Journal of Neuropsychopharmacology* described what happened when eight patients with difficult-to-treat major depressive disorder, dysthymic disorder, or bipolar disorder were given chromium supplements. In every case, the patients enjoyed "dramatic improvements in their symptoms and functioning." None of the patients had previously experienced a satisfactory response to standard antidepressant therapy. With chromium, they all enjoyed clinical remission of depression.

This news was encouraging but limited, because the eight patients were individual case studies rather than one large, placebo-controlled clinical study. Subsequent, larger studies have shown promising results.

For one of these studies, researchers from Duke University Medical Center enlisted fifteen people suffering from major depressive disorder, atypical type. The study participants were randomly assigned to receive either 600 μg of chromium picolinate or a placebo daily for eight weeks. At the end of the study period, 70 percent of those taking the chromium responded to treatment, compared to 0 percent of the placebo group. Although this was a small study, the researchers concluded that chromium shows "promising antidepressant effects" against this form of major depressive disorder.

A larger study involved 110 people suffering from either major depressive disorder or dysthymia. The participants were randomly assigned to take 400 μg/day of chromium picolinate for two weeks, then 600 μg/day for another six weeks, or a placebo for the entire eight weeks. The HDRS was used to gauge the severity of the patients' depression at the beginning and the degree of improvement at the end of the study. Among those who began the study with carbohydrate cravings, chromium was shown to be superior to placebo in reducing both depressive symptoms and cravings.

As with so many medications and supplements, we don't know exactly how chromium works against depression. It is known to increase insulin sensitivity, and depression has been linked to insulin resistance. Perhaps restoring insulin sensitivity also enhances the activity of serotonin and noradrenaline activity. This large study reinforced the theory that chromium is an effective antidepressant for patients with carbohydrate cravings. These findings also reinforce my conviction that each patient must be treated as an individual: Chromium may be an effective treatment for some, while another approach may be necessary for others. We must break away from the "one medicine fits all" concept of psychiatry and view the patient as an individual with unique biochemistry and unique needs.

Most primary care physicians and psychiatrists do not check chromium levels in their patients. I believe we should do so routinely, and if the levels are low or low-normal, we should recommend chromium supplements. Chromium picolinate at a dose between 400 and 600 μg/day is usually sufficient to replete a chromium deficiency.

Iodine and Depression

Iodine is discussed in Chapter 8 in relationship to thyroid function. An essential trace mineral found naturally in food and in the human body, iodine is used to manufacture the thyroid hormones T_3 and T_4. The thyroid gland "snatches" iodine that is circulating in the blood and incorporates it into these hormones. The human body needs relatively small amounts of this mineral, but should it run low, the thyroid enlarges in size as it tries harder and harder to get the iodine it needs, eventually growing large enough to be a visible goiter. And, of course, no matter how large the thyroid grows, if there simply is not enough iodine available, it cannot manufacture the precious hormones.

Iodine is found in ocean water and in soil, although the amount in the soil varies from region to region. It's also found in iodized salt, which is a major source of the mineral for many people.

We have long known that problems with the thyroid gland and thyroid hormones can trigger psychiatric symptoms, and that even mild problems with thyroid function can increase the risk of developing a psychiatric disorder. We also know that in as many as 25 percent of those with depression, there is a weak response to a "request" for more thyroid hormone coming from the pituitary gland. In addition, researchers have found that when thyroid hormone is added to standard antidepressant therapy, the response can be better than that seen with the medication alone. This suggests that iodine levels should be monitored in depressed patients and, if low, pushed up to well within the normal range.

There is not a large body of scientific evidence showing that simply taking iodine relieves depression. But I remind you that depression is a multifaceted disorder, with many factors contributing to its onset and continuation. As I point out in Chapter 8, the standard tests for thyroid deficiency are potentially misleading, so it's not enough to perform a standard TSH test and assume that everything is okay. Instead, I suggest the full thyroid screening (checking free T_3 and T_4 levels), plus the monitoring of iodine intake and levels. For a certain number of people, simply bringing iodine up to an adequate level and restoring proper thyroid function can go a long way toward resolving depression.

Iron and Depression

Finally, let's look at the mineral iron. It's rare that a psychiatrist or physician considers iron deficiency as a potential cause of depression. However, this connection is common. Iron is important for regulating cell growth and serving as part of the hemoglobin molecule within red blood cells that carries oxygen through the blood. A shortage of iron results in a lack of fresh oxygen being brought to body cells, leading to fatigue, a weakened immune system, and many psychological problems, including poor attention. Signs of iron deficiency include weakness, fatigue, digestive problems, fragile bones, difficulty maintaining body temperature, increased infections, and poor performance at work or school.

Iron is found in red meat, fish, poultry, beans, lentils, iron-fortified cereals, and other foods. Iron deficiency is caused by low consumption of these foods and/or high consumption of foods rich in iron inhibitors (such as fiber and phytate). Worldwide, iron deficiency is the number one nutrient deficiency. Those at greatest risk of an iron deficiency include the following:

- Pregnant women (more iron is required during pregnancy)
- Older infants
- Toddlers
- Teenage girls
- Women of childbearing age (especially if they have heavy menstrual bleeding)
- Those with celiac disease or other gastrointestinal disorders that interfere with iron absorption

How does iron deficiency affect depression? Iron deficiency can depress the mood, as was demonstrated in a 2007 study involving 192 young women in Tehran. Of these women, 77 were depressed, and the 125 who were not served as controls for comparison. After measuring iron levels, the researchers found that the average iron level in the depressed women was significantly lower than in the healthy women.

Iron-deficiency anemia also affects the emotions of women after they have given birth. This was demonstrated in a 2005 study involving depressed South African women (some of whom were iron deficient and some of whom were not) who had just given birth. Some of the new mothers were given daily doses of vitamin C and folate; others received C, folate, and 125 mg of iron. The women and their babies were monitored, with testing conducted ten weeks after birth and again at nine months. Among the iron-deficient women, iron supplementation resulted in a 25 percent improvement in depression and stress scales over the course of the study.

Depressed mood and other behavioral problems associated with low iron status can show up even before iron levels are low enough to fall into the iron deficiency anemia category. But emotional problems that begin to surface as iron levels drop into the low-normal range are often overlooked by physicians and psychiatrists, who don't become alarmed until levels fall far enough to qualify as a "real problem."

I recommend that all patients have their iron and ferritin levels checked. Levels of ferritin, a protein that binds to iron, are checked because most of the iron stored in the body is bound to ferritin. If levels of both iron and ferritin are low, more iron-containing foods should be eaten and/or iron supplements should be taken. I like to see ferritin levels close to 100 μg/L and iron levels higher than 50 μg/dL.

I generally recommend starting supplementation with a form of iron called ferrous bisglycinate, which does not cause the typical side effects of iron supplementation, including nausea, constipation, and gastric upset. I also recommend taking 10 mg of ferritin supplements twice per day until iron and ferritin levels return to normal.

However, caution must be exercised when supplementing, for excess iron can be harmful. Iron supplements should not be taken by men or postmenopausal women unless there is a clear indication of a deficiency, as neither has an ongoing means of disposing of excess iron.

Take-Home Message

In this chapter, we've looked at a lot of studies examining the link between zinc, copper, magnesium, lithium, chromium, iodine, and iron. The key points to remember are that

- minerals and other nutrients influence brain function and mood;
- doctors should always consider the possibility of a deficiency of or excess or imbalance in trace minerals when assessing patients for depression;
- everyone with depression should be evaluated for trace mineral deficiencies;

- everyone is unique, and each person's needs must be assessed individually;
- taking too much of any trace mineral sets up imbalances among minerals, and supplementation should always be done under the guidance of a health professional;
- it is always best to obtain minerals from nutrient-dense whole foods or whole-food supplements.

Many Americans eat an overabundance of food but do not consume nutrient-dense whole foods. There may be plenty of calories, but too many of us are lacking in the nutrients we need for optimal mental and physical health. Although vitamins and vitamin deficiencies receive considerable attention today, I believe it is our deficiencies in trace minerals that have more effects on mental health, in particular depression. Fortunately, in many cases our suboptimal nutrient status can be corrected fairly quickly and easily. Restoring the balance in any of these trace minerals can even help resolve long-standing depression that has been resistant to medication and psychotherapy.

11

E – Essential Fatty Acids and Cholesterol

The human brain is a very fatty organ that simply does not work unless it is supplied with plentiful amounts of EFAs, cholesterol, and other naturally occurring fatty substances called lipids. If you were to wring the liquid out of a brain and analyze what's left, you'd find that about 60 percent of its dry weight consists of fat and at least 25 percent of its white matter is made from fatty acids. But despite its high fat content, the brain doesn't resemble a steak, with chunks of fat that can be sliced off and discarded. Instead, the fat is integrated into every brain cell, where it takes different forms and performs numerous tasks that keep us alive, healthy, and—we hope—happy.

Fatty Acids, the Building Blocks of Fat

Fats belong to a larger group called lipids, which also includes sterols such as cholesterol. When we talk about fats in the body, we're usually referring to fatty acids, which are organic compounds made up of chains of carbon and hydrogen atoms that promote and maintain the health of the body in countless ways. Fatty acids are to fat what amino acids are to proteins: They are the building blocks. Just as various amino acids can be combined to produce different proteins, various fatty acids can be joined together in specific combinations to create different kinds of fat.

The body uses numerous fatty acids, most of which it can manufacture on its own by disassembling fats from the food we eat and recombining them in different configurations. However, there are two fatty acids—linolenic acid and linoleic acid—that the body cannot synthesize on its own, which makes them EFAs, or fatty acids that must be obtained from food sources.

Fatty acids, both those we can synthesize and those we must get from food, are necessary for the proper construction and maintenance of every single cell in the body. They also play roles in promoting the health of the nervous system, immune system, skin, and joints, as well as in normalizing appetite, burning body fat, manufacturing hormones, and controlling inflammation. But perhaps even more interesting, and more relevant to this book, is the link between fatty acids and depression. Before we go further, let's take a look at the fatty acid itself: What it is, how it's named, and how it affects the body.

What's a fatty acid?

A fatty acid is basically a line of carbon atoms, each of which is hooked to the one in front and in back of it, except for those at the head or tail of the line. Think of a train, with each car hooked to two others (one in front and another in back) except for the engine and the caboose. Every carbon atom in the chain (except those on each end) has an "arm" protruding from either side, and at the end of each arm is a "hand" that can hold onto a hydrogen atom. When all of the carbons in the line are holding onto two hydrogen atoms, the fatty acid is considered *saturated*. Unable to hold any more hydrogen atoms, it is completely full, like a saturated sponge.

But if a carbon atom should let go of a hydrogen atom, meaning that it now holds onto just one hydrogen atom, the fatty acid is considered either *monounsaturated* or *polyunsaturated*, depending on how many times this occurs in the line of carbons *(mono* for once; *poly* for more than once.) If the first missing hydrogen occurs on the third carbon in the line, the configuration is called an *omega-3* fatty acid. If it occurs on the sixth carbon, it's called an *omega-6* fatty acid. This may not seem like much of a difference, but in the three-dimensional world of biochemistry, the position of a single atom can make a world of difference, by allowing a molecule to interact with others or by preventing it from even getting close.

Omega-3 fatty acids are concentrated in fish, fish oil, flaxseed oil, and walnuts, while omega-6s are found primarily in corn, soy or sunflower oil, margarine, eggs, and meat. Both play crucial roles in brain function; thus, both are necessary components of a balanced diet. However, because omega-6 fatty acids can promote inflammation under certain circumstances, while omega-3s can help quell inflammation, it's important to have the proper ratio of omega-6s to omega-3s. The recommended ratio is 4:1. Shockingly, the Standard American Diet is not only low in omega-3s, it can contain up to twenty-five times more omega-6s than omega-3s, skyrocketing the ratio from 4:1 to 25:1. The omega-6 fatty acids are certainly essential, healthful, and necessary, but not in that amount.

A tremendous overload of omega-6s coupled with a deficiency in omega-3s is believed to contribute to a large number of diseases and conditions, including depression, allergies, angina, arthritis, behavioral disorders, cancer, diabetes, dementia, heart disease, reduced immune function, hyperactivity, inflammatory conditions, autoimmune disorders, obesity, psoriasis, schizophrenia, stroke, and vision disorders. The imbalance between omega-6s and omega-3s is primarily due to our typical diet, which is extremely heavy in foods containing omega-6 fatty acids, especially oils used in cooking, fried foods, processed foods, and junk food. The decrease in overall levels of omega-3 fatty acids in the diet is, in part, the result of eating cage-raised cattle and farm-raised fish, which contain up to five times *fewer* omega-3s than their wild counterparts.

Not only is the omega-6 to omega-3 ratio skewed, but we're also taking in fewer of the EFAs than we need, even though our diets are high in fats. So although fat is too plentiful in our diets, we can't seem to get the right kind of fat in the proper ratios to enjoy healthy lives.

Essential fatty acids and depression

Two specific omega-3 EFAs are important to brain health: EPA and DHA. Both provide fuel for the brain and help control the chronic inflammation seen in degenerative brain diseases such as Alzheimer's disease. EPA plays a major role in the maintenance of nerve cell membranes, while

DHA is the main structural fatty acid in the brain's gray matter and in the retina. DHA also improves the transmission of brain signals and, thus, communication between brain cells.

When it comes to the brain, you are indeed what you eat, for diet affects the levels and kinds of fat that the brain contains. Experiments with rats have shown a difference in the contents of their brain fats after only a few weeks on experimental diets. And in humans, an inadequate supply of omega-3s during early neural development (in the embryonic/fetal stages) leads to lower levels of DHA in the brain.

But does the level of EFAs in the brain have an effect on brain function? A great many studies suggest that it does. Babies bottle-fed without DHA supplements or born to mothers who are omega-3 deficient may not achieve optimal visual and cognitive development. An omega-3 deficiency may render children less likely to sit still and pay attention in school. Too few omega-3s later in life may increase the risk of memory problems, dementia, or stroke. And low levels of DHA and other omega-3s have been linked to depression and bipolar disorder.

DHA is highly concentrated in the area of brain cells where the mood-altering neurotransmitters are stored, and it may help regulate mood by increasing levels of serotonin, a neurotransmitter that relieves depression. Several studies have found links between low blood levels of omega-3 EFAs and depression. Consider the following examples:

1. As the EPA content of red blood cells decreases, the severity of depression increases, and vice versa. Similar results were found for EPA and DHA levels in fat tissue. Mildly depressed people were found to have 34 percent less DHA in their fat tissue than nondepressed people.
2. Low blood levels of EFAs may be related to postpartum depression. A mother transfers a significant amount of EFA to her developing fetus, and her EPA levels have to be restored after the baby is born. The longer this restoration process takes, the greater the risk of postpartum depression.
3. Compared to healthy people, patients with bipolar mood disorder have lower levels of EPA, DHA, and alpha linolenic acid, a plant-based omega-3 that the body uses to manufacture EPA.
4. Suicide attempts are correlated with low plasma levels of DHA, as well as a high ratio of omega-6s to omega-3s.

If low levels of EFAs are correlated with depression, will increasing the intake of EPA and/or DHA reverse the condition? Many studies say the answer is yes. For example, a study published in the prestigious medical journal *Lancet* compared the intake of fish (a key source of omega-3 fatty acids) to the rates of depression in various population groups. The study found that higher fish consumption was linked to lower levels of depression, and vice versa.

Here's a sampling of the positive results found in other depression/omega-3 studies:

1. Consuming fish or seafood is correlated with protection against postpartum depression, bipolar disorder, and SAD.
2. In a double-blind, placebo-controlled trial, depressed people who took 9.6 g/day of DHA and EPA for eight weeks experienced improvement in mood with significantly decreased scores on the HDRS.
3. Improvement in symptoms of major depressive disorder was seen in six- to twelve-year-olds given EPA and DHA supplementation, as measured by the Children's Depression Rating Scale, Children's Depression Inventory, and Clinical Global Impression rating scale.
4. One study of patients with bipolar disorder showed that taking 9.6 g of omega-3 fatty acids each day in addition to medication helped stabilize their conditions.
5. In another study, twenty children and adolescents diagnosed with juvenile bipolar disorder were given daily doses of 360 mg of EPA and 1,560 mg of DHA. At the study's end, symptoms of mania and depression were significantly reduced.
6. In 2002, British and Scottish researchers enlisted seventy people suffering from depression who did not respond to standard medication in their randomized, double-blind study. In addition to the medication, patients were randomly assigned to receive either a placebo or ethyl-eicosapentaenoate (another form of EPA) at dosages of 1, 2, or 4 g/day for twelve weeks. Ethyl-eicosapentaenoate at the 1 g/day dosage was effective in treating depression with beneficial effects on the patients' anxiety, sleep, libido, and suicidality. Higher doses of ethyl-eicosapentaenoate in the study did not show any greater effectiveness than the placebo.

7. Omega-3 fatty acids were compared to fluoxetine (Prozac) in a 2008 study involving sixty people suffering from major depressive disorder. The study subjects were randomly assigned to take 1,000 mg of EPA, 20 mg of Prozac, or both, every day. By the end of the eight-week study, EPA proved to be as effective as Prozac in treating major depressive disorder, although the combination of the two was even better.

Not all of the omega-3 studies have yielded positive results. Sometimes EPA, DHA, or some combination of the two doesn't seem to be particularly beneficial. This happens often when a new treatment is being investigated, and it can lead to conflicting claims of efficacy. Are omega-3 fatty acids helpful in treating "straight" depression, depression with anxiety, bipolar depression, postpartum depression, or other forms of the illness?

In an attempt to advance our understanding, Canadian researchers conducted the largest "effectiveness" study to date, enlisting 430 adults suffering from a major depressive episode that had lasted at least four weeks. A little more than half of them also suffered from anxiety disorder. The subjects were randomly assigned to take either a combination of EPA and DHA or a placebo and then the intensity of their depression was tracked for eight weeks. The results were intriguing: The omega-3 fatty acid supplements were somewhat more helpful than placebo in treating depression overall. But the omega-3s produced a "clear benefit" among those who simply had a major depressive episode, without anxiety. This study suggests that while not everyone suffering from depression benefits from omega-3s, those who have certain types of depression may enjoy substantial relief. As the research progresses, we'll undoubtedly learn who will most likely benefit from omega-3 fatty acids in cases of depression.

The core concept of THE ZEEBrA approach is individualized treatment. If you have low levels of EFAs, determined via testing or the presence of deficiency symptoms described previously, then supplementation is more likely going to help.

A young woman named Julie had been suffering from bipolar disorder for ten years. As I reviewed the thick files sent to me by her various physicians, I was struck by the fact that she intermittently complained of dry skin, fatigue, allergies, and being thirsty all the time. These, along with depression, are symptoms of omega-3 fatty acid deficiency, so I asked

Julie about her diet. She explained that she tried to eat healthy foods, but her diet was unbalanced. Testing her levels of nutrients revealed dramatically low levels of omega-3s in addition to other nutrient deficiencies. Within a few months of correcting her diet, Julie's dry skin cleared. She stopped feeling thirsty all day long, and she started to notice an improvement in her mood and energy levels.

Add essential fatty acids to your diet

Although consuming sufficient fat is not a problem for most Americans, getting enough of the right kind of fat is. Here's what you can do to help ensure you're providing your body with adequate amounts of EFAs, particularly EPA and DHA:

1. Eat seafood at least twice a week, especially salmon, mackerel, herring, sardines, halibut, and albacore tuna. Grill or bake the fish without adding oils and avoid deep-frying, as this can destroy the omega-3s.
2. Eat "wild" rather than "farmed" fish; the farmed varieties typically have far fewer omega-3 acids than their wild cousins.
3. Eat meats from grass-fed animals whenever possible, as these contain a higher omega-3 to omega-6 ratio.
4. Eat foods containing omega-3s, such as walnuts, pecans, pumpkin seeds, sesame seeds, tahini, hummus, tofu, and fresh spinach.
5. Check levels of EFAs to determine proper ratios for supplementation.
6. Take an omega-3 supplement. These may come in different forms, labeled Omega-3, Fish Oil, EPA, DHA, Essential Fatty Acids, or Cod Liver Oil. Be sure to read the label carefully, for it can be confusing. If you have not been tested for EFA levels, look for a supplement that contains EPA, DHA, and gamma-linolenic acid, which supplies all of the EFAs.

Although omega-3 fatty acids are good for mental and physical health, overdoing it is not recommended. Beyond a certain point, omega-3 fatty acids disrupt the omega-6 to omega-3 fatty acid ratio, and perhaps push certain necessary fats out of the diet. Excessive amounts of omega-3 fatty acids can cause the blood to thin, leading to excessive bleeding and delayed clotting time. Be sure to check with your physician before taking omega-3 supplements, particularly if you are taking blood-thinning medicines.

My recommendations

A wealth of scientific literature supports the use of omega-3 fatty acids for depression, and many of my colleagues are prescribing higher dosages of omega-3s for their patients. I've been testing levels of EFAs in my patients for almost twenty years and have been struck by individual differences in EFA levels that are often not predicted by dietary intake.

I'm a strong advocate for individual laboratory testing to develop a personalized program for each patient. The omega-3 fatty acids are so important that it's fine to take up to 3 g/day for up to three months without testing or while waiting for tests to be ordered and performed. That's enough to eliminate a deficiency without upsetting the level of omega-6 fatty acids and possibly other substances. But beyond the three-month period, I recommend no more than 2 g/day.

Interestingly, many patients I see have deficiencies of omega-6 fatty acids after EFA testing. This is common when high doses of omega-3 supplements are taken for months without monitoring or testing. This is surprising to many, since usually the problem is an elevated level, especially in relation to the omega-3 fatty acids. I routinely recommend both omega-3 and omega-6 fatty acids from the outset, especially for those who have eczema, rashes, or other skin conditions that suggest an omega-6 fatty acid deficiency. In these cases, I often suggest that patients take the omega-6 fatty acids in the form of borage oil or evening primrose oil (which can be rubbed right on the skin).

A final word

EPA and DHA, the two key EFAs, are not magical cures for depression; neither is fish, fish oil, or cod liver oil. However, there is enough scientific evidence and practical experience to show that inadequate levels and ratios of EFAs may interfere with normalizing moods. Psychiatrists and other physicians should ensure that their patients understand the importance of taking in sufficient EFAs, in a ratio of 4:1 (omega-6 fatty acid to omega-3 fatty acid). Unless you are taking blood-thinning medications, there is no risk of significant side effects.

With so many patients still suffering from depression despite standard treatment, it is worthwhile to address EFA status as a potential factor in this complex disorder.

Cholesterol and Depression

Most people are aware that elevated cholesterol levels are a risk factor for cardiovascular disease (primarily heart attacks and strokes caused by blockages in the arteries). The U.S. government and various health organizations have been pounding that message home for decades, and cholesterol has developed a reputation as a dangerous substance. But cholesterol is also a valuable and necessary part of human chemistry and optimal brain function. The brain is the most cholesterol-rich organ in the body.

Technically speaking, cholesterol is a waxy steroid metabolite that is found in body cells and is transported through the body in the bloodstream. It is absolutely essential for life. Cholesterol ensures that cell walls function properly, is converted into vitamin D, is used to make sex and stress hormones, and serves as a major part of the coating of nerve cells, making it crucial to a functioning nervous system.

The body manufactures cholesterol as necessary, with the bulk of the production occurring in the liver. Relatively little cholesterol, about 15 percent, comes from the food we eat. The body responds to cholesterol absorbed from food. If more is consumed, less is made internally. If less is consumed, the body produces more.

The lipid hypothesis, proposed by the German pathologist Rudolf Virchow in 1856, received renewed attention in the latter half of the twentieth century. It argues that elevated levels of total cholesterol and LDL "bad" cholesterol set the stage for cardiovascular disease by damaging the interior linings of the arteries. On the other hand, the HDL "good" cholesterol can protect the arterial linings by carrying cholesterol away, so higher levels of HDL are considered to be good. Current guidelines for total cholesterol are as follows:

Desirable	less than 200 mg/dL
Borderline	200 to 239 mg/dL
High Risk	240-plus mg/dL

There's been a major effort to reduce these numbers in recent years, despite the fact that our understanding of the causes of cardiovascular disease has grown more sophisticated since cholesterol was singled out as the chief cause of heart attacks several decades ago. Many studies have shown, for example, that some people with elevated cholesterol levels do not have heart attacks or strokes, while many people who do have heart attacks or strokes do not have elevated cholesterol. Still, we are constantly exhorted to reduce our levels of total cholesterol and LDL.

This recommendation may not be a good thing for mental health, for low levels of total cholesterol have been linked to depression and suicide. Studies in the 1980s suggested that when the total cholesterol level is too low, people face an increased risk of developing depression, as well as death from suicide, accidents, and homicide. People with low cholesterol *are* at risk of death by homicide (coincidentally, low cholesterol is also seen in homicidal offenders).

Low cholesterol and depression

Several studies have linked low cholesterol levels to an increased risk of developing depression. Consider the following examples:

1. A 1993 paper published in the *Lancet* reported, "Among men aged seventy years and older, categorically defined depression was three times more common in the group with low total plasma cholesterol . . . than in those with higher concentrations."
2. A 2000 study published in *Psychosomatic Medicine*, researchers compared cholesterol levels to depressive symptoms in men ranging in age from forty to seventy. They found that men with long-term, low total cholesterol levels "have a higher prevalence of depressive symptoms" compared to those with higher cholesterol levels.
3. Women with low cholesterol levels are also vulnerable to depression. In 1998, Swedish researchers reported the results of their examination of cholesterol and depressive symptoms among 300 healthy women, ages thirty-one to sixty-five, in and around Stockholm. Women in the lowest cholesterol group (the bottom tenth percentile) suffered from significantly more depressive symptoms than did the others.
4. A 2001 study published in *Psychiatry Research* looked at primary care patients in Ireland, finding that low levels of cholesterol were linked to higher ratings on depression rating scales.
5. Italian researchers measured the cholesterol levels of 186 patients hospitalized for depression and found an association between low cholesterol and depressive symptoms.

This research is supported by other studies, including a 2008 meta-analysis, which found that a higher total cholesterol was associated with lower levels of depression. A recently published, very interesting study looked at the levels of HDL in depressed people and found that low levels of HDL were linked to "long-term depressive symptomatology."

Low cholesterol and suicide

Suffering through a depressive episode can be very difficult, and one of the great fears is that someone in the throes of depression does not see any point in continuing to live.

Early evidence of a link between low cholesterol and suicide came from the Multiple Risk Factor Intervention Trial study, a large-scale, long-term look at various health factors involving hundreds of thousands of volunteers. Data from the study was analyzed by researchers from the University of Minnesota, who found that people with total cholesterol levels lower than 160 mg/dL were more likely to commit suicide than those with higher cholesterol levels. Other studies are equally alarming:

1. A 2008 study looked at forty men who were hospitalized due to bipolar disorder. Twenty had attempted suicide at some point in the past, and the other twenty had not. Both cholesterol and blood fat levels were lower, on average, among those who had attempted suicide.
2. A paper published in the *Journal of Clinical Psychiatry* in the same year reported the results of an examination of cholesterol levels in 417 patients who had attempted suicide at some point, 155 hospitalized psychiatric patients who had not, and healthy controls. Results of the study suggest that low cholesterol may be associated with suicide attempts.
3. The suicidal method of choice, self-inflicted fatal gun wound versus pills, for example, may also be related to cholesterol levels. A 2008 study published in *Psychiatry Research* compared nineteen people who had attempted suicide using violent methods to sixteen who had attempted to kill themselves nonviolently, as well as to twenty healthy controls. The researchers found that "violent suicide attempters had significantly lower total cholesterol and leptin levels compared with those with nonviolent suicide attempts."

The strong connection between low cholesterol and suicide is highlighted in a 2004 study, which concluded that a low total cholesterol level can be used as an indicator of suicide risk. This study, involving suicide attempters with major depressive disorder, nonsuicidal depressed patients, and normal controls, found significant differences in cholesterol levels among the various groups.

The average total serum cholesterol level was 190 mg/dL among the normal controls, 180 mg/dL in nonsuicidal depressed group, and 150 mg/dL among the suicidal depressive patients. This study showed that the total cholesterol level can be used to gauge possible suicide risk (less than 180 mg/dL) and probable risk (150 mg/dL and lower).

Numerous studies investigated the possibility that low cholesterol levels can drive people to commit, or attempt to commit, suicide. The research is not unanimous in its conclusion, but a strong body of evidence indicates that low cholesterol and suicide, particularly violent suicide, are linked.

Suicide is not the only type of violence associated with lower cholesterol levels. Homicide and other violence committed against others is also associated with low cholesterol. Swedish researchers compared one-time cholesterol measurements on nearly eighty thousand men and women, ranging in age from twenty-four to seventy, to subsequent arrests for violent crime. The researchers reported that "low cholesterol is associated with increased subsequent criminal violence."

What's the cholesterol-depression link?

The studies linking low cholesterol to depression, suicide, and violence looked at the serum cholesterol level, which is the amount of cholesterol in the blood. But what about the amount of cholesterol in the brain?

Canadian researchers were the first to examine this question in their 2007 study published in the *International Journal of Neuropsychopharmacology*. The researchers measured and compared the cholesterol content in various parts of the brains of forty-one men who had committed suicide and twenty-one men who had died of other, sudden causes that had no direct impact on the brain. The results were intriguing: When the suicides were categorized as violent or nonviolent, those who had committed violent suicide were found to have less cholesterol than the others in the gray matter of their brains. This was seen specifically in the frontal cortex, a part of the brain that handles "executive functions," including processes involved in planning, cognitive flexibility, abstract thinking, initiating appropriate actions and inhibiting inappropriate actions, and selecting relevant sensory information. The frontal cortex essentially controls the ability to make good decisions.

As is the case with so much of psychiatry, we don't know exactly why a low cholesterol level is linked to depression. Cholesterol is a critical precursor to many essential physiological molecules in the human body that directly and indirectly affect our moods and optimal brain function. Some researchers theorize that low levels of cholesterol alter brain chemistry, suppressing the production and/or availability of the neurotransmitter serotonin. In Chapter 8 you learn that cholesterol is essential for the synthesis of all steroid and sex hormones, including DHEA, testosterone, and estrogen. And in Chapter 13 you learn that vitamin D is synthesized with the help of cholesterol and ultraviolet light.

Another hypothesis, based on the knowledge that cholesterol has a role in inflammation, suggests that the link between low cholesterol and depression is chronic, low-grade inflammation. More ideas have been proposed, and future research will undoubtedly find the "missing link" between low cholesterol and depression.

A dangerous trend

In the meantime it's critical that we become aware of a dangerous trend. For years now, I've been looking into the depression-low cholesterol link, and I'm becoming increasingly alarmed as more and more people are put on statin medications that cause their cholesterol levels to plummet.

> Daniel, a forty-two-year-old executive, came to see me for depression and anxiety. After struggling with depression in college, he had been doing well until this past year. Reviewing his laboratory tests, I shared with him my concern about his total cholesterol level of 125 mg/dL. A year ago he had been placed on a statin for "preventative" reasons when his cholesterol levels reached 200 mg/dL. As his cholesterol levels declined with the statin, so did his mood. His physician agreed to discontinue Daniel's statin. Within three months, Daniel's cholesterol levels normalized and his depressed mood "miraculously" disappeared without medications.

One drug company has received the FDA's approval to begin advertising its statin as a preventive measure for *people who do not even have high cholesterol levels.* If, however, they have elevated levels of inflammation within their body plus another risk factor for cardiovascular disease, such as high blood pressure, they would be considered eligible for the medicine.

Currently, about 80 million Americans can be prescribed statins, according to the old criteria. The new criteria for prescribing statins increases the number of eligible Americans by an estimated 6.5 million people. Many of my patients have told me that they're pressured by their family practitioner or cardiologist to take statins or other cholesterol-lowering medicines, even if their cholesterol is only slightly elevated or in the higher ranges of normal. Doctors often do prescribe cholesterol-lowering medications to patients with normal cholesterol levels, especially if they have diabetes, a family history of heart disease, or another cardiovascular risk factor. That may be reasonable from the point of view of cardiology, but not so wise from a psychiatric perspective. The "cholesterol culture" calls for pushing cholesterol numbers down, without taking into account potential psychological consequences.

If a patient's total cholesterol is less than 165, the psychiatrist should suspect that it may be a contributing factor to depression. If it's 140 or less, I recommend that the cholesterol level be pushed back up above 165. For some patients, raising cholesterol levels is simply a matter of adjusting their cholesterol medication and allowing cholesterol levels to rise naturally. For others, it means changing their diet to include eggs and other cholesterol-rich foods. This should be done in cooperation with the patient's personal physician to ensure that cardiovascular risk factors are properly monitored.

Too Important to Overlook

Cholesterol and EFAs are intimately linked to depression, although the links are not immediately obvious and often require a bit of detective work. Understanding the consequences of deficiencies in essential fats and cholesterol is important for the effective treatment of depression. Whether it is drug induced, genetic, or a result of dietary patterns, low cholesterol prevents our brains from functioning optimally. Low cholesterol may contribute to the development of depression and stand in the way of successful and sustained recovery from depression.

12

E – Exercise and Energy

"Yes, I know it's good for me," Marissa said when I suggested that she start exercising. "I think about it a lot and I keep paying my health-club fees, but I don't have the energy. I just don't have the energy."

Many patients struggling with depression have a hard time summoning the motivation and energy needed to exercise, even though they know it helps reduce symptoms of depression. However, I believe it's vital for those suffering from depression to exercise. What you do is not nearly as important as simply doing something, whether it is walking, swimming, weight lifting, dancing, bike riding, gardening, tai chi, or aerobics.

Later in this chapter, I describe specific supplements I recommend to help patients gain the energy they may need to get started. But first, let's take a look at the antidepressive effects of exercise.

Science Supports Exercise

The idea that exercise can help relieve the symptoms of depression is not new. If you look through the online National Library of Medicine, you'll find studies dating back to 1970 that look at the psychological effects of exercise. Here are the findings from some recent studies:

1. A Columbia University Department of Epidemiology researcher examined data on exercise habits and mental status taken from 8,098 subjects participating in the National Comorbidity Survey. The 60.3 percent of adults in the survey who engaged in regular physical activity were significantly less likely to suffer from major depression and anxiety disorders.
2. The National Institutes of Health assessed the effects of exercise in 5,451 men and 1,277 women, ages twenty through eighty-eight. This study looked specifically at walking, jogging, and running as exercise, ranking the participants according to how often they exercised. Those who exercised more were less likely to have depressive symptoms, but it didn't take running a marathon to chase away the blues. In fact, the "dose response" peaked at 11–19 miles per week, which amounts to 1.6–2.7 miles per day.
3. Eight adults, ranging in age from twenty to forty-five and all suffering from mild to moderate major depressive disorder, were enlisted in a study that tested whether aerobic exercise was an effective treatment for major depressive disorder, as well as how much exercise was necessary. Researchers measured the severity of depression by scores on the widely used HDRS test for depression. The participants were randomly assigned to four different exercise groups, with the most active group exercising five times a week at a level consistent with public health recommendations (thirty minutes of moderate-to-vigorous exercise most days per week). After twelve weeks, depression scores on the HDRS dropped 47 percent for those in the most active exercise group, an improvement comparable to what's seen with some medications.
4. The benefits of exercise were tested in new mothers, 13 percent of whom develop postpartum depression. Eighty volunteers were enlisted, all of whom had a score of ten or more on the Edinburgh Postnatal Depression Scale. They were assigned to one of two groups: An exercise support group that had three supervised exercise sessions per week (one at the hospital, two at home) for three months or a control group that just received standard care. Five

months postpartum, the women in the exercise group were less likely to have high scores on the depression scale than the women who did not exercise.

5. Duke University researchers compared the long-term effects of exercise to a standard antidepressant in a study of 156 adults suffering from major depressive disorder. The volunteers were randomly assigned to either a four-month aerobic exercise program, treatment with sertraline (Zoloft), or both. At the end of the four-month period, results were comparable in all three groups. In other words, exercise alone, Zoloft alone, or the two together were equally effective in reducing symptoms of depression. However, six months later, those who had exercised and whose symptoms of depression had improved were less likely to have relapsed than those who had not exercised. The researchers noted that exercise is a feasible treatment for major depressive disorde and is "associated with significant therapeutic benefit."
6. Weight lifting can also be an "antidepressive exercise." A Harvard Medical School researcher examined the effects of weight lifting in senior citizens (average age seventy-one) who were randomly assigned to either the exercise group, which performed ten weeks of supervised weight lifting followed by ten weeks of unsupervised weight lifting, or the control group, which did not receive any active treatment. Twenty weeks later, those who had been lifting weights had significantly lower depression scores, compared to those in the no-exercise group. The volunteers were left alone for about two years, allowed to exercise or not exercise as they pleased. When they were retested, those who had originally been in the exercise group continued to enjoy lower depression scores, indicating that exercise may have a long-term benefit.
7. The antidepressant effects of yoga have long been reported, and several studies have shown that this mind-body exercise is effective. In one such study, young adults suffering from mild depression were randomly assigned to yoga classes or to take no yoga and serve as a control group. At the end of the five-week study period, those who had participated in the yoga classes showed significant drops in depressive symptoms. A similar study evaluated the mental health symptoms of professional musicians, who often suffer from elevated

stress and performance anxiety. Fifteen musicians practiced yoga and meditation; an additional fifteen practiced yoga and meditation plus group classes and discussions emphasizing a "yogic lifestyle"; and a final group of fifteen, serving as the control group, practiced neither yoga nor meditation. Two months later, the volunteers in both the yoga and meditation groups enjoyed significantly less depression, general anxiety and tension, and anger compared to the control group.

8. The ancient Asian movement form called tai chi is also effective in reducing symptoms of depression. This has been demonstrated in studies of people with osteoarthritis and rheumatoid arthritis, senior citizens, and others. Part of tai chi's antidepressant effects may come from the exercise itself and part from the fact that it is usually practiced in a group, so participants benefit from social interaction.
9. The antidepressant effects of exercise are so widely known that the June 2009 issue of *Current Psychiatry* even ran an article titled *Exercise Prescription*, reviewing the studies and recommending that psychiatrists help their depressed patients to begin exercising and to stay with it. Specifically, the article suggested that psychiatrists "counsel patients about exercise as a plan or prescription, and discuss exercise at each visit." This is excellent advice, because, as noted recently in *U.S. News & World Report*, exercise does the following:

    Reverses the detrimental effects of stress
    Lifts depression
    Improves learning
    Builds self-esteem and improves body image
    Leaves you feeling euphoric

Exercise may improve mood in ways similar to antidepressant medications by regulating neurotransmitters. Recently, University of Georgia researchers demonstrated that exercise can activate genes that increase the level of the neurotransmitter galanin in the brain, which, in turn, influences norepinephrine and reduces the body's stress response.

A newly published study indicates that exercise can even help the brain heal from damage caused by early childhood trauma. Researchers from

Australia's University of New South Wales separated newborn rats from their mothers for specific periods of time in order to cause high levels of stress. Once they were weaned, the young rats were randomly assigned to either eat regular chow, eat a high-fat diet, exercise voluntarily on an exercise wheel, or both exercise and eat a high-fat diet, for eleven weeks. Separating the young animals from their mothers caused measurable changes in the brain, which were reversed in the rats that were allowed to exercise over a long period of time (as well as in those who ate a high-fat diet). The researchers concluded that exercise "produced beneficial effects on both the behaviour and metabolic outcomes following early life stress induced by maternal separation."

How does exercise work?

We haven't yet identified the exact way(s) in which exercise relieves depression. The several possibilities include the following:

Physical factors

- Spurring the release of endorphins or other "feel good" hormones
- Changing the levels or effects of norepinephrine, serotonin, or other brain chemicals
- Lowering the levels of cortisol, a "stress hormone"
- Increasing body temperature

Psychological factors

- Getting the mind off daily activities and stress
- Improving self-esteem as you accomplish exercise goals
- Improving self-image as you become stronger, more flexible, or slimmer
- Encouraging interaction with others (in some exercise activities)

The ultimate answer: just exercise

Even though exercise has been proven to help relieve symptoms of depression, questions remain. Exactly which type of exercise is best? How often should one exercise, how long, and how intense should each session be? Studies have examined these questions, and more, without coming to definitive answers.

Meanwhile, start exercising! If you love to jog, jog. If you prefer ballet or yoga class, great. If you enjoy playing baseball or gardening, lifting weights or shooting baskets, do so. The most important thing you can do is get started. Yes, the studies show that there is a certain level of intensity necessary to get the antidepressant value, but many depressed people are lacking in energy and motivation and are out of shape, which is why I say just start exercising. Even if the benefits are relatively small in the beginning, they'll begin to add up, making it easier to step it up to the next level in time.

Don't wait for the definitive study to answer all the exercise questions and don't try to devise the "perfect" exercise plan. Don't try to figure out exactly how many calories you're burning and don't compare yourself to anyone else or to what you think you should do. Just get started. It is always helpful to discuss your plans for exercise with your primary care physician.

How Can You Exercise without Energy?

Exercising improves brain chemistry and boosts energy, but if you haven't got the energy to begin with, how do you get started? Overcoming depression-caused inertia can be very difficult. "It's like I'm a car with no gas; I can't move," is how one patient described it. "I'd like to, but it ain't gonna happen."

Psychiatrists have long been aware that a great many of our depressed patients complain of a lack of energy. A paper published in the *Journal of Affective Disorders* in 2008 used data from nearly twenty-two hundred patients suffering from major depressive disorder to determine which physical symptoms were most commonly afflicting those with major depressive disorder from a moderate to a more severe degree. The top five were as follows:

Complaint	Percent of Patients
Feeling fatigued, weak, or tired all over	78
Feeling not in as good physical health as friends	59
Not feeling well most of the time in past few years	54
Feeling weak in parts of body	45
Headaches	45

Psychiatrists tended to dismiss these physical symptoms hoping they would resolve with medication and therapy. However, as you learned earlier, more than two-thirds of patients treated for depression continue to suffer from symptoms such as fatigue. New research is now looking into the physical symptoms of depression, including fatigue. Their findings suggest that the body's mitochondria may be implicated.

Mitochondria are tiny structures within the body's cells that serve as "cellular energy factories" generating most of a cell's adenosine triphosphate (ATP), which acts as a form of "gasoline" for the cell's "engines." Mitochondria also participate in other cellular functions, such as regulation of cellular growth and death. Damage to the mitochondria can result in less energy available to the cells. This, in turn, can hamper their function. In 2008, a team of researchers from Sweden and the United States compared the mitochondrial function in muscle tissue and "body complaints" of twenty-one people suffering from major depressive disorder to that of ten healthy controls. This was the first time such a study had been undertaken, and the results were intriguing. In the words of the researchers, "Mitochondrial function correlates very strongly with self-reported data related to somatic symptoms." In other words, weakened mitochondrial activity, translates into less cellular energy, which is linked to physical discomfort.

Is it possible that poor mitochondrial function is also linked to psychiatric distress? The human brain, which requires a lot of energy, contains a large number of mitochondria. It would be no surprise to find that damage to the vital mitochondria may be an underlying cause of depression and other psychiatric disorders. This theory has been investigated in animal studies, which show that stress interferes with mitochondrial energy production.

Understanding the importance of mitochondria for energy production in every cell of the human body offers us a new way to treat depression. It also gives us a way to deal with the relentless fatigue and other physical symptoms associated with depression: Support the mitochondria. The strategy for doing so is threefold: First, keep the body as healthy as possible; second, use natural substances that are known to support the mitochondria; and third, use energy-boosting supplements to overcome fatigue so that you can start exercising. This breaks the terrible "depression-fatigue-can't move-more depression-more fatigue" cycle.

The entire THE ZEEBrA program is a synergistic program that strengthens the body and builds energy. Better sleep garners energy, as does reducing stress, improving digestion, optimizing hormone levels, eliminating foods that sap energy, and taking in generous quantities of all the necessary nutrients. Simply working through THE ZEEBrA recommendations will lead to better health and increased energy, which will be boosted even further with exercise. In addition, selected supplements help boost energy.

Overcoming "Antiexercise Inertia" with B_{12}

One of the key elements in THE ZEEBrA program, as far as energy is concerned, is vitamin B_{12}, otherwise known as cyanocobalamin. B_{12} works in concert with other members of the B-family of vitamins to perform a variety of tasks within the body, including strengthening the nervous and immune systems and helping to maintain muscle tone and healthy skin. B_{12} plays a vital role in energy metabolism, and a shortage of the vitamin can lead to a lack of energy. Indeed, fatigue is one of the most common symptoms of B_{12} deficiency. (Another symptom is depression.) At one time in history, doctors regularly gave B_{12} injections to their patients who felt tired or run down. As was the case with many other natural remedies, B_{12} was pushed aside by the wave of new medicines and never subjected to the extensive testing it deserves.

I have found that B_{12} does indeed boost energy in people with low, low-normal, and even "normal" serum B_{12} levels. There are times B_{12} has even helped boost energy when B_{12} levels were completely normal. But there's disagreement about what constitutes optimal levels. The "normal" range is usually given as 200–900 picograms per milliliter (pg/mL). That's quite a wide range, with the larger number being four-and-a-half times larger than the smaller. Can you really say that someone whose level is 200 is as healthy as another person with a 900 level? Is 250 really just as good 850?

Some doctors pick a middle range, saying that "normal" is between 400 and 500. However, I have found that people have much better energy levels when their B_{12} is much higher, up in the 800–900 range. I talk more about vitamin B_{12} in Chapter 13. For now, I simply want you to be aware that low levels of B_{12} can lead to low energy and that increasing the amount of B_{12} available for energy production can be very helpful, especially for senior citizens, vegans, and people taking acid-blocking medicines for GERD or other reasons. Those taking acid blockers may have trouble absorbing the vitamins. Vegans, who do no eat animal or dairy products, do not ingest B_{12}, which is found in foods of animal origin.

Other medications can also interfere with the body's ability to use vitamin B_{12}, including amoxicillin and other antibiotics, as well as the colestipol used to reduce cholesterol levels.

Energizing the Cellular Energy Factories with Carnitine

While B_{12} helps with overall energy levels, a supplement called carnitine can be specifically helpful for revving up the mitochondrial energy factories.

Carnitine is a natural substance, made from amino acids, found in most cells in the human body. Its name comes from the Latin word for flesh (*carnus*), because it was first isolated in meat. One of carnitine's key functions is helping to produce energy in the mitochondria. It does so by carrying fatty acids into the mitochondria, where they are "burned" to release energy.

Several studies have investigated the use of carnitine as an energy booster. One of these involved centenarians (people who are one hundred years old or older), for they frequently suffer from fatigue. Sixty-six centenarians were randomly assigned to receive either 2 g of carnitine (levocarnitine) daily or a placebo for six months. Those taking the carnitine showed less physical and mental fatigue, compared to those taking the placebo. Carnitine supplements have helped restore energy levels in people with chronic fatigue syndrome, which is characterized by low blood levels of carnitine. Carnitine has also been used to treat fatigue related to cancer, adult celiac disease, and other ailments.

We get some carnitine from food (the best sources are meat, milk, poultry, and fish) and some is made in the liver and kidneys from the amino acids lysine and methionine. Carnitine supplements come in different forms: L-carnitine, acetyl-L-carnitine, and propionyl-L-carnitine.

The U.S. government has not set a daily minimum intake of carnitine, assuming we get enough from our food and internal production, and people are not generally tested for carnitine deficiency. Thus, we typically don't know if a patient is producing enough internally and, even if they are, whether their bodies are able to transport and use the carnitine. Lacking simple tools to determine if someone is carnitine deficient, I often recommend carnitine supplementation to patients with depression. Without it, a fifty-seven-year-old patient of mine named John stated, "I couldn't summon the energy to exercise if you held a gun to my head."

Many depressed people benefit greatly from carnitine. It gives them the energy boost they need to exercise and otherwise change their lifestyle to combat depression. It worked well for John, who after taking carnitine and other nutritional supplements for three months told me, "You don't need a gun to get me to exercise any more. You don't even have to tell me to do it. I look forward to my daily strolls."

To ensure they have generous supplies of energy-producing carnitine, I typically recommend that patients start by taking 500 mg twice a day and then work their way up to 1 g of carnitine before breakfast and another before lunch in a few weeks. Side effects of excessive carnitine supplementation, which typically show up if one is taking 3 g/day or more, include nausea, diarrhea, and abdominal cramps. Keep in mind that medicines such as carbamazepine and Depakote, used for seizures, and the chemotherapy agent doxorubicin can deplete the body of carnitine.

Strengthening the carnitine effect with CoQ10

The effect of carnitine is enhanced when taken with Coenzyme Q10 (CoQ10), a natural, vitamin-like substance found in the energy-producing mitochondria. As part of the "cellular energy factory," CoQ10 helps to manufacture ATP, the major source of cellular energy. In addition to boosting energy, CoQ10 has antioxidant properties and strengthens the immune system.

Several studies have shown that CoQ10 helps boost energy levels. In a double-blind placebo-controlled study, seventeen healthy subjects, averaging 37.5 years old, were randomly assigned to one of three different groups: the 100 mg CoQ10, the 300 mg CoQ10, or the placebo groups. They took their supplements daily for eight days, their ability to exercise on a bicycle was measured, and then they switched to a new group.

By the time the study was completed, all of the subjects had taken all of the substances (100 mg CoQ10, 300 mg CoQ10, and placebo), although neither they nor the doctors knew when they took each preparation until the study was completed. While taking either dose of CoQ10, the volunteers suffered from less fatigue than when they were taking the placebo, and they were better able to exercise.

CoQ10 supplements are used to treat chronic fatigue syndrome, and I have found them to be very helpful in overcoming depression-related fatigue. Newer studies have shown that CoQ10 supplements help improve athletic performance. In addition to carnitine, I often recommend CoQ10 to patients who complain about lack of energy. CoQ10, a fat-soluble molecule, is available in two forms: ubiquinone and ubiquinol. Ubiquinol is the most active form of CoQ10 in the body and is synthesized from ubiquinone. For the treatment of depression, I recommend ubiquinol, if available, in capsules of 100 mg/day or ubiquinone up to 200 mg/day. Because these are fat soluble, they should be taken with food that contains some fat.

The body uses tyrosine and numerous nutrients to manufacture CoQ10, and it is also found in food. Dietary sources of CoQ10 include whole grains, salmon and other oily fish, and organ meats such as liver. Certain medicines, including the statin drugs used to lower cholesterol, some beta-blockers used primarily for heart rhythm disorders and high blood pressure, and imipramine (Tofranil) used for depression, can deplete the body of CoQ10.

Creating Cellular Energy with Ribose and Whey

The special sugar ribose, which is found in the body, produces the ATP that energizes cells. Ribose is an essential ingredient in the ATP-manufacturing process, but it is more than a building block, for its presence in the cells encourages the production of ATP. Thus, it is serves as both a raw material and "production manager," ordering the creation of more cellular energy.

The use of ribose as an energy-generating supplement was tested in a study examining whether ribose (in the form of D-ribose) could improve energy levels in people suffering from chronic fatigue syndrome or fibromyalgia. This was an open-label study, so both the participants and the doctors knew that all of the volunteers were receiving the "real thing" and not a placebo. The forty-one volunteers took 15 g of D-ribose daily, and at the end of the study period they showed significant improvement in energy, sleep, mental clarity, and well-being, and they experienced reduced pain intensity. The average increase in energy, as perceived by the participants, was 45 percent.

Ribose's energy-generating properties can also been seen in athletes. Danish researchers had eight healthy athletes take either ribose or a placebo for three days following a week of heavy intermittent exercise. The level of ATP in the muscles of the participants fell by nearly 30 percent after the exercise period, but in those taking ribose, it returned to normal three days later. In those taking the placebo, ATP recovery took noticeably more time.

I typically recommend 5 g of ribose powder in addition to carnitine and CoQ10. I also recommend that patients take whey protein amino acids, which are protein building blocks taken from the clear liquid that develops during the cheese-making process. Whey protein supplies the amino acids necessary for the body to produce CoQ10 and other substances used in the energy-generating process.

These energy-boosting nutrients can be taken twice a day in what I have called THE ZEEBrA Shake.

Each of these shakes can be made using a blender. The 5 g of ribose makes these shakes truly "natural" energy drinks.

Chocolate/Banana THE ZEEBrA Shake

(Recipe yields 1 serving)

1 scoop of purified chocolate whey protein (or protein substitute)
1/2 cup milk (regular, almond, or soy)
1/2 cup plain yogurt
5 grams ribose
1/2 frozen banana
Crushed ice as needed

Mixed Berry THE ZEEBrA Shake

(Recipe yields 1 serving)

1 scoop of vanilla or berry whey protein (or protein substitute)
1/2 cup milk (regular, almond, or soy)
1/2 cup plain yogurt
5 grams ribose
1/2 cup frozen berries (raspberries, blueberries, strawberries)
Crushed ice as needed

Getting Energized!

While some people with depression seem to generate the energy they need to begin exercising, others need assistance from B_{12}, carnitine, CoQ10, ribose, and pure whey protein. Whatever way works for you is fine, as long as you begin exercising. And you needn't exercise for hours on end. New research is showing that several smaller bursts of exercise are as effective for reducing the risk of cardiovascular disease as are fewer, longer sessions, and I have found that for my patients, smaller bursts of exercise help to break the depression cycle and generate additional energy.

Get started!

13

B – B Vitamins and Other Vitamins

An ample supply of vitamins and minerals is absolutely necessary, not only for physical health but also for psychological well-being. But it's not just a matter of staving off the terrible deficiency diseases such as scurvy or beriberi. Optimal psychological health requires generous amounts of nutrients to manufacture neurotransmitters, stabilize blood sugar, ease mood swings, improve sleep, and help the body rid itself of toxins.

Nancy, a fifty-seven-year-old homemaker and grandmother, had been taking what she described as a "small dose of antidepressants" for three decades. "They helped, I guess," she told me. When I checked her diet and blood tests, I found she was moderately low in vitamin B_{12}; that is, she was at the low end of the recommended range. I suggested she increase her B_{12} intake, but she challenged me, saying that there was no point in doing so if her level was in the recommended range. I pointed out that everyone is biochemically unique and that what was acceptable for the imaginary average person may be way too low for her. She agreed and increased her B_{12} intake. Soon afterward her depression lifted.

This chapter focuses on vitamins that can affect your mood: the B vitamins and vitamin D, plus the neurotransmitter-regulating substance S-adenosyl-L-methionine, or SAMe. The B family of vitamins, which includes thiamine, riboflavin, niacin, vitamin B_6, vitamin B_{12}, folate (folic acid), and inositol, works as a team that performs several vital tasks in the body. Some of the most critical jobs involve controlling the release of energy in the brain cells and manufacturing those all-important brain chemicals, the neurotransmitters. Niacin and B_6, in particular, help support the production of serotonin, a neurotransmitter that regulates mood, sleep, and appetite. The B vitamins also aid in mood regulation through their role in carbohydrate metabolism. They help stabilize blood sugar, ease mood swings, and improve sleep. In addition, they assist the liver in deactivating and disposing of old estrogen, which might otherwise build up and contribute to estrogen excess, a suspected cause of mood changes.

The B vitamins are also critical to the energy-generating process that turns nutrients into energy, known as the Krebs cycle. Without ample supplies of these vitamins, energy levels run low, contributing to the feelings of fatigue that are so commonly seen in depression.

Deficiencies in B vitamins can actually harm the brain, leading to depression, anxiety, irritability, and difficulty concentrating. Studies have shown the following:

- Too little thiamine can interfere with the uptake of glucose in the brain, leading to mental fatigue and poor moods.
- A lack of folate can contribute to depression.
- A deficiency of B_6, which is necessary for the manufacture of serotonin and dopamine, can bring on depression and mental confusion.
- Inadequate B_{12}, which is necessary for red blood cell formation, leads to problems transporting oxygen through the body and can cause fatigue, mood swings, irritability, dementia, or mania.

Let's take a closer look at some of the key B vitamins (and other substances) to see how they influence mood.

Folate (Vitamin B_9)

Folate, commonly referred to as folic acid, is required for normal cell development and the manufacture of DNA and RNA. It's also necessary for the formation of SAMe, which, in turn, is needed for neurotransmitter metabolism. Folate may protect against colorectal, breast, and cervical cancers. It also protects the heart by breaking down a harmful substance associated with heart disease called homocysteine. For years, doctors have recommended that pregnant women take folate supplements to reduce the risk of fetal brain and spinal cord defects, as folate is necessary for closing the neural tube in the fetus, a tube that will become the spinal cord.

Folate and depression

The link between folate and depression has been discussed in the medical literature since the 1960s. As the decades have passed, hypotheses have been replaced by facts based on significant research conducted by highly regarded academic institutions across the country. Here's what they have found:

Folate factors into the depression equation in a number of ways. First, studies have found that many people with depression have lower levels of folate than those who are not depressed. Red blood cell folate levels are significantly lower in depressed patients than in those suffering from other psychiatric disorders. Conversely, a recent study found that people whose diets contain greater amounts of folate report less depression. Thus, for some people with depression, the problem—and the solution—may be dietary.

Second, studies have also found that antidepressant treatments, including medications and ECT, do not work as well for people who are folate deficient. One such study looked at 213 adults with major depressive disorder who were treated with fluoxetine (Prozac) for eight weeks, finding that low folate levels correlated with a lack of response to the medicine. This shows that a certain level of folate must be present if antidepressants are to be effective, and it may explain some instances of medication failure in depression treatment.

Third, depressed people with lower levels of folate have higher rates of relapse. That is, depression may lift with treatment, but it is more likely to return if there is inadequate folate. This was demonstrated by researchers from Massachusetts General Hospital in their study of depressed individuals who had improved after taking fluoxetine. The researchers checked patients' folate levels to determine prestudy levels and then monitored their progress for about seven months as they continued to take fluoxetine. The baseline folate levels played a role in whether depression returned: 43 percent of those with low folate levels relapsed, compared to only 3 percent of study subjects with normal folate levels.

Building on this knowledge, researchers explored the addition of folate to standard antidepressant treatment. In a ten-week study, men and women diagnosed with a new episode of depression were treated with daily doses of fluoxetine. In addition they received either 500 μg of folic acid or a placebo every day. At the end of the study, the women (but not the men) who had taken folic acid with their medication were significantly happier than those on the placebo plus medication. The researchers noted that "Folic acid is a simple method of greatly improving the antidepressant action of fluoxetine and probably other antidepressant agents."

Another study from pscyhiatrists at Massachusetts General Hospital corroborated the benefits of taking folate with antidepressant medications. Patients with depression, who had remained depressed despite taking antidepressant SSRI medications such as Prozac, Zoloft, Effexor, and Paxil were given a folic acid supplement to take with their medication for eight weeks. At the end of the eight weeks, the patients' depression improved.

The following sums up the results of the studies:

- Low folate levels are associated with an increased incidence of depression.
- Low folate levels are linked with poor response to antidepressants.
- Low folate levels are correlated with a higher relapse rate.
- Folate supplementation enhances the effect of antidepressants.

Folate, folic acid, and L-methylfolate

I have been using the words "folate" and "folic acid" interchangeably, as if they were exactly the same thing. But the truth is that they are different forms of the same vitamin, and as a result the body handles them differently:

- Folate is the naturally occurring form of the vitamin found in various foods.
- Folic acid is the synthetic form of the vitamin used in supplements and fortified foods.
- 5-methyltetrahydrofolate (also known as L-methylfolate) is the natural, active form of folate used at the cellular level for DNA reproduction, regulation of homocysteine, and other functions.
- L-methylfolate easily crosses the blood-brain barrier.

The form of folate that people commonly take as a supplement is folic acid, the synthetic form. This type of folate can exert activity in the body but not in the brain. In order to affect the brain and influence mental well-being, folate must first be converted into L-methylfolate. This form of folate is capable of crossing the physiological "wall" separating the rest of the body from the brain, the so-called blood-brain barrier. The blood-brain barrier surrounds and protects the central nervous system (the brain, spinal cord, and their fluids) allowing certain substances to cross it, while fencing others out. Folate crosses the blood-brain barrier in the form of L-methylfolate. After entering the brain, this form of folate is changed into yet another form that helps create the mood-altering neurotransmitters serotonin, dopamine, and norepinephrine. Maintaining the proper amounts and ratios of these neurotransmitters is crucial for warding off depression.

Many people's bodies easily and efficiently convert the folate they get from food and folic acid from supplements into the active forms needed for optimal body and brain function. But others do not, due to their unique genetics. For example, genetic mutations called *MTHFR* polymorphisms prevent the body from easily converting folate into the active form that crosses the blood-brain barrier. People with this genetic alteration may eat plenty of folate-containing foods and take folate supplements, but the amount of folate in the brain or brain area is still insufficient. Not surprisingly, studies have found that people with the *MTHFR* alteration are more likely to develop depression compared to those without the mutation, and that people with depression are more likely to have the *MTHFR* alteration.

Determining if there is enough folate

No single test can determine if your body's folate levels are sufficient. You can measure folate levels in the blood, but these do not always accurately reflect the folate levels in the CSF surrounding the brain. A blood level may be in the normal range, but because there is not enough folate in the brain, an individual can have a "functional deficiency." Another way to assess a person's folate status is to measure the levels of an amino acid called homocysteine. Folate helps break down homocysteine in the body: If a person is folate deficient, homocysteine levels rise.

How much to take

For some depressed patients, especially those on severely restricted diets, simply adding folate-rich foods to the diet can make a difference. Good sources include asparagus, citrus fruit, fortified cereals, green leafy vegetables, and legumes (peas, beans, and lentils). Moreover, many brands of cereal and flour are fortified with folic acid.

However, it's possible for people to become folate deficient even if there's plenty of this nutrient in the diet. As stated earlier, some people have a genetic abnormality that prevents them from converting folate to a form that can cross the blood-brain barrier. Others may have difficulty absorbing folate. In addition, oral contraceptives, anticonvulsants, antacids, certain antibiotics, alcohol consumption, and tobacco use can interfere with folate metabolism.

In many cases of depression, supplementation may be necessary. I typically recommend folate in the form of L-methylfolate, the form of folate that crosses the blood-brain barrier, which is especially helpful for those individuals with a *MTHFR* polymorphism. L-methylfolate can also be purchased over the counter in some pharmacies, vitamin stores, and health-food stores. A prescription-grade L-methylfolate is available as well. The good news is that with a pharmaceutical company backing a nutritional supplement, growing research now supports the use of L-methylfolate for the treatment of depression. L-methylfolate can be used in conjunction with antidepressants or, for many, it can be a core supplement in a treatment plan that does not include antidepressant medication.

The results of studies exploring the relationship between folate and depression are clear and compelling. When supplementing, avoid synthetic forms of folate such as folic acid and use L-methylfolate instead. Eat plenty of foods containing the natural forms of folate.

Everyone should also be aware of the concern that folic acid supplementation may have potentially serious side effects, such as enhancing cancer risk and increasing the rate of cognitive decline. Due to its role in DNA synthesis, folate is required for cell division and growth. It has been suggested that increased amounts of folate in the body may speed up the growth of cells leading to cancer. Furthermore, if there is underlying cancer, folate may facilitate its development.

Another concern is folate's potential role in cognitive decline. A study conducted among older community-dwelling residents found that high folate intake, both from food sources and supplementation, was associated with a faster rate of cognitive decline. Although it's not clear how folate may increase cognitive decline, one study suggested that high folate intake may mask a deficiency of vitamin B_{12}, which is vital to proper brain and spinal cord functioning. A more recent study has shown that when seniors had low vitamin B_{12} status, high serum folate was associated with cognitive impairment. Once their vitamin B_{12} levels were normal, high serum folate was associated with protection against cognitive impairment.

Folate in the form of L-methylfolate has been shown to have fewer potential health risks than the synthetic folic acid supplement commonly used. I recommend 3–5 mg of L-methylfolate per day for depression.

Remember that when you are using supplements, your physician should monitor you carefully to ensure that you are getting ample amounts, but never too much, in accordance with your biochemical individuality.

Vitamin B_{12}

Vitamin B_{12} is not a single substance. Instead, it is a family of compounds manufactured by bacteria, fungi, or other organisms. Best known for its role in forming red blood cells, B_{12} also works in conjunction with B_6 and folic acid in the manufacturing of serotonin and dopamine. Low levels of this vitamin are associated with infertility, osteoporosis, heart disease, and stroke. B_{12} is also critical for normal functioning of the central nervous system (brain and spinal cord).

People who are vitamin B_{12} deficient may suffer from numerous neurological problems, including tingling in the hands and feet and difficulty with coordination and walking. If not recognized and treated, some of these symptoms can be irreversible. A vitamin B_{12} deficiency can also lead to a range of psychiatric conditions, including depression, anxiety, paranoia, hallucinations, memory loss, confusion, outbursts of temper, and behavioral changes.

Vitamin B_{12} and depression

Even slightly lower-than-normal levels of B_{12} may be linked to depression, fatigue, and poor memory in some individuals, and if levels drop further a condition known as *pernicious anemia* can develop. A combination of vitamin B_{12} and folic acid is required for the synthesis of SAMe, which in turn is necessary for the metabolism of the neurotransmitters that regulate mood. And studies have shown that up to 30 percent of those hospitalized for depression are deficient in vitamin B_{12}.

In one study, researchers assessed vitamin B_{12} levels in almost three hundred elderly people with depressive symptoms or clinical depression and compared them to those of people who were not depressed. They found that people with a vitamin B_{12} deficiency were significantly more likely to be depressed.

Another study assessed the vitamin B_{12} levels of 115 people diagnosed with major depressive disorder and then followed them for six months, at which time researchers measured the levels again. Higher vitamin B_{12} levels were correlated with better long-term psychological functioning. Those whose depression improved the most had the highest vitamin B_{12} levels in their blood after six months. Those whose depression had not improved at all had the lowest vitamin B_{12} levels.

Determining if there is enough vitamin B_{12}

Vitamin B_{12} blood levels of 200–600 pg/mL are generally considered normal, but "normal" is not high enough for many people. Even if this "normal" level were adequate for physical function, the amount of vitamin B_{12} in the blood does not necessarily equate with the amount in the brain, so brain levels could be low even though blood levels are fine. Tests for blood and urine methylmalonic acid or homocysteine can also be used to gauge whether B_{12} levels are optimal. I recommend supplementation to anyone with a level under 600 pg/mL.

How much to take

It's best to get ample amounts of B_{12} from foods such as beef liver, cheese, eggs, milk, fish, and yogurt. However, as with folate, some people may consume plenty of foods containing B_{12} yet still suffer from a deficiency because they cannot absorb the vitamin well. This can happen if the stomach is not producing enough hydrochloric acid to release B_{12} from the food. Hydrochloric acid production falls with age and can be artifically depressed through the use of antacids and ulcer medications. B_{12} levels also recede should the body fail to produce enough intrinsic factor, a natural substance necessary for B_{12} absorption. Intrinsic factor levels tend to fall with age, so many people who are middle aged and older do not have enough. Without enough intrinsic factor, intestinal bacteria consume most of the available B_{12} and the rest may be excreted.

I recommend that all depressed patients have their B_{12}, methylmalonic acid, and homocysteine levels checked. If B_{12} levels are low (less than 500 pg/mL) and homocysteine levels are high (more than 12 micromoles per liter [μm/L]), then I recommend B_{12} shots of 1 mg to quickly increase levels as patients start taking daily supplements of sublingual B_{12}, a form of the vitamin absorbed under the tongue.

There are three forms of vitamin B_{12}: methylcobalamin, hydroxycobalamin, and cyanocobalamin. All three forms increase blood levels of B_{12} and improve symptoms. My preference is the hydroxycobalamin or the methylcobalamin, if available.

Assessing a patient's B_{12} level is simple and safe, and the rewards can be immense for many patients. In my opinion, most physicians believe that B_{12} deficiency is a problem of the elderly. Yet, I have seen B_{12} deficiencies in children, adolescents, and young to middle-aged adults suffering from depression as well as in those who are suffering from anxiety. Get your levels checked.

Vitamin D

Vitamin D comes from two very different sources: food and sunlight. Cholesterol is the precursor to vitamin D. Upon exposure to ultraviolet light, cholesterol is converted to this vitamin photochemically in the skin and is then absorbed by the body. Vitamin D is crucial for the absorption

ation of calcium and phosphorus and for the growth of bones and teeth. It is also very much involved in brain function. Vitamin D receptors are found in both neurons and glial cells, brain *cells* that "support" neurons by providing nutrition and insulation.

Like other nutrients, vitamin D comes in different forms. These include vitamin D_2, known technically as ergocalciferol, which is manufactured by plants and enters the human body when those plants are eaten, and vitamin D_3, also known as cholecalciferol, which is created by the human body when the skin is exposed to sunlight.

Vitamin D was originally believed to be of use only in preventing rickets and osteomalacia, which are the classic diseases of vitamin D deficiency, and other diseases of the bone. Accumulating evidence, however, has demonstrated that vitamin D does much more, influencing the health and function of tissues and organs throughout the body. Thanks to research conducted over the past several decades, we can now say with conviction that low levels of the vitamin are associated with psoriasis, muscle pain and weakness, elevated blood pressure, some forms of cancer and autoimmune disease, and other ailments. As the scientific evidence mounts, more and more health experts are calling for an increase in the recommended allotment of vitamin D.

I have seen supplement fads come and go but never have I been as impressed as I am by research about vitamin D effectiveness and importance to human health. There is an avalanche of solid scientific information showing that vitamin D is much more than a way to keep the bones strong. Although psychiatry has been slow to acknowledge the importance of this vitamin, the consensus is now clear: Ample amounts of vitamin D are necessary for optimal mental health.

Vitamin D and depression

Health experts suspect a link between vitamin D and mood, observing the fact that SAD arises in the dark times of the year when there is relatively little sunshine available to create vitamin D in the body. For example, researchers from the Washington University School of Medicine in St. Louis, Missouri, examined the relationship between vitamin D and depression in senior citizens. Both vitamin levels and emotional status were established in eighty research subjects, 59 percent of whom had abnormally low vitamin D levels. When vitamin levels and mood were compared, it was clear that "vitamin D deficiency was associated with low mood. . . ."

The weight of scientific evidence suggests that low vitamin D levels are associated with major depression and that depression has increased during the last century as we have reduced our exposure to sunlight consequently leading to decreased vitamin D levels. Here's a quick look at just a few of the studies published in 2010:

1. Vitamin D levels were measured in 7,358 people with cardiovascular disease, aged fifty and older. Based on the results, they were placed in either the Optimal, Normal, Low, or Very Low vitamin D groups. They were also evaluated for depression. When compared to those in the Opitmal vitamin D group, those in the Normal, Low, and Very Low groups were more likely to be depressed.
2. Italian researchers checked the vitamin D levels and mental-health status of 954 senior citizens at the beginning of their six-year study. The level of depression, if any, was assessed again after three and six years. Both men and women with lower levels of vitamin D were more likely to experience worsened depression, or to develop depression if they did not have it at the beginning, compared to those with higher levels.
3. British researchers used data from the 2005 Health Survey for England to compare vitamin D levels to depression in 2,070 people. They found that "[d]epressive symptoms were associated with clinical vitamin D deficiency. . . ."
4. A pair of Duke University Medical Center researchers looked at forty-two different studies and found that vitamin D deficiency was quite common among seniors living in the community (rather than in nursing or retirement homes) and that lower levels of the vitamin were linked to a greater likelihood of having depression.
5. Vitamin D deficiency may even set the stage for depression while one is still in the womb. An intriguing paper published by Danish researchers noted that "patients with both schizophrenia and bipolar condition are more frequently born in winter and spring, the periods which have the largest maternal decline in plasma concentrations of vitamin D."

Research has also demonstrated that vitamin D treatment can relieve symtpoms of depression. For example, a 1999 study of patients with SAD found that those given a one-time oral dose of 100,000 international units (IU) of vitamin D experienced greater relief from depression than those given light therapy (a standard treatment for SAD). A 2009 pilot study arrived at similar results, finding that supplemental vitamin D given to women with lower levels of the vitamin in their blood caused their D levels to rise and their depression ratings to fall. The vitamin has even been used to improve the mood of healthy, nondepressed people during the winter months when there is less sunshine available to spur the body's production of vitamin D.

I was recently asked to see a seventeen-year-old depressed adolescent whose family did not want her to take any medications. Her depression was overwhelming, causing her to drop out of her athletic activities and affecting her ability to complete her coursework at school. When I checked her vitamin D levels I found that she was severely deficient, with a level of 7 nanograms per milliliter (ng/mL). I quickly started her on 3,000 IU of vitamin D for two months. As her vitamin D level rose to 35 ng/mL, her mood improved and she was able to return to her schoolwork and her activities. This case is striking, as vitamin D supplementation was the only biological intervention needed to treat her depression.

Determining if there is enough vitamin D

For a long time, vitamin D blood levels between 20 and 30 ng/mL have been accepted as normal and healthy. We now know that this range is too low, and even people who were thought to be safely in the middle of range may need more of the vitamin. And, given the quirks of biochemical individuality, some people in the upper reaches may need more. Vitamin D is measured with a simple blood test assessing the 25-hydroxyvitamin D level. I prefer to see a 25-hydroxyvitamin D between 40 and 60 ng/mL in my patients.

How much to take

Vitamin D is found in foods such as mackerel, salmon, sardines, and vitamin D-fortified milk. The body also manufactures its own vitamin D when the skin is exposed to sunlight, so it would seem that a deficiency in the vitamin would be rare. However, in truth millions of people are deficient in vitamin D, especially those living in areas where there is not year-round sunshine, and those who avoid exposure to sunlight.

I recommend vitamin D supplementation only after testing the 25-hydroxyvitamin D levels. Supplementation is based on blood levels and may range from 2,000 IU to 10,000 IU. Vitamin D supplementation needs to be monitored by blood testing every few months until levels are no longer below 60.

As is always the case when you take vitamin supplements, your physician should monitor you carefully to ensure that you are getting ample amounts but never too much, in accordance with your biochemical individuality.

Biochemical individuality plays a substantial role in vitamin D status. Although environmental factors, such as nutrition and sun exposure, are considered the major determinants of vitamin D status, genetics are responsible for a large portion of the variation seen in serum 25-hydroxyvitamin D. A Swedish study involving 204 same-sex twins between the ages of thirty-nine and eighty-five years living at northern latitude 60 degrees found that genetic factors were responsible for one-fourth of the variation in serum 25-hydroxyvitamin D, independent of season. During the summer season alone, genetics was responsible for half of the variability in 25-hydroxyvitamin D.

SAMe

The body uses the amino acid methionine to create a substance commonly called SAMe, which, in turn, aids in the synthesis of neurotransmitters, proteins, and hormones. Among the neurotransmitters it helps create is the mood enhancer serotonin.

SAMe and depression

Several studies have shown that supplemental SAMe can help relieve depression. A 1988 study conducted by researchers from the University of California at Irvine tested the effects of SAMe on eighteen adults who had major depression. The study subjects were randomly assigned to receive either a daily infusion of 400 mg SAMe plus a placebo capsule or the antidepressant imipramine in capsule form plus a placebo infusion. After two weeks of treatment, about 66 percent of those receiving the SAMe plus placebo enjoyed a significant reduction in their depression, compared to 22 percent of those who had received the medicine plus placebo.

In 2002, an article in the *American Journal of Clinical Nutrition* described the results of two studies comparing SAMe to the antidepressant imipramine in adults suffering from major depression. In one study the participants were given either 1,600 mg SAMe or up to 150 mg imipramine daily; in the other, they were given either daily injections of 400 mg SAMe plus a placebo capsule or up to 150 mg imipramine in capsule form plus a placebo injection. In both studies, SAMe performed as well as the medicine in reducing symptoms of depression.

A meta-analysis looking at the efficacy of SAMe for treatment of depression was published in 1994. The authors of this meta-analysis reported that the ability of SAMe to relieve depression "is superior to that of placebo and comparable to that of standard tricyclic antidepressants." In 2008, National Center for Complementary and Alternative Medicine published their own meta-analysis on SAMe and depression. Combining the results of twenty-eight different studies, they found that SAMe produced a statistically significant improvement in depression compared to placebo.

More recently, a 2010 study found SAMe to be an effective adjunct to traditional medication for patients with major depression who failed to respond to antidepressant treatment. In the study, seventy-three SSRI nonresponders with major depression were given either an oral dose of SAMe (800 mg twice daily) or a placebo in addition to their current medication regimen. At the end of six weeks they were evaluated based on the HDRS. Patients treated with adjunctive SAMe showed more improvement in their Hamilton scores and had higher rates of remission than those receiving adjunctive placebo. SAMe was effective as an adjunct to medication.

Reading studies is reassuring, but there's nothing like seeing the positive effects in a patient. I remember a fifty-seven-year-old artist who was reluctant to take antidepressants because of a side effect he'd had several years previously. "I'd rather be sad than go through those side effects again," he said. He agreed to try SAMe and within a few months reported that his depression was "almost entirely gone," without any apparent side effects.

How much to take

SAMe is available as a supplement; no prescription is required. A standard dose for SAMe has not been set: SAMe studies have used doses ranging from 400 to 1,600 mg/day.

I recommend 800 to 1,600 mg SAMe per day for depression.

Potential side effects of SAMe include insomnia, anxiety, and gastrointestinal upset. The combinatin of SAMe and certain antidepressants may trigger serotonin syndrome, which is characterized by rapid heartbeat, agitation, tremors, and other symptoms. Although SAMe is available without a prescription, it should always be taken under the supervision of a physician.

Remember, with SAMe—as with any other supplements—you should collaborate with a physician or a healthcare professional.

Inositol

Inositol (also known as vitamin B_8) helps form healthy cell membranes and maintains proper electrical energy and nutrient transfer between the cells. Inositol is converted into a substance that regulates the action of serotonin, the lack of which is linked to depression, panic disorder, and OCD. Restoring normal levels of this vitamin may help alleviate psychiatric symptoms, including depression, feelings of panic, and obsessive thoughts.

Inositol and depression

Low levels of inositol in the CSF have been found in depressed people. Several studies have demonstrated that the vitamin can help improve symptoms of depression at dosages of 12 g/day. In some studies, patients took inositol in addition to antidepressant medications; in others, they took only inositol or a placebo. The results were the same: Depression significantly improved when inositol was taken. One study went one step further, showing that when inositol treatment was stopped, the depression returned. Then, when inositol treatment was reinstated, symptoms of depression disappeared again.

Two studies support the use of inositol in reducing the frequency and severity of panic attacks, a problem that sometimes arises in conjunction with depression. One reported that a group of patients taking inositol had significantly fewer panic attacks compared to a group taking a placebo pill. The other compared inositol to the psychiatric medication fluvoxamine (Luvox). Subjects with active panic disorder were treated with up to 18 g/day of inositol or up to 150 mg/day of fluvoxamine. The researchers found that both inositol and fluvoxamine were equally effective in treating panic disorder, but inositol was superior in reducing the number of panic attacks experienced.

Inositol can also be helpful in reducing obsessive thinking, another feature commonly seen in depression. One study found that people with OCD who took 18 g/day of inositol reported experiencing fewer obsessions and compulsions.

How much to take

Ideally, everyone would get enough inositol from foods such as wheat germ, brewer's yeast, grapefruit, liver, raisins, and unrefined molasses. But there is always the chance that the body cannot absorb or use the vitamin efficiently, which increases requirements. In many cases, eating too much sugar may impair absorption. Inositol is a carbohydrate that can be produced by the body from glucose, but eating too much sugar can disrupt the inositol shuttle system and other messenger pathways, leading to deficiency.

There is no RDA for inositol, but it is estimated that most people ingest about 1 g per day.

I recommend patients start with 1/2 teaspoon (1.4 g) of inositol powder twice a day. Over the course of four weeks I suggest increasing the dose by 1/2 teaspoon every five days until you reach 12 g of inositol per day. Inositol can be taken alone or with medications.

Supplemental inositol appears to be safe, even in high doses. Common side effects include nausea, bloating, insomnia, and fatigue. Because it may stimulate contractions of the uterus, caution is strongly advised when adminstering it to pregnant women.

Vitamins B_1 (Thiamine), B_3 (Niacin), and B_6 (Pyridoxine)

These three B vitamins play supportive roles in maintaining emotional health and generating energy.

Thiamine helps the brain convert glucose into fuel. It also stimulates brain action, is necessary for the health of the nervous system, and aids in digestion.

Niacin helps maintain healthy nervous and digestive systems. The vitamin also stimulates circulation, causing the blood vessels and red blood cells to become more flexible. This flexibility makes it easier for blood to flow through the body and especially the brain, which may be one reason that niacin helps ease depression. A severe niacin deficiency causes a disease called pellagra. Symptoms of pellagra include depression, anxiety, and apathy.

Vitamin B_6 is involved in processing amino acids and converting nutrients into energy and is necessary for the synthesis of the mood-modulating neurotransmitters serotonin and dopamine. In addition, B_6 is needed for normal brain function, synthesis of RNA and DNA, and formation of the myelin sheath around the nerve cells, which helps speed signals through the brain.

Vitamins B_1, B_3, B_6 and depression

Thiamine. The brain rapidly loses energy when thiamine is in short supply, leading to depression, fatigue, anxiety, irritability, insomnia, and memory problems. Decades ago, studies demonstrated that thiamine is critical for normal brain function and that those who are deficient often become depressed and irritable and have difficulty concentrating and sleeping. In 1942, eleven women participated in a study in which they consumed a diet that contained only half of the recommended amount of thiamine for eight to twelve weeks. They developed troubling symptoms, which grew worse the longer they remained on the diet, including a decreased appetite and lower food intake. Most notably, most of the women became depressed. When the women began taking thiamine supplements at the conclusion of the study, the symptoms gradually subsided.

Niacin. The "feel good" neurotransmitter serotonin is produced from an amino acid called tryptophan, which is usually plentiful in the food supply. However, when niacin is in short supply, tryptophan is used to manufacture niacin instead of serotonin. Since synthesizing just 1 mg of niacin takes 60 mg of tryptophan, the body can easily run short of the "raw material" it needs to make serotonin when it is forced to synthesize niacin. No wonder, then, that a niacin deficiency can result in depression, agitation, and anxiety, all of which are linked to inadequate amounts of serotonin.

Pyridoxine. Psychological and psychiatric conditions such as depression, confusion, and irritability can result from vitamin B_6 deficiency. This is most likely because B_6 is needed to make the neurotransmitters serotonin, dopamine, norepinephrine, and GABA—all of which have potent effects on the brain. Depressed patients often have low B_6 levels. One study found low blood levels of B_6 in 21 percent of 101 depressed outpatients. Another found significantly lower levels (48 percent lower) of active vitamin B_6 in depressed patients compared to controls.

Interfering with these three Bs

The body's supply of B vitamins can be depleted by the overconsumption of refined carbohydrates, which are the simple sugars found in white flour, cakes, candy, pies, syrups, sweetened breakfast cereals, and many processed foods. Alcoholics and those with kidney failure may also be lacking in the vitamins.

How much to take

In a perfect world, everyone would absorb ample amounts of these vitamins from foods, including bananas, beans, lentils, broccoli, brown rice, eggs, fish, lean meat, oatmeal, soybeans, spinach, sunflower seeds, nuts, pork, whole-grain cereals, yeast, and poultry. But since an unknown number of people have inadequate diets or absorption difficulties, supplementation is often wise.

I recommend a B-complex vitamin containing 50–75 mg of these three B vitamins per day for depression.

Check and Replenish Based on Your Unique Biochemical Needs

Through the early part of the twentieth century, numerous articles appeared in the medical literature documenting successful treatment of depression with B vitamins and other nutrients. Building on new understandings of the body and nutrition, pioneering physicians were developing a new approach to treating depression that showed great promise. However, as public health officials used this scientific knowledge to fortify our food supply, vitamin-deficiency disease states started slowly disappearing. In the 1950s, pharmaceutical companies introduced prescription medications for depression, and in the decades following, interest in nutritional treatment of mental disease waned.

Although the lion's share of research funds has been allocated to pharmaceuticals over the past fifty or sixty years, research into vitamins and other nutrients has continued, and impressive evidence that folic acid, B_{12}, vitamin D, and other nutrients can be effective treatments for many people has slowly accumulated. Today, we can offer nondrug treatments that we know are successful. This is not to say that supplements are better than medicines, or vice versa. For certain people, vitamins or other supplements, or even a simple change in diet, is exactly what's needed. For others, medicines or a combination of medicines and nutrients is the right prescription.

My experience has shown that better nutrition and supplements are a must for almost everyone because modern agricultural, processing, shipping, and selling practices have resulted in foods that are relatively devoid of nutrients. And not only are we not getting the nutrition we should, but refined foods filled with sugars can also force the body to "use up" the B vitamins and other nutrients it has. In the Standard American Diet, we do not get enough of the nutrients we need. As a result, many people suffer from serious nutritional deficits. Often, depression can be helped by simply restoring nutritional health.

As we add nutrients to the list of effective treatments, we have a greater opportunity to find the treatments that work best with each person's unique biochemistry and genetic inheritance. Instead of always blindly prescribing pharmaceuticals, we can easily identify nutritional deficiencies and then correct them, simply and safely. If doing so improves or eliminates the psychiatric distress, terrific. If not, we've narrowed the range of possible causes and can move ahead with that much more confidence.

Because this chapter covers a lot of information, I want to emphasize the most important idea: Every depressed person should take L-methylfolate and a B-complex vitamin with no more than 400 μg of folic acid.

Vitamin B_{12} and vitamin D levels need to be checked and supplemented accordingly. Everybody is biochemically and genetically unique, so it is vital that you have a health professional test your nutrient levels. If any deficits are discovered, they should be treated aggressively. The treatment of nutritional deficiencies may be the way out of depression.

14

r – referenced-EEG

Many patients I see are painful reflections of the failure of our current treatments for depression.

Janet is a thirty-five-year-old police officer. The police department referred her to me because depression was interfering with her work. Janet entered my consulting room, made no eye contact, and slumped in the chair across from my desk. When I encouraged her to talk, Janet seemed listless. She complained that she was unable to concentrate at work, she tossed and turned throughout the night, and the future in front of her seemed an expanse of nothingness.

Janet was no stranger to a psychiatrist's office. In fact, I learned that she had suffered from major depressive disorder since her early twenties and that through the years she had undergone five trials of different SSRI medications and two trials of tricyclic antidepressants. Each of these trials, of course, involved several months. First, she would have to stop taking all medication. Then there was an induction phase where she was started on a low dose followed by an increase to a full therapeutic dose of the medication. During all this time she was under the care of a psychiatrist and would dutifully keep office appointments for progress checks. She was also vigilant about diminished symptoms. Nothing. Janet's symptoms showed no significant improvement on any of these medication trials.

To have sought treatment and to continue faithfully under a psychiatrist's care and still suffer without relief discouraged Janet. She had been hospitalized once after she attempted suicide. Just before the police department referred her to me, her family had taken her to the emergency department because she was again thinking of killing herself.

Janet's story is not rare. Instead, Janet's story is familiar to many patients and professionals.

I began seeing these "treatment failures" when I was a psychiatry resident. My colleagues clung to the notion that patients were to blame: They must be taking their medicines improperly, withholding important information, or just clinging stubbornly to their depression to avoid something difficult in their lives. I must confess that I bought into the argument that the practice of psychiatry was not the problem. But as the years passed, I couldn't help but wonder why so many patients were not helped by our best medicines when they were prescribed according to the guidelines produced by the latest studies.

I still had too many patients like Frank, a thirty-year-old attorney who had taken thirteen different medications for major depression over the course of eight years. Or fifty-five-year-old Dorothy, who told me she "couldn't count that high" when I asked her about the different medications she had taken for her depression. Or nineteen-year-old Jody, a college student who had been on and off nine different medications for bipolar disorder during the previous five years. In each case I went back to the beginning and took a complete history in order to create the perfect symptom list so I could select the ideal medicine. But too many times the patients and I were disappointed.

Reluctantly, I came to the conclusion that we simply did not know which medicines would work in any given patient. Although study after study appeared to "prove" that a certain medicine was best suited to certain types of psychiatric disorders, the results continued to be disappointing. I continually searched for an objective guide to match patient to prescription.

We have finally discovered an objective way to match patient to medicine. We now have a tool that produces a personalized profile of the brain's physiology. In most cases it allows us to match certain clearly defined brainwave patterns with the medicines best suited to normalize them. This, in turn, reduces or eliminates the patient's symptoms. The tool, rEEG, has been available for the past eight to ten years. As more and more psychiatrists around the world are becoming aware of its power, rEEG has the potential to revolutionize the practice of psychiatry.

"Reading" the Brain

Chapter 6 briefly discusses the EEG, a device first used in the 1920s to monitor the electrical activity of the human brain. It's similar to the ECG, a machine that monitors the movement of electrical current through the heart and that provides a lot of information about heart health.

You can think of the EEG as an ECG for the brain, charting the waves of electrical impulses that brain cells use to communicate with each other. These waves, including delta waves, theta waves, alpha waves, and beta waves, change depending on what one is doing (concentrating, relaxing, looking at pictures, or sleeping). They also vary with age and in the presence of certain diseases, such as epilepsy.

Soon after it was invented, the EEG rapidly proved useful for diagnosing epilepsy, studying sleep disorders, documenting brain death, and dealing with other issues related to the physical status of the brain. Some early researchers thought it might also be possible to link certain brainwave patterns to specific psychiatric disorders and to use the EEG to diagnose illnesses such as depression or anxiety. They hoped, for example, to find a "depression brainwave profile," a "schizophrenia brainwave profile," and so on. But it soon became clear that there were no such profiles. In truth, the EEGs of two depressed people, for example, often looked very different from each other. And in many cases the EEGs of people with long-standing psychiatric illness looked quite normal, while those of perfectly healthy people looked unusual. In other words, there seemed to be no correlation between the EEG and psychiatric disorder, and the EEG appeared to be of little use to psychiatrists.

This began to change in the 1970s, when the EEG was melded with computer technology to create a much more detailed and complex look at brainwaves. Researchers began compiling EEGs of healthy people and were able to determine what "normal" brainwave patterns looked like. The first publication on rEEG was in 1995. A pair of researchers named Hamlin Emory, MD, and Stephen Suffin, MD, performed EEGs on large numbers of psychiatric patients and made an astonishing observation. They didn't find the hoped-for "depression brainwave pattern" or "schizophrenia brainwave pattern," or any other such disorder pattern, but they did find that when EEG brainwave patterns diverged from the norm in similar ways, the patients with similar deviations responded well to the same medications, no matter *what* their psychiatric disorders were.

Emory and Suffin reported that 87 percent of patients with a pattern called "frontal cortex alpha relative power" responded well to antidepressants, 100 percent of those with "excess frontal cortex theta relative power" responded well to stimulants, and 80 percent of those with "frontal theta excess and hypercoherence" responded well to lithium or anticonvulsants, *regardless* of their *DSM* diagnoses.

This observation flew in the face of all that was known to be true about psychiatric disorder. Everyone "knew," for example, that depression and panic disorder were completely different disorders that had nothing in common. It made no sense that the same medicine would work for both of them. Or that the same medicine could help treat OCD and premenstrual mood changes. Or that another medicine could ease depression and help curb smoking addiction. Yet that's exactly what happened when the same medicines were given to people with the same EEG divergences.

In many cases these drug choices were counterintuitive. Few psychiatrists would have considered anticonvulsants, for example, to treat depression.As more and more patients received EEGs and their responses to medicines were recorded, these records formed a large database of individual brainwave patterns and medicine responses. This database enabled us to finally see which medicines could be matched to which brainwave patterns in order to correct the patient's symptoms. This led to the development of the rEEG, which allows doctors to submit a patient's EEG for comparison to those in the database of more than seventeen thousand medication trials where it can be matched to those with similar brainwave patterns. The psychiatrist can then prescribe the medicine(s) that have been found to work best with that particular brainwave pattern.

Referenced-EEG was a phenomenal discovery because it finally gave psychiatry a measurable, objective treatment target. Identify the brainwave deviation, use the appropriate medicine(s), and the symptoms will recede. Instead of relying on a patient's subjective feelings and the psychiatrist's or family's subjective observations to guide treatment, psychiatrists could assess the effectiveness of their treatments by correlating brainwaves with known positive responses.

The EEG test itself is simple and noninvasive. It records electrical signals coming from the brain, but no electricity is put into the brain or body. To prepare for the test, the patient must taper off his or her medications. Otherwise, the measured brainwaves will reflect the effects of the medications rather than the brain's fundamental signature. During the test, a mesh hat that looks like a bathing cap is placed on the patient's head. This hat is embedded with about twenty small electrodes. Clips that look like clip-on earrings are placed on the ears. Through these electrodes the electrical activity of the patient's brain is measured and recorded. During the test, which takes between thirty minutes and an hour, the patient is alert and seated in a chair.

The rEEG converts the signals it receives to digital form and analyzes brain biomarkers to identify abnormalities in brainwaves. The rEEG analyzes seventy-four different biomarkers to compile the unique brain signature for each patient.

I have seen firsthand the power of rEEG for targeting psychiatric treatment and how effective this can be.

Rachel came to my office after struggling with depression for more than two decades. At forty-three, she tried to remember a time when she hadn't felt depressed. She told me that college had been a roller coaster during which she suffered several depressive episodes. Although she was able to function—she regularly attended therapy and did well academically—she remained depressed most of the time. She remembers an intense sadness that left her with "a loneliness even when [she] was with supportive friends." When she was twenty-four, her primary care physician prescribed Prozac, and, according to Rachel, "My life changed."

But the change did not last. Within a year, even though Rachel had everything she had dreamed of—close friends and a boyfriend—she felt herself slipping back into the dark hole of depression.

Having been helped once by medication, Rachel sought help quickly. That was the beginning of a fifteen-year period of medication trials—sometimes one after another, sometimes up to three at a time. The drugs prescribed for Rachel included Lexapro, Zoloft, Paxil, lithium, Abilify, Klonopin, Wellbutrin, and Ativan. Despite all these interventions, she found no relief, and her depression spiraled downward.

When she came to me, I immediately ordered an r-EEG. Rachel's EEG was compared with those showing similar brainwave patterns, and the results predicted that Wellbutrin in combination with Lamictal could restore her brainwave patterns to normal range. After all the years of trial-and-error prescriptions, Rachel is now doing well on this combination of drugs. "The rEEG saved my life," she claims.

Backed by Science

Research studies reinforce what I've seen in my clinical practice. One study focused on fifteen people suffering from refractory eating disorders and co-occurring depression. They had suffered from serious depression during the two years before beginning the study, had taken psychiatric medications, and had spent an average of 37.2 days in the hospital.

The patients were given EEGs, and the results were used to determine which medicines were most likely effective in the individual patients. Each had a different medication regimen. Some were given antidepressants, others a stimulant plus an anticonvulsant, and still others different combinations, depending on the rEEG recommendations. Although these medication regimens were not standard, they led to an impressive reduction in symptoms and in the need for hospitalization during the two years after the rEEG: Only six of the fifteen were hospitalized during the post-rEEG period and only for an average of seven days each.

The HDRS was used to monitor improvements in the patients' depression. The severity of their depression diminished from incapacitating to slight. In some cases they even returned to normal mood.

A recent study, published in the *Journal of Psychiatric Research* in July 2010, was conducted by researchers from Harvard Medical School, Stanford University School of Medicine, and other prestigious medical centers. This study included eighty-nine people suffering from refractory depression. All of the volunteers had failed to respond to at least one treatment with antidepressants selected in the usual way, with most failing to respond to two or more treatments. The participants, none of whom had been helped by previous antidepressant therapy, were randomly assigned to have treatment guided by rEEG results or to receive antidepressants chosen the standard way. After twelve weeks of treatment, the results were clear-cut: Patients who underwent "rEEG-guided pharmacotherapy exhibited significant improvement" in their depression, compared to those who were given medicines selected in the usual manner.

Correcting the Marker Eliminates the Symptoms

I've been using rEEG for more than six years. The results have been consistently gratifying.

The EEG allows me to make an objective analysis of the problem and the rEEG selects the medications best suited to help the patient. This information, combined with the patient's feedback and my own observations, helps me guide treatment to a successful conclusion in most cases.

I'd like to share with you one more story of a patient whose life was turned around by rEEG.

After college, Brad began work in his family's insurance business. He married, and he and his wife had two sons and enjoyed a comfortable life. After knee surgery, however, Brad began to take prescription painkillers. He couldn't stop. He began to use alcohol heavily, and his life became a frantic search for drugs acquired through doctor shopping and Internet purchases. Brad was in trouble. For ten years, he battled depression and substance abuse. His wife left him, and he had little contact with the sons he had adored.

Brad sought help. Despite his unrelieved depression, he managed to be persistent enough to seek out a half dozen psychiatrists through the years. He knew the names of the smorgasbord of psychiatric medications he had tried as well as any psychiatrist does. But nothing had helped relieve his symptoms.

When Brad found his way to my office, I arranged for an EEG right away. The rEEG predicted that a combination of medications, including a stimulant, would help normalize Brad's brainwave pattern. I prescribed a nonaddicting form of the stimulant Provigil. That was three years ago.

Brad has been free of depression, and he has not taken a drink or misused drugs since starting his rEEG-based treatment.

Not a Magic Bullet

I don't want to suggest that the rEEG is a magic bullet that will eliminate all psychiatric symptoms by indicating absolutely which medicine will be effective in every single case. Even when a patient receives the best available medicine, it may not be possible to completely restore health or eliminate every symptom.

However, the rEEG gives us our first objective tool for targeting treatment. We can now select the medicines most likely to be effective and measure the results of treatment simply by looking at brainwave patterns. As an x-ray is to the body, the rEEG is to the brain: a way to "see" into the patient and devise a more effective treatment strategy.

Without the rEEG, patients sometimes feel like guinea pigs as they endure the trial-and-error process with medications. They may lose hope and motivation to recover. They may believe that their lack of improvement signals a moral fault in themselves, or doctors may label them with negative language like "treatment resistant." All of these are hidden costs of depression and of psychiatry's inability to treat it effectively. It's not unusual for years and even decades to slip by as one medication combination after another is prescribed for a suffering patient. The rEEG offers patients and psychiatrists the promising possibility of finding effective treatment for depression in an efficient manner.

15

A – Amino Acids and Proteins

Finally, we've reached "A," the last of the components I advocate as part of THE ZEEBrA approach to treating depression. "A" stands for amino acids, which are important for their potential effect on neurotransmitters.

We don't completely understand the way antidepressants and similar medicines work, but we do know that they influence neurotransmitters, important brain chemicals that help regulate mood and behavior. Prozac, for example, increases the amount of serotonin available in the brain. But antidepressants don't work for everyone, which is why it's important to know there are other ways to affect neurotransmitters.

One approach is to use amino acid precursors, which are foods or supplements that supply the body with extra amounts of the amino acids that influence neurotransmitter levels or activity. Over many years of practice, I've found these to be an invaluable aid in the treatment of depression. I've seen many depressed patients with low levels of amino acids whose moods improve dramatically when they are given the proper amino acids.

I'm going to begin this chapter by making a statement that will sound heretical to most psychiatrists: *Sometimes the most significant intervention for the treatment of depression is supplying the patient with amino acids.*

These "building blocks" of protein can be some of the most powerful antidepressants in existence. I've seen for myself that many depressed patients have low levels of amino acids and that frequently their moods improve dramatically when they are given amino acids. The basis of all psychiatric medications involves enhancing neurotransmitters. Amino acids are capable of doing the same thing, as they are the building blocks of the vast majority of neurotransmitters.

The Pieces that Make a Protein

Amino acids are the building blocks of protein. These molecules, which contain carbon, hydrogen, oxygen, and nitrogen atoms in specific configurations, can be strung together in unique sequences to form a huge variety of proteins. In addition to building proteins, amino acids build and repair muscle tissue, form enzymes and hormones (which are also proteins) crucial to the regulation of body processes, and provide the "raw material" for the production of neurotransmitters.

The liver manufactures eleven of the twenty amino acids necessary for human health, while the remaining nine must be obtained through the diet. These nine are called the "essential" amino acids, since consumption of them is essential to good health. The nine essential amino acids are as follows:

histidine
isoleucine
leucine
lysine
methionine
phenylalanine
threonine
tryptophan
valine

The other amino acids are considered "nonessential." Since the body makes them, consuming them is not necessarily crucial to health.

Amino Acids and Mood

Certain amino acids, including GABA, glutamine, phenylalanine, taurine, tryptophan, and tyrosine, have been shown to influence the mood.

Some are converted into neurotransmitters that are critical to brain function and disposition, others affect the way the brain works, and one is actually a neurotransmitter itself.

GABA. Gamma-aminobutyric acid is, itself, a neurotransmitter, one of the main substances that helps brain cells communicate with each other. GABA helps brain cells calm down and become less excited, aids in the control of muscle activity, and plays an important part in vision. Because it reduces brain-cell excitability, GABA acts as a natural tranquilizer, reducing stress and anxiety while increasing alertness and helping to keep other neurotransmitters in check. People with low levels of GABA often experience anxiety, depression, irritability, headaches, and hypertension.

Glutamine. The most abundant amino acid in the body, glutamine increases GABA levels in the brain. Glutamine also helps remove excess ammonia from the body, improves immune-system function, protects the intestinal lining, and appears to be needed for normal brain function. Although the body usually makes enough glutamine on its own, extreme stress (e.g., heavy exercise or an injury) can increase the need for this amino acid beyond the amount naturally manufactured. Some experts believe that low levels of glutamine may contribute to depression, fatigue, and alcohol cravings.

Phenylalanine. The endorphins, natural substances that help modulate the mood and block chronic pain, occur naturally in the body and are continually built and destroyed. Phenylalanine appears to protect the endorphins from routine destruction, increasing their levels and improving depressed moods. This essential amino acid also plays a part in creating the neurotransmitters dopamine and norepinephrine.

Taurine. A nonessential amino acid, taurine works with GABA to help prevent overactivity of the neurotransmitters, easing anxiety and hyperactivity. Taurine can also function as a neurotransmitter, helping to prevent the reuptake of serotonin and other neurotransmitters such as dopamine, epinephrine, and norepinephrine, thus preserving their levels in the brain.

Tryptophan. Tryptophan is the amino acid from which serotonin (the "feel-good" neurotransmitter) is created in the brain. Some studies have shown that taking 5-HTP, a form of tryptophan, boosts brain levels of serotonin and can be an important adjunct in treating depression.

Tyrosine. Tyrosine is a precursor of the neurotransmitters norepinephrine and dopamine. When levels of tyrosine are optimal, energy, alertness, and improved moods may follow.

Amino Acids and Depression

While there's no doubt that low levels of amino acids are linked to depression, anxiety, and other negative moods, no one has yet figured out all of the connections. We cannot say, for example, that an X percent drop in tryptophan absorption will lead to a Y percent increase in one's depression rating. Researchers have, however, been able to put several pieces of the puzzle into place. For example, they have learned the following:

1. Changes in amino acid levels affect mood. In particular, tryptophan depletion has been associated with depressive symptoms and negative mood. In one study, researchers deliberately depleted the tryptophan levels of fifteen women who had suffered from repeated episodes of major depression. Within a short time, ten of the fifteen study subjects suffered "clinically significant depressive symptoms." Another study found that adding tryptophan to fluoxetine (Prozac) treatment decreased depression scores more than fluoxetine plus placebo.
2. Amino acid levels change when depression sets in, and the severity of depression may be linked to amino acid and protein levels. One study found highly significant differences in blood protein levels (total serum protein) between people with major depression (without melancholia) and healthy controls and between those with major depression (with melancholia) and dysthymia. Another study examining depressed and healthy patients found that blood levels of the amino acids glutamate, glutamine, glycine, and taurine were significantly changed in depressed people, compared to the healthy people.

3. The relative levels of certain amino acids in the blood and platelets may make a person more or less likely to respond to treatment with fluvoxamine (Luvox) for major depression and, undoubtedly, other medications as well.
4. Complex fatigue, which includes both mental and physical fatigue, causes changes in amino acid levels and metabolism in multiple organs. A study of animals with complex fatigue found decreases in total amino acid levels and low levels of glutamine in the plasma, skeletal muscle, and liver; in the animals' brains, researchers found low levels of phenylalanine, tyrosine, arginine, and threonine.

Many mysteries remain, but the following is clear:

- Low levels of certain amino acids can set the stage for depression.
- Depression is often accompanied by alterations in amino acid metabolism.
- The levels and ratios of certain amino acids may make psychiatric medicines more or less effective.

What Makes Amino Acid Levels Decrease?

A lack of sufficient amino acids can result from several problems, which I'll discuss further below, but perhaps the most common cause is the poor digestion of protein. The breakdown of protein occurs in the stomach, which secretes the powerful gastric acid called hydrochloric acid. But hydrochloric acid doesn't simply "burn through" proteins. It also converts a substance called pepsinogen into pepsin, an enzyme that cuts up protein into smaller pieces known as polypeptides. In a sense, hydrochloric acid takes the "dull" pepsinogen and turns it into the "razor-sharp" pepsin. Without pepsin, the human body cannot digest protein, so a decrease in the production of hydrochloric acid means that protein digestion will be less efficient. In addition, hydrochloric acid aids in the absorption of vitamin B_{12} and various minerals, the destruction of bacteria that enter the body through the digestive tract, and the triggering of satiety signals, letting the brain know the belly is full. Thus, too little hydrochloric acid can translate to a decrease in nutrient absorption, greater exposure to bacteria, impaired satiety signals, and hampered digestion in general.

Who's at Risk for Declining Hydrochloric Acid Levels?

The amount of gastric acid produced by the stomach falls sharply with age, dropping by roughly 40 percent from the teens to the thirties, and almost half again by the time a person reaches the seventies. This means that the ability to digest protein also decreases markedly with age.

Stomach acid levels are also lower in those who regularly use antacids and other medicines that interfere with acid production, whether prescription or over the counter. And that means that nutrient absorption and digestive capabilities can decrease in younger people, as well.

Besides poor digestion of protein, low hydrochloric acid levels are associated with many chronic digestive complaints, including pain or discomfort after eating, gas, bloating, and food sensitivities and allergies. Low hydrochloric acid levels can also contribute to iron-deficiency anemia, osteoporosis, gallstones, skin conditions, rheumatoid arthritis, periodontal disease, asthma, and chronic stress.

Low Acid Levels

We generally think of acid indigestion, heartburn, or GERD as problems caused by excess acid in middle-aged and older adults. What many people (including quite a few health professionals) don't realize is that *low* acid levels can also trigger symptoms of GERD, which include burning pain in the middle of the chest, nausea, and regurgitation.

Rather than avoid the foods that seem to cause the problem, most people are inclined to pop a pill to "cool the burn." Thanks to ongoing ad campaigns as well as the "educational materials" provided by pharmaceutical companies, some sixty million prescriptions for GERD medicines are written every year, in addition to the sale of millions of over-the-counter remedies, such as Prilosec, Rolaids, Tums, Maalox, and Nexium. This means untold millions of people may be attempting to treat symptoms of low stomach acid by lowering it even further, exacerbating problems with protein digestion and poor nutrient absorption. Low levels of stomach acid can also impair absorption of zinc, magnesium, and other minerals, as well as vitamin C and certain B vitamins. Of these, poor absorption of zinc may be the most important.

As you learn in Chapter 10, zinc is involved in more than two hundred different enzyme reactions, including several having to do with digestion. All of the digestive enzymes, including hydrochloric acid, depend on zinc to function properly.

Low acid can equal low mood

Low levels of stomach acid and digestive enzymes can also cause psychological consequences. When protein molecules are not broken down efficiently, sufficient levels of key amino acids may not be released into the bloodstream. Among the amino acids "missing in action" can be tryptophan, tyrosine, and phenylalanine, all of which play an important role in mood regulation. For example, tryptophan serves as "raw material" for serotonin, while phenylalanine is necessary for the production of dopamine and norepinephrine. In addition, in order to create neurotransmitters, ample supplies of zinc, copper, magnesium, folic acid, vitamin B_6, vitamin B_{12} and other nutrients are required.

Making sure the body has enough nutrients, then, plus ample amounts of stomach acid and digestive enzymes, is a first and crucial step in helping to normalize neurotransmitter levels. If any of these nutrients is in short supply, the manufacturing of neurotransmitters can falter. This can occur even when a patient is taking a medicine such as Prozac, which lowers the reabsorption of serotonin by brain cells in order to boost serotonin levels. If the body has so few raw materials that it can only make meager amounts of serotonin, the "Prozac boost" won't do any good.

Melinda, a thirty-six-year-old mother of two, was very concerned about her weight and was constantly trying the latest diet. Her worries about her weight were accompanied by depression. She had suffered from depression since college but had stopped taking antidepressants due to sexual side effects. She also suffered constantly from bloating, gas, and what she described as chronic indigestion. To handle these problems, she continually took over-the-counter antacids, popping them like candy. Even though Melinda was careful about her diet and ate plenty of protein, including fish and chicken, her tests revealed low levels of all essential amino acids. Without changing her diet, Melinda started taking hydrochloric acid and digestive enzymes. She not only noticed an improvement in her mood and energy, but her chronic digestion problem resolved.

Pumping Up the Acid

If you have stomach problems, heartburn, gas, bloating, or other digestive complaints, and depressed mood, your problems might be caused by *low* levels of stomach acid, resulting in deficiencies in amino acids, zinc, or other nutrients.

Despite the potential harm antacids can cause to your body, it's important to taper off antacids gradually rather than stopping all at once. Begin by taking the proper digestive enzymes with hydrochloric acid and pepsin and eliminating anything that upsets your stomach, such as alcohol, coffee, and soft drinks. Once your digestive symptoms are under control, you can speak to your physician about substituting the prescription antacid medication with over-the-counter antacids. Over-the-counter antacids, such as Tagamet, are not as strong as their prescription counterparts. To slowly ease your body back to its normal production of acid, gradually decrease the dose of over-the-counter antacid until you no longer require any. As internal acid production normalizes, many of my patients find that they are able to stop using antacids completely.

Maintaining Proper Amino Acid and Protein Levels

Sometimes amino acid levels are low for dietary reasons, especially in diets that include no meat or exclude all animal products. Other fad diets or crash weight-loss diets can also be protein deficient. Depression itself may play a role in amino acid deprivation, as some depressed people lose interest in food, eat fewer kinds of food, and eat less food overall.

Amino acid supplementation

Some people can erase a protein deficit by simply making sure they eat adequate amounts of meat, poultry, fish, or dairy products, with adequate hydrochloric acid and digestive enzymes.

Others, especially those with dietary restrictions, malnutrition, or diseases that interfere with absorption, may need amino acid supplements. These come in the form of whey protein powder or free-form amino acids.

Whey protein powder. This is the type of protein powder I recommend to my patients for THE ZEEBrA energy shake. Whey, a liquid byproduct of the cheese-making process, contains β-lactoglobulin, α-lactalbumin and other highly bioavailable proteins. These bioavailable proteins contain all the essential amino acids and are rapidly digested. As I suggest in Chapter 12, whey protein can be made into a shake with energy-generating ribose powder. Drinking this for breakfast is a great way to get energy levels up early in the morning and to keep them up through the afternoon hours when energy tends to lag. Whey protein powder is an excellent protein supplement for anyone who's not allergic to dairy.

Free-form amino acids. These are amino acids that are not attached to other amino acids, so they can be readily absorbed and easily used by the body to strengthen mental and physical health. Free-form amino acids are available in capsules or powders. If testing reveals low levels of fasting amino acids, I routinely recommend 4 g of amino acids mixed with a THE ZEEBrA shake or juice twice daily, before breakfast and before dinner.

It is always best to work with a physician or registered dietitian who is well versed in the proper usage of amino acids, as well as in potential drug interactions and side effects.

When should protein be consumed?

Even when a diet contains ample amounts of protein, it's often skewed toward nighttime delivery of the protein. A typical breakfast might consist of cereal and buttered toast, while dinner might include a large piece of meat or fish, meaning that relatively little protein is consumed in the morning, while a large "shipment" is delivered to the stomach in the evening. Indeed, the latest government dietary guidelines "produce meal patterns with over 65 percent of protein consumed in a single large meal after 6:30 p.m." Contrary to the way we typically eat, it is important for a significant amount of protein to be present in the diet throughout the day, especially in the morning.

Consuming an adequate amount of protein in the morning (much more than is contained in the typical American breakfast) is vital for, among other things, regulating a cascade of hormones necessary for mood control and many other tasks. Waiting until dinner to do so may dampen the mood of susceptible people. This means that a source of high-quality protein, such as meat or eggs, should be part of breakfast every morning. Eliminating the high carbohydrate breakfast is a simple, effective first step in THE ZEEBrA approach to treating depression.

Remember, the body disassembles the protein from food into amino acids, absorbs them, and then recombines them in new ways to create proteins.

Increasing neurotransmitters with amino acid precursors

An initial goal of depression treatment should be to discover any deficiencies in essential amino acids that can be corrected with dietary changes, digestive enzymes such as hydrochloric acid, protein shakes, or free-form amino acid supplements.

It's not enough for psychiatrists to ask patients about their diets and then stop investigating if patients say they consume adequate amounts of protein or even describe what are obviously amino acid-rich diets. I have frequently seen patients who eat healthful diets containing plenty of essential amino acids, yet they continue to struggle with depression.

For these people, targeted amino acids are excellent pharmacological aids to enhance the synthesis of neurotransmitters and to produce an antidepressant effect.

As I mentioned earlier, the amino acid L-tryptophan is a precursor to serotonin, while phenylalanine and tyrosine are precursors to dopamine and norepinephrine. We know that providing more L-tryptophan via the diet increases serotonin levels in the brain, while increasing tyrosine and phenylalanine in the body can increase dopamine synthesis.

For years, scientists have studied depression in both animals and humans by putting them on tryptophan-limited diets: The goal, routinely achieved, is to deplete their bodies of the amino acid, to lower serotonin levels, and to induce a state of depression. Given that tryptophan depletion is so commonly used to trigger depression, I have never quite understood why the idea of giving additional tryptophan has never been considered a potential treatment. If deliberately lowering tryptophan is so effective at triggering depression, why aren't we giving it to depressed people, especially those with already-low levels? Why aren't we at least checking those levels in every patient? Why isn't the medical community encouraging the research to answer these questions?

In my practice, I use a combination of 5-HTP and tyrosine. Normally, the body uses tryptophan to manufacture 5-HTP, which easily crosses the blood-brain barrier to enhance the synthesis of serotonin. Giving 5-HTP saves a step and, because 5-HTP is not incorporated into various proteins, more is available to increase brain serotonin levels. We usually see a response to this treatment in less than two weeks. It's true that there is only limited research supporting the use of 5-HTP in combination with tyrosine, but psychiatrists and clinicians around the country have been successfully using this combination for many years.

I have been using 5-HTP and tyrosine together for more than ten years, and my patients have enjoyed significant improvements from this combination. I typically prescribe them in a ratio of 10:1 (tyrosine to 5-HTP), so a typical prescription would be 500 mg of tyrosine and 50 mg of 5-HTP taken three times a day. However, individuals may need more of one amino acid or the other. Individual dosing is critical for successful treatment. I have found that patients with low energy tend to do better with higher doses of tyrosine and patients with obsessive ruminations need higher doses of 5-HTP.

Although 5-HTP can trigger some side effects, including gastrointestinal distress, gas, and cramping, these can be eliminated by starting slowly with just 50 mg/day and gradually increasing to 300 mg in divided dosages: for example, 100 mg at breakfast, 100 mg at lunch, and 100 mg at dinner. Some people become slightly tired after taking 5-HTP, so they may want to take smaller doses during the day and a larger dose in the evening before bed.

Despite the occasional side effects, using 5-HTP together with tyrosine to enhance the body's production of mood-lifting neurotransmitters is an effective strategy for many patients. Sometimes it's enough to banish depression, while other times it's an effective adjunct to antidepressants.

It's Worth Repeating

Sometimes, the most significant intervention for the treatment of depression is the repletion of sufficient amino acids. I can't stress this enough. The diet and nutritional status of every depressed patient should be checked and corrected if necessary. For many, this first step is the only one they'll ever have to take.

16

Laboratory Tests Your Doctor May Order

Traditionally, reviewing nutritional status has not been a part of a psychiatric evaluation. Although you might be tempted to skip a comprehensive metabolic evaluation, it is a critical part of understanding potential treatable causes of depression. Results from this evaluation are used as a basis for developing a personalized nutritional program that optimizes functioning and helps ensure your recovery and long-term health.

Rather than treating symptoms, it makes more sense to treat the nutritional and metabolic imbalances that are getting in the way of positive mood and healthy functioning. By restoring balance, the symptoms should lessen, or even vanish. But first we must discover where those imbalances lie. One of the best ways to do so is through laboratory tests.

In the nutritional assessment of a person with depression, a number of tests are critical. Some are conventional and commonly performed in a doctor's office, while others are not as well known. It's also possible that they won't be covered by health insurance. However, all are important. Discovering nutrient deficiencies and correcting them with the proper amounts of supplements can do much to help you feel better mentally and physically and to make it easier for you to participate in your recovery.

Getting Started

For all patients I recommend the following tests, which can be ordered by any physician:

- Fasting amino acids
- Complete Blood Count (CBC) with differential
- Celiac disease screening (antitissue transglutaminase antibody and antigliadin antibody tests)
- Lipid panel
- Comprehensive chemistry panel
- Copper level
- DHEA-S
- EFAs
- Folate and vitamin B_{12}
- Food allergies
- Homocysteine
- Iron and ferritin
- Magnesium
- Methylmalonic acid
- Red blood cell trace minerals
- Testosterone
- Thyroid
- Urinary organic acids
- Urinary peptides (including casomorphin and gliadorphin)
- Vitamin D (25-hydroxyvitamin D)
- Zinc

Amino acids

Building blocks of the proteins found in every tissue and organ of the body, amino acids help regulate neurotransmitters, form antibodies, and produce energy inside the cells. Deficiencies, then, especially in the nine essential amino acids, can cause serious health problems, including some related to mood and cognitive function. For example, too little tryptophan can lead to depression, while a lack of tyrosine or phenylalanine can contribute to fatigue and difficulty concentrating. Both blood and urine tests can be used to detect amino acid levels. Blood tests may mean a blood draw or just a finger stick. If amino acid levels prove to be abnormally low or high, they can usually be adjusted through supplementation or diet.

Complete blood count with differential

The CBC measures white blood cell count and types (called differential), red blood cell count and characteristics, hemoglobin, hematocrit, and platelets. Anemia, which can lead to depression, is indicated by low red blood cell count, low hemoglobin, and low hematocrit. Certain characteristics of the red blood cell, designated MCH, MCV, or MCHC, can pinpoint the nutrient deficiency causing the anemia, whether it's copper, folate, iron, or vitamin B_{12}.

White blood cell levels can be abnormally high due to an infection, an allergic reaction, or leukemia or abnormally low due to medication reactions or low levels of zinc, which is needed for white blood cell production. Platelets play a role in blood clotting, and both high and low levels are abnormal. Low levels can cause excessive bleeding and bruising.

Celiac screening

Celiac disease is a sensitivity to the gluten found in wheat and other grains, meaning that the body mistakenly identifies gluten as a foreign invader and launches an immune attack. A good amount of evidence suggests that people with celiac disease have higher rates of anxiety and depression than the general population. It appears that an activation of the inflammatory response system accompanies major depression and that certain proinflammatory substances like cytokines can actually trigger symptoms of depression.

Screening for celiac disease involves examining a blood sample to determine the presence of two antibodies that the body manufactures in response to gluten: antitissue transglutaminase and antigliadin. To confirm a positive result, a biopsy of the small intestine can be performed. An endoscope is inserted down the throat, through the stomach, and into the small intestine. Tissue samples taken from its lining are examined under a microscope to identify characteristic changes seen in celiac disease, including shrunken, flattened villi, the hairlike projections lining the intestine.

Lipid panel

A lipid panel measures the levels of total cholesterol, triglycerides, HDL, and LDL through a blood test. As discussed in Chapter 11, recent studies suggest that low total cholesterol levels are associated with depression and suicidal thoughts. One study published in the *Journal of Psychiatric Research* in 2009 found death from suicide, accidents, and other unnatural causes was seven times more likely to occur in men with low total cholesterol (below 165 mg/dL). Some experts have theorized that having low levels of cholesterol results in lowered production of serotonin and fewer serotonin receptors. And low serotonin levels are linked to depression as well as to decreased levels of progesterone and testosterone (both of which are also associated with depression.)

Comprehensive chemistry panel

This group of blood tests is used to evaluate organ function and is a preliminary check for diabetes, liver disease, and kidney problems. The test results give important information about electrolyte status, acid-base balance, kidney function, liver function, blood sugar, and protein levels. This panel can also assess a person's zinc status by measuring alkaline phosphatase, an enzyme produced in the presence of zinc. A low alkaline phosphatase level is frequently an indicator of a zinc deficiency.

Copper

Low copper levels can lead to symptoms of depression, which is not surprising considering that copper is required for the synthesis of the neurotransmitters norepinephrine and dopamine. A deficiency of a form of copper called ceruloplasmin can cause anemia, which itself can bring on symptoms of depression. On the other hand, abnormally high levels of copper can be associated with psychological symptoms such as aggression, paranoia, and anxiety. Copper levels are determined by blood tests or, in some cases, a urinary test. Levels that are abnormal may be treated with supplementation or modification to the diet.

DHEA

Low levels of DHEA, a hormone produced by the adrenal glands, have been linked to depression. DHEA levels typically peak in one's twenties and slowly fall during subsequent years. In men, DHEA levels typically rise as high as 650 μg/dL in the twenties, falling to 30–175 μg/dL in the senior years. In women, comparable figures are approximately 380 μg/dL in the twenties and 20–90 μg/dL in the senior years. Levels are checked by measuring a form of the hormone called DHEA-Sulfate in the blood.

Essential fatty acids

Two kinds of fatty acids are considered essential because the body cannot manufacture them itself: the omega-3s and the omega-6s. The omega-3s, EPA and DHA, help fuel the brain and control the inflammation seen in degenerative brain diseases such as Alzheimer's. EPA helps maintain nerve cell membranes, while DHA improves communication between the brain cells. The omega-6s are also crucial to brain function. People who have essential fatty acid deficiencies are at risk of developing many symptoms, including depression. In addition, depression can result from omega-6 levels that are too high relative to omega-3s.

Tests of the blood serum and the red blood cells can indicate levels of omega-3s and omega-6s, as well as the ratio between the two. Abnormally high or low levels of various fatty acids can be treated with supplementation or through dietary modification.

Folate and vitamin B_{12}

Folate and vitamin B_{12} are essential for normal psychological function. Deficiencies are often found in depressed people. Folate is necessary for the production of brain neurotransmitters, while B_{12} is necessary for the manufacture of red blood cells. Folate deficiencies have been linked to depression and anemia, while vitamin B_{12} deficiencies can contribute to many psychiatric and neurological symptoms, including depression, anxiety, hallucinations, memory loss, and confusion.

Food allergies

Food allergies may be contributing factors to many psychiatric illnesses, including depression, ADHD, and anxiety. It is clear that many people with food allergies tend to suffer from depression more so than their healthy counterparts.

These food allergies, as you recall from Chapter 9, lead to the overproduction of IgG antibodies. There are now several ways to test for the presence of IgG antibodies. For many years, the standard test for allergies to various kinds of foods was a skin-prick test. This consisted of scratching the patient's skin and then dropping an extract of a particular food into the wound. If a reddened bump that looked like a mosquito bite arose, the person was considered to be allergic to that food. More recently, a blood test, either taken from a blood draw or a finger prick, has become popular. For this test, blood is drawn from a patient and sent to a laboratory, where extracts of individual foods are introduced to see if specific elements of the immune system in the blood, the IgG antibodies, react to them. The test measures whether IgG antibodies are produced. If so, the person is thought to be allergic to that food.

Homocysteine

Homocysteine, an amino acid produced by the body, is normally converted quickly to another amino acid called cysteine. But if this conversion is somehow impaired, homocysteine levels rise. High homocysteine levels are detrimental to the body, as they are associated with an increase in free radical activity, the formation of blood clots, and coronary artery disease. A link also exists between elevated homocysteine and major depression. Although not all depressed people have elevated homocysteine, and not all of those with elevated homocysteine are depressed, data from the Health in Men Study, which involved 3,752 men aged seventy years and older, found that higher levels of homocysteine increased the risk of depression. Conversely, lowering homocysteine by 0.19 mg/L reduced the odds of depression by about 20 percent.

Because folate, vitamins B_{12} and B_6, and zinc are responsible for converting homocysteine to the nonharmful cysteine, those deficient in these nutrients can develop a buildup of homocysteine. In fact, elevated homocysteine levels can indicate an early-stage deficiency of folate, or vitamins B_6 or B_{12}, before blood levels of these nutrients reflect these problems. Oral doses of folic acid, B_6, and B_{12} may be of help in improving treatment outcome in depression.

Iron and ferritin

Depression is often a symptom of chronic iron deficiency. Iron deficiency can cause depression, fatigue, and weakness because iron is necessary for the production of hemoglobin, which helps the red blood cells ferry oxygen to the cells. Without adequate iron intake, the cells can become starved of oxygen, leading to weakness, fatigue, and general malaise.

There are many tests used to evaluate an individual's iron status: Two common tests screen levels of serum iron and ferritin, a protein that stores iron. They are often ordered together. Sometimes, blood levels of iron appear normal, but the stored supplies are low. If ferritin levels are below normal, or even in the low-normal range (less than 100 ng/mL), I recommend additional iron supplements. Taking iron with vitamin C can help with absorption.

Magnesium

The mineral magnesium is essential to several hundred bodily functions, including the conversion of carbohydrates, fats, and proteins into energy and the maintenance of normal heartbeat, blood coagulation, insulin production, and muscle and nerve function.

Magnesium deficiency can result in depression, anxiety, weakness, cardiac complications, insomnia, and difficulty concentrating, among other problems.

Testing for magnesium deficiency is not as simple as taking a blood sample. The majority of the body's magnesium is stored within our cells; only about 1 percent of the body's total magnesium is present in the blood. In other words, a blood test may not be the most accurate indicator of the body's magnesium levels. A person may have a normal blood level but still not have enough magnesium to smoothly run other biological functions.

While the most common test for magnesium is a blood test, an alternate method is to perform a twenty-four hour urine test to determine the amount of magnesium excreted from the body. Once that amount is known, the doctor injects the patient with a specified amount of magnesium and collects urine for another twenty-four hours to determine the change, if any, in the amout of magnesium the patient's body has retained. If the patient retains more magnesium than normal, he is magnesium deficient because the body retained the injected magnesium in order to compensate for the deficiency. Testing magnesium levels in the cells is yet another option. For this method, the doctor scrapes under the patient's tongue to obtain cells, which are then tested for magnesium.

Red blood cell trace minerals

When assessing any disorder associated with a zinc deficiency, including depression, a red blood cell analysis is recommended. This test evaluates levels of a number of nutrients, including calcium, phosphorous, zinc, selenium, boron, chromium, and vanadium plus potentially toxic elements, all of which have important effects on blood cells or blood cell membranes. The toxic elements include arsenic, cadmium, lead, and mercury. The results of this test can help pinpoint exactly which nutritional supplements are necessary for that person to attain optimal health.

Testosterone

All depressed men should have their testosterone levels checked. There is a strong association between depression and low levels of testosterone, and in some men depression cannot be relieved until low testosterone levels are raised. Testosterone levels are checked via a simple blood test. The "normal" values vary from laboratory to laboratory, with a range of about 270–1,000 ng/dL being considered normal for men between the ages of twenty and forty. The top of the range declines as men age, falling to the 700s for most men age sixty and older. Remember, however, what may be "normal" for one man can be low for another, so the test results must be interpreted in light of all other findings.

Thyroid

The thyroid, an endocrine gland located at the front of the base of the neck, responds to the release of a hormone manufactured by the pituitary gland called TSH. The thyroid gland produces its own hormones: T_4 and T_3, which help the body use energy at a specific rate. Levels of thyroid hormones that are too high (hyperthyroidism) or too low (hypothyroidism) cause problems. While hyperthyroidism can cause increased heart rate, palpitations, anxiety, hair and muscle loss, and insomnia, hypothyroidism can cause depression, fatigue, sluggishness, forgetfulness, increased sensitivity to cold, and weight gain. Screening for thyroid problems, then, is an important step in diagnosing and treating depression. The levels of thyroid hormones are assessed through a simple blood test.

Urinary organic acids

Abnormally high levels of organic acids result from the blockage of one or more of the body's metabolic pathways, which prompts excretion of these acids through the urine. Organic acids in the urine indicate problems with biological processes, including neurotransmitter function, detoxification, digestive imbalances, energy production, and nutrient deficiencies.

For example, high levels of a urinary organic acid called methylmalonic acid can indicate a vitamin B_{12} deficiency in its early stages, before it's detected through other methods. B_{12} is necessary for various chemical reactions that keep methylmalonic acid levels in check, so when B_{12} levels drop, methylmalonic acid levels rise. When combined with the results of a homocysteine test, high methylmalonic acid levels can confirm a mild or early vitamin B_{12} deficiency even if blood levels of B_{12} appear normal.

Similarly, high levels of an organic acid called kynurenate may indicate a deficiency of vitamin B_6, a vitamin required for the synthesis of all major neurotransmitters. When there are inadequate amounts of B_6, kynurenate levels increase in the urine.

Testing for urinary organic acids necessitates a first-morning urine sample. Diet modification, nutrient supplementation, or antifungal/antibiotic medications may be used to correct the underlying conditions leading to any abnormally high levels.

Urinary peptides

The opiate peptides casomorphin and gliadorphin appear in the urine when the naturally occurring proteins casein (found in milk) and gluten (found in wheat, rye, barley, and certain other grains) are broken down incompletely. These problems in breakdown occur because the protease enzyme *DPP* IV occurs in insufficient quantities in the small intestine or is simply inactive. Abnormally high levels of the opiate peptides cause psychological symptoms, including depression.

The test requires a first-morning urine sample. Normally, test results should be negative, meaning that casomorphin and gliadorphin are not present in the urine. If they are present, casein and/or gluten should be eliminated from the diet. Supplementation of the diet with the enzyme *DPP* IV helps to completely digest these neuroactive peptides.

Vitamin D

A deficiency in vitamin D may be associated with depression, an increased stress response, high blood pressure, high blood sugar levels, or a host of diseases including heart disease, cancer, and multiple sclerosis.

Vitamin D is converted in the liver to 25-hydroxyvitamin D, the form found in the bloodstream and typically used to evaluate an individual's vitamin D status. Low levels of 25-hydroxyvitamin D indicate that a person is not getting enough dietary vitamin D or exposure to sunlight or has a problem absorbing the vitamin. Low levels should be treated with Vitamin D_3 supplementation and the 25-hydroxyvitamin D status should be monitored every three months until levels are within the target range.

Zinc

Low levels of zinc have been correlated with depression, and the lower they are, the worse the depression. Conversely, taking zinc supplements has been shown to improve depression and to complement antidepressant therapy. However, measuring blood levels of zinc is not always a reliable way to detect a zinc deficiency. A better way to assess zinc status is to take the zinc taste test (described in Chapter 10). This test can identify even a subtle deficiency.

It's Worth the Effort

Very few psychiatrists routinely request these laboratory tests. That's an oversight, for they don't take much time and cost relatively little when compared to the monetary costs of paying for the wrong medicine and the emotional toll of remaining in the grips of depression. I have found that running a few blood tests can guide you toward the right treatment. I believe we need to investigate the potential causes of depressed mood with the same energy and passion that we use medical testing to detect causes of other ailments. If we find all the factors causing depression, then we are closer to finding the correct therapies to facilitate complete recovery and permanent remission.

17

Beyond Biochemistry

Earlier, I reviewed basic but often-ignored causes of the nutritional and biochemical triggers of depression. Restoring healthy nutrients to the body is the foundation of effective treatment. Therefore, I have focused this book primarily on nutritional interventions. I have identified many ways to address vitamin and mineral deficiencies that restrict the capacities of both body and mind. These interventions help the body to work the molecular magic that restores psychological health. Reading a magazine article on a new supplement is very different from looking at your unique metabolic profile compiled through laboratory testing. Biochemical individuality is the cornerstone of health and well-being.

Here, I focus on the big picture. Depression is clearly a complex problem involving body, mind, and soul. Nutrition is clearly a neglected approach to treating it. But treatment should also involve building an individual's inner strengths and exploring the potential of meaningful and healing connections with the outside world. So now let's shift the focus from nourishing the brain to nurturing the mind.

Western medicine tends to see only part of the depression picture. Its primary emphasis is identifying pathology at the neurotransmitter level. According to this view, if the levels of neurotransmitters are properly adjusted through pharmacological treatment, the patient's brain will return to normal and both physical and psychological symptoms will disappear. But even after trying to manipulate neurotransmitter levels with multiple medications, the problems are not necessarily solved. That's because the individual is more than just a brain. After all, to a person you value deeply, you say, "I love you" not "I love your brain."

It is important, then, to look at depression within the context of a complete, unique individual. What causes and sustains depression and influences when or even whether a person gets better depends upon the interaction of psychological, social, and cultural factors combined with biochemistry. We must remember that a person's biochemistry is not a discrete entity separate from his or her style of thinking, personal values, and life experience. And just as beliefs, personality traits, and expectations can make people sick, they can also heal. Whereas Western biomedicine views the patient as a passive entity who must follow treatment advice in order to diminish symptoms, recovery from depression often requires an understanding of a patient's beliefs and expectations about his or her condition.

One hallmark feature of depression is the depressed person's habit of focusing on negative feelings and thoughts. Depressed patients typically think obsessively, with one negative thought following another, a process called rumination. The past is tinged with regret; the present is empty; the future is unpromising. This pattern of thinking is described by Dr. Daniel Amen as Automatic Negative Thoughts, or ANTs. Amen encourages patients suffering from depression to become aware of repetitive negative thoughts. By becoming aware of and challenging ANTs, one can begin to take away their power. Amen describes this as "feeding your emotional anteater."

Cultivating positive behaviors that increase peace of mind helps lift the fog of depression more quickly. Peace of mind is not just the absence of depression but a positive state of being. A copy of Joshua Liebman's book *Peace of Mind* was given to me as a gift by my parents when I was growing up. Since peace of mind was an elusive quality, I read the book with interest. "Many men do not understand that the need for fellowship is really as deep as the need for food, so they go through life accepting many substitutes for genuine, warm, simple relatedness," wrote Liebman.

An inner sense of completeness, Liebman asserted, can be cultivated. In the decades since Liebman's book was published, research has shown that the inner resource of optimism—viewing the glass as half full instead of half empty—can not only lift a depressed mood but also lengthen life.

Becoming aware of habitual negative thinking is a critical component of a concept called "mindfulness." This concept, developed by Harvard psychologist Ellen Langer and other doctors and therapists, involves increasing one's self-awareness and living deliberately. This means turning off the "automatic pilot" that steers us mindlessly through our lives and paying attention to our thoughts, feelings, and bodily sensations. Once we are no longer "zoned out," we can start to notice variability, question knee-jerk decisions that rob us of choices, and reclaim our vitality. Langer calls this the power of possibility and encourages us to become more aware of what could be, rather than assuming that what is or what has always been is the way things have to be. Langer writes that one of the most painful aspects of depression is the belief that it has lasted since the beginning of time and will continue forever. If we pay closer attention, even when we are depressed, we realize that we are not depressed every minute of every day. Seeing that depression is not relentless helps us regain some of our ability to manage it.

Numerous practices involving mindfulness can be helpful in overcoming depression. In Chapter 19, I discuss several "mindfulness" strategies that can be started immediately. Any of these can help a person break the habit of negative thinking and become more open to healing life experiences.

One of the best ways to become mindful and self-aware, and to lift depression, is through psychotherapy, sometimes referred to as "talking therapy." Cognitive-behavioral therapy (CBT) is a form of psychotherapy that helps the individual to identify negative thoughts that sustain a depressed mood and to replace them with more positive, realistic thoughts. It offers a guided process for dealing with the self-defeating tendency to ruminate. CBT is based on the observation that depressed people tend to have negative views of themselves and the future. Instead of being considered unpleasant but haphazard events, unhappy circumstances become confirmation of the person's "essential worthlessness." CBT has been shown to be as (or nearly as) effective in treating depression as antidepressant medication and appears to be superior to antidepressants at warding off relapse. CBT also provides strategies for changing unhealthy patterns of thinking, should they re-emerge.

Researchers have also studied various types of psychodynamic therapy, which explores the roots of a patient's emotional state, often focusing on unconscious motives and defenses. Several studies demonstrate the effectiveness of psychodynamic therapies in resolving depression. However, scientists have concluded that no particular methodology produces significantly better results than any other. In a 2010 article in *American Psychologist*, J. Shelder calls this the "Dodo-bird verdict," based on the Dodo bird's exclamation in the book *Alice in Wonderland.* At the end of a contest, the Dodo bird proclaims, "Everybody has won, and all must have prizes!"

The lack of a clear winner among styles of psychotherapy may be because a patient's ongoing, trusting relationship with a therapist is more important than therapeutic content. Indeed, many researchers believe that this relationship is key to overcoming depression. While depression leads to passivity and social withdrawal, the act of participating in a therapeutic process can restore confidence and a sense of control. If interpersonal difficulties have been a factor in the depression, the opportunity to work some of these out with someone who does not react in the predictable and sometimes dysfunctional ways seen in family members can help the patient achieve a more positive resolution. Psychotherapy helps patients understand the meanings and dimensions of their depression and makes them partners in regaining health and recovery.

The experience of telling one's story is itself important, as identity is shaped by the stories we tell about ourselves. Recent research reveals that the way people describe an event shapes the choices they see. The opportunity to rework one's personal narrative in collaboration with a therapist can allow an individual to see his or her life in a new way and to envision a more hopeful future.

Family and friends can also help an individual emerge from the isolation of depression. In my clinical practice, I have observed that some patients—often busy, successful professionals—come to my office alone and are fairly secretive about their struggles with depression. Others come with a spouse or other family member. Almost invariably, those who are accompanied by supportive family members are more likely to continue with their treatment and eventually achieve relief from the symptoms of depression.

Some researchers believe that depression itself can have some positive aspects. According to James Gordon, MD, chair of the White House Commission on Complementary and Alternative Medicine Policy, "Symptoms of depression, lethargy, pessimism, and helplessness should serve as a wake-up call . . . these are actually signs that let us know we're out of balance: physically, psychologically, spiritually. They alert us that we need to do something to restore balance."

This chapter introduced some of the psychological issues that fuel depression. Chapter 18 discusses other potential forces in recovery: religious tradition, or spirituality, and the belief in healing.

18

Prayer and Placebos

Recently, researchers have studied the connections between depression and religious or spiritual life. For a long time, psychiatry tended to view patients' attitudes toward God and religion as proof of obsessional tendencies and obstacles to healing. Fantasies about an angry, punitive God, for instance, could impede rather than bolster a patient's recovery. More recently, however, researchers have found that there are benefits conferred by a patient's religion and spirituality. Being part of an established religious tradition can help a person connect with and feel part of a larger whole. A personal sense of spirituality often gives people a comforting perspective about their place in the world and the meaning of life.

Many studies that have taken place in different settings, with people of different ethnic backgrounds and across different age groups, have concluded that people who have faith in religion seem to cope better with stress and to suffer from less depression than those who do not define themselves as religious or spiritual. Research also shows that symptoms of depression dispel more quickly in religious people. Belief in a caring God, a basic tenet of many religions, appears to help people recover more quickly from depression and even improves their response to medical treatment. Praying to a God who is perceived as a source of unconditional support may help depressed people find a way out of their prison of isolation. Religious belief seems to be especially important in elderly people who are depressed. Although membership in a church or synagogue may provide the patient with social support (which, in itself, is a good thing), scientific research has demonstrated that religious belief alone helps older people recover from depression more quickly than social support alone.

Because of the potential for religion to bolster recovery from depression, I find it important to explore and understand religious beliefs and practices. Perhaps these current connections, or some renewed connections, can be mobilized to help alleviate depression. Religious beliefs can offer opportunities to see meaning in life beyond the narrow constructs of success and failure, satisfaction, and disappointment. For the therapist, a patient's religious beliefs provide a window into the way patients see themselves in relation to the world at large. Like psychotherapy, religious beliefs often give patients hope to move beyond depression.

As is the case with religious beliefs, the "placebo effect" offers insight to how a person operates; in this case, how he or she may be able to heal from depression. "Placebo effect" used to have negative connotations. At best it was an annoying variable to be controlled for in clinical trials; at worst, it implied that patients were somehow mystified or fooled. Our increased knowledge of the effects of expectation and desire on physiological processes has shown that the placebo effect can be a positive force used for healing purposes.

The placebo effect is a result obtained from a treatment that contains no medication or other substances that confer a known physiological effect on the body. For example, a placebo may simply be a sugar pill or an injection containing nothing but water. The effect may be the result of a conscious belief in the power of a drug or a subconscious association between the experience of being treated for an illness and recovery. The placebo effect occurs often in the treatment of depression—far too often to be a coincidence—with an amazing 35–45 percent of patients improving even if they are given only a sugar pill. These findings suggest that just deciding to do something can help lift depression. Because of the very positive effect of placebos in depression treatment, the FDA requires the testing of all new drugs against placebos to make sure they demonstrate greater effectiveness than a placebo alone.

In people with severe depression, the benefit of medication over placebo is significant. But with moderate depression, antidepressants do not show much more benefit than a placebo. This may make it sound like antidepressant drugs aren't worth the cost or the risk of side effects for mild to moderate depression. Exactly how much of the benefit of depression treatment comes from the placebo effect is difficult to assess in subjective states such as depression. There are no biochemical markers for depression and no blood tests to confirm its presence. And pharmaceutical companies aren't especially interested in funding studies on the benefits of placebos. But the placebo effect clearly brings relief from depression in some cases, and it is a testament to the power of belief in the healing process. After studying the results of many drug trials, psychiatrist Irving Kirsch estimates that 75 percent of the improvement is due to the experience of being in treatment for depression and 25 percent is due to a true drug response.

Worldwide by the year 2020, following heart disease, depression is predicted to be the second greatest source of disability of any kind. My experience with patients convinces me that it would be difficult to overestimate the toll depression takes on them. Many are cut off from the wellsprings of vitality in themselves and the comfort of other people. To escape, they may attempt suicide or seek refuge in alcohol or other drugs. In his memoir, *Darkness Visible*, writer William Styron describes his own experiences with depression and the absence of faith and hope: "In depression . . . faith in deliverance, in ultimate restoration, is absent. The pain is unrelenting and what makes the condition intolerable is the foreknowledge that no remedy will come—not in a day, an hour, a month, or a minute . . . It is hopelessness even more than pain that crushes the soul."

Depression presents complex challenges to those who suffer from it and to those who treat it. Unlike diseases due to a single cause such as a poison or infection, depression springs from many sources. Happily, there are also many ways to help resolve it. Strengthening or renewing contact with a religious community and connecting with the spiritual dimension of life are promising paths to recovery that spur the emergence from depression and the re-engagement with life.

19

Letting Go

Depression can be compared to being smothered by a heavy weight or confined to an airless room. Many describe it as pressure bearing down on the chest, restricting movement and freedom. Some have likened it to the lead vest worn when getting dental x-rays, to heavy ankle weights, or to a backpack filled with one hundred pounds of rocks. Shakespeare's Macbeth describes what we now know as depression as the feeling of being closed in, claustrophobic: "I am cabin'd, cribb'd, confined, bound in/to saucy doubts and fears." These images illustrate the profound physical and psychological burdens brought on by depression.

And yet the burden of depression *can* be lifted. As the brain becomes well nourished, the biochemical processes underlying depression have an opportunity to heal. For some people, nutritional restoration is enough to bring relief from depression. For others, the journey is more complicated. In addition to nourishing the body, they need to focus on the tangle of thoughts, emotions, and behaviors that have contributed to the disorder. They may need to address the cognitive vulnerabilities that fuel depression and to find ways to build inner strength.

Despite all the knowledge gained through scientific research, some aspects of emotional and mental health remain a mystery. We can understand the biochemical processes that make the disorder wax or wane, but how do people heal? Treating depression is anything but an exact science, and it lacks the tangible physical outcome seen when treating, say, strep throat. So while two therapists practicing different styles of therapy may both help a patient find relief from depression, there is still much we don't understand about how people get better.

What we do know is that those who suffer from depression understandably want relief *now.* And there are various strategies that can help lift the burden of depression immediately. I have found in my clinical practice that relief often comes through a process of letting go of whatever keeps you stuck. This can be a job in which you feel trapped, a relationship that undermines your confidence, or extra weight that saps your energy and drags down your self-esteem. Sometimes people cling for a long time to a demeaning job, a toxic relationship, or extra pounds because they lack the hope or energy to let go.

Make a decision to let go of the things that restrict you.

Only when you let go can you truly embrace the present and create your future.

The following are just a few of the many strategies you can use right now to help you let go of whatever has sustained your depression.

Visualization

Imagery is the language we use to describe feelings the the mind engages with at a level deeper than it does conscious thought. Patients and creative writers have used many images throughout the years to convey the experience of depression: the heavy weight, the Slough of Despond (John Bunyan), a dark dungeon (Nathaniel Hawthorne), the noonday demon (Andrew Solomon). All of these convey a sense of entrapment. However, it is possible through visualization to reprogram your mind with positive images. You can harness your imagination to visualize something positive—an image of lightness and fluidity that reinforces the sense of letting go.

Sports figures engage in positive visualization all the time. They may imagine the arc of the tennis ball as they slam it into the corner of their opponent's court or conjure up a detailed map of the fairway as they swing a golf club. In his book *The Seven Habits of Highly Effective People,* best-selling author Steven Covey suggests visualizing an image that is personal, positive, and in the present tense.

Breathing and Meditation

Focused breathing is another practice you can begin right away. It costs nothing and takes only a few minutes a day. Long known to practitioners of yoga, the importance of breathing as a sign of well-being is increasingly accepted by medical science. Breathing is the only aspect of the autonomic nervous system that is both voluntary and involuntary, allowing us to practice deep breathing to elicit a relaxed state. Interest in Eastern breathing practices is growing, and breathing techniques are being adapted to diverse cultures and medical settings for the health of both body and mind.

Western medical researchers are now studying the potential role of yoga-breathing in treating disorders such as depression. In small studies, after just four days of yoga-breathing practice, depressed patients showed an improvement in symptoms according to the Beck Depression Inventory. Moreover, the benefits were sustained as the volunteers were periodically rechecked.

Yogic breathing facilitates meditation, which is central to yoga practice, but is not the exclusive domain of any particular practice or philosophy. All the meditative practices encourage focused control over one's thinking, which in turn affects not only the mind but also physiological processes such as blood pressure and serotonin levels. According to the philosophy of yoga, the greatest stress in life comes from the mind's fluctuations, which allow it to become mired in thoughts about past frustrations and mistakes, also known as rumination. Deep mindful breathing, called *pranayama* in yoga, helps train the mind to stay in the present moment. In other words, it helps the individual let go. Focusing on breathing can interrupt the negative cycle of thinking, lower stress levels, slow down both body and mind, and encourage patience.

Laughing

We know instinctively that a sense of humor encourages a pleasant state and is a wonderful asset in life, contributing to resilience and helping us weather the inevitable indignities. In one study, recently widowed spouses rated humor and laughter as very important in their daily lives and in their adjustment to bereavement. Humor involves the whole person, on cognitive, emotional, behavioral, and social levels, and is associated with favorable adjustments to life losses and depression. Evidence shows that humor can also play a positive role in physical healing.

The importance of humor to mental health has led to the study and cultivation of laughter. A type of yoga now centers around laughter. The concept of Laughter Yoga was popularized as an exercise routine by Indian physician Madan Kataria. In 1995, Kataria launched his first Laughter Yoga Club. Now more than six thousand laughter clubs exist in sixty countries. Practitioners begin by simulating laughter that develops into real, contagious laughter. In this form of yoga, the laughter is physical and does not involve humor or comedy. Just the act of laughing leads to increased oxygen consumption and can stimulate the immune system.

Chanting

Chanting is another practice that may bring relief from depression. Defined as singing repetitive devotional invocations, the discipline of chanting has been shown to improve both breathing function and a sense of well-being in depressed people. Chanting a daily mantra, which is typically seen in practices like Transcendental Meditation, may lessen symptoms of depression, particularly in those people who tend to be restless.

All of the above-mentioned practices, from focused breathing to chanting, involve little cost, are easily and immediately accessible, and can help you begin to let go of emotional burdens that prolong your depression.

Forgiveness: The Ultimate Way to Let Go

The ultimate form of letting go is forgiveness. In order to forgive, you must let go of feelings of indignation and fantasies of revenge toward people who have wronged you. This doesn't mean you must behave as if you were never hurt or let people who have caused you harm back into your life. It merely means releasing the negative emotions that prevent you from moving forward. This is often accompanied by a lessening of anxiety and depression.

The ability to forgive confers many benefits. Forgiveness is strongly associated with well-being. An inverse relationship exists between a forgiving nature and depression, and forgiveness is correlated with higher satisfaction in life. According to the Heartland Forgiveness Scale, a forgiving disposition predicts relationship satisfaction and overall positive affect. Moreover, forgiveness is a factor in resilience, or the ability to recover from illness and stress and to adapt to change. Forgiveness of others seems to be even more important to middle-aged and older adults than to young adults.

Perhaps most important of all is forgiveness of self. It is the self, after all, who supplies the critical voice, with every imperfection and transgression held up to an inner magnifying glass. Be sure to let go of these negative feelings toward yourself.

Forgiveness is not a strategy or a practice in itself but a goal. We can't exactly force ourselves to forgive but just trying to let go can help make it happen. One research study showed that mindful meditation enhances the capacity to forgive.

Whatever you can do to let go of life circumstances that sustain your depression, do it. Depression can feel like living in a dark dungeon but the keys to unlock the door belong to you. The rest of your life is waiting for you!

Conclusion

Personalized Medicine

So many patients arrive at my office for the first time, already discouraged. They are tired of promised treatment and tired of being depressed. That they are still depressed is not for lack of trying: Most have tried at least one medication (and sometimes as many as seven) and every new therapy or self-help guide promising relief and recovery. Although their individual stories differ, the common theme is helplessness and the sense of being let down by the confused profession of psychiatry.

It is for these patients that I have written this book.

I've covered a lot in this book, looking at everything from amino acids to zinc. I've discussed current psychiatric practices and focused on biochemical individuality and the rEEG. It's difficult to absorb all this information in a single reading, so in this chapter I'd like to review and summarize some of the central features of THE ZEEBrA approach.

1. Every individual has unique biochemistry. Levels that are normal in one person may be high or low in the next. Indeed, a measure that may be normal or healthy for thousands or even millions of patients may be terrible for the patient who happens to walk into a

psychiatrist's office at any given moment. Benchmarks, averages, and standard ranges are good starting points, but they are just a start. Every patient has unique psychological and nutritional needs.

2. Depression is a full-body disorder, encompassing body, mind, and spirit. Depression is a complex state influenced by body chemistry and metabolism, genetics and epigenetics, nutrient intake and absorption, hormones, food sensitivities, life events, social support, and many other factors that define our lives.
3. Treatment for depression must begin with testing to identify all contributing factors. No stone should be left unturned, because even a slight mineral deficiency or hormone imbalance can result in symptoms of depression.
4. Antidepressant medications are not a magic bullet to treat depression. Although they belong in the doctor's little black bag, they must share space with other treatments, including improved nutrition, balanced hormones, and elimination of coexisting diseases. Antidepressants clearly help some patients, but not all.
5. Referenced-EEG provides reliable guidance for prescribing antidepressants and is now available. Millions of Americans have been forced to endure one medication or combination of medications after another until something works or they give up in frustration. The rEEG finally allows us to identify which classes of medications are likely to help a particular patient. The test is noninvasive, rapid, and reliable.
6. Integrative psychiatry offers the best approach for treating depression. This discipline focuses on each person's unique personality, metabolism, and environment. It treats the whole person rather than the disease alone, striving to restore the patient to good health rather than simply eliminating symptoms.

All of these principles are incorporated in THE ZEEBrA approach, a program for treating the whole patient through personalized medicine.

The Most Vulnerable Patients

As I conclude this book, I'd like to briefly discuss groups of patients who tend to be the most vulnerable. These are the individuals at each end of the age spectrum, children and seniors. Depressed children and seniors are often poorly served by psychiatry, although they comprise a significant percentage of the patients seeking help for depressed moods.

Adolescents

At any given time, as many as 15 percent of adolescents are depressed, making depression a more common ailment than asthma and most other chronic problems in this age group.

Hayley's story illustrates the cost of psychiatry's hit-or-miss prescription patterns. At sixteen, Hayley was brought to my office by her worried mother, who explained that Hayley had been an active, engaged child who did well in school and played on the school lacrosse team until her sophomore year. When Hayley failed to make the cut for the varsity team, she stopped playing lacrosse altogether and no longer spent time with her friends, most of whom she had met through the sport. Instead she began to isolate herself in her room, spending her time online. While she had always been an honor student, she began to get Cs and Ds on her report card, just when grades were becoming increasingly important to her future.

Hayley's parents were painfully aware of her downward spiral, and they had taken her to see a psychiatrist a year before. The psychiatrist diagnosed Hayley with major depressive disorder and prescribed Lexapro. This drug made Hayley agitated and unable to concentrate. Consequently, the psychiatrist prescribed Paxil instead. Hayley's agitation subsided, but she began to experience dramatic shifts in mood. The drug Abilify was added to stabilize Hayley's mood. This drug combination made Hayley sleepy all the time, and a stimulant drug was prescribed in addition to the two medications Hayley was already taking. Hayley continued to be depressed, and her parents were concerned that their adolescent daughter was taking three drugs, none of which were approved by the FDA for her illness. They brought her to me for a second opinion.

I tested Hayley for nutritional deficiencies, and, based on the results, I prescribed a diet higher in protein than what she was eating. Testing also found Hayley deficient in zinc, magnesium, and vitamin B_{12}; supplements of these minerals and vitamin were added to her diet. After conducting an rEEG, I determined that the drug Wellbutrin was more likely to be effective on Hayley's brain chemistry than any of the medications she had been taking.

Hayley got steadily better on this new regimen. In time she was able to turn her record around before applying to college, reconnect with old friends, and derive some pleasure from her remaining time in high school.

So many depressed adolescents do not get effective treatment even when they are under psychiatric care, and the stakes for them are high. Three-fourths of lifetime psychiatric disorders first emerge in adolescence or early adulthood. Depressed young people are also more likely to have conduct problems, to underachieve, and to engage in substance abuse than other adolescents. More depressed college students have used alcohol than their peers who do not suffer from depression. Moreover, once adolescents have participated in high-risk behaviors, they are more likely to continue to engage in them as they become adults. For all of these reasons depression in adolescents is of special concern.

The elderly

Depression is also of special concern for the elderly. Diagnosis in this group is more challenging because these patients often do not manifest the "typical" signs of depression. Depressed seniors may express no feelings of sadness; they can simply appear apathetic or uninterested in activities that formerly brought them pleasure. They may not be as forthcoming about their feelings in general as those who have grown up in an era of relatively free personal expression. Instead, the elderly may report more physical symptoms than painful feelings, so that symptoms of depression are cloaked in other medical complaints. A shuffling gait may suggest arthritis, while difficulty breathing can raise the suspicion of pulmonary disease. The erosion of cognitive processes can look like Alzheimer's disease. But all these symptoms can be signs of depression.

How often do you hear that an elderly relative has little interest in food? Or that food doesn't taste good? If you remember, poor taste is a symptom of zinc deficiency. Zinc deficiency, a treatable contributing factor in depression, is common in the elderly.

Medications

Elderly and young patients are particularly vulnerable to psychiatric medications. The use of these drugs is studied in young and middle-aged adults, not in adolescents and seniors. For seniors these drugs may interact with other medication they take to treat other chronic conditions.

For adolescents even greater dangers may be involved. Because antidepressant drugs can increase agitation and suicidal thinking in adolescents during the early phase of treatment, the FDA has required since 2004 that these drugs contain a "black-box warning," the most serious warning placed on medication labels. In addition, the effects of these powerful drugs on the developing brain are not fully understood. Most clinical trials assessing their effectiveness have been of short duration and have been conducted on small numbers of participants.

Some psychiatrists concerned about the burgeoning use of antidepressant drugs argue that this treatment model could actually be fueling an epidemic of mental illness among adolescents. The prescription rate of antidepressant medication for young people has increased sevenfold since 1990, and the rate of mental illness in young people itself continues to accelerate. If antidepressants continue to be prescribed at the current rate, within a generation half of American children will be taking psychiatric medication. Some studies show that even if young patients experience symptom relief when they begin to take these drugs, the depression comes back. Instead of an episodic problem, then, depression becomes a chronic one.

Medical professionals can no longer continue treating vulnerable patients like adolescents and seniors as if there is but one answer to depression: medication.

Given that many members of these groups are malnourished, do not exercise enough, lack support, and have concurrent diseases, it's vital that treatment addresses all of these areas. Indeed, for these groups and for all patients, we need to use every tool available to treat depression.

The Future of Treatment for Depression

Although THE ZEEBRA is the most complete, personalized, and integrative approach for dealing with depression, medical science is continuing to advance, offering new hope for successful diagnosis and treatment.

The most exciting new treatment technique, recently approved by the FDA for major depressive disorder, is called transcranial magnetic stimulation (TMS). TMS sends carefully targeted magnetic field impulses into the prefrontal cortex, an area of the brain that plays a major role in regulating mood and that has been specifically linked to depression. Researchers believe that depression alters the prefrontal cortex. The mild electrical current generated by the magnetic impulses appears to improve the function and behavior of the prefrontal cortex.

Studies involving more than ten thousand TMS treatments show that it is safe and effective. In an open label trial, about 50 percent of patients enjoyed significant improvement in depression symptoms, with the symptoms being completely resolved in 33 percent of the participants. The benefits lasted through the six months that the patients were monitored. Side effects included mild to moderate scalp discomfort and headache, with the problems occurring less frequently after the first week of treatment.

The treatment sessions are easy and uneventful for the patient, who sits in a large chair with a small "arm" that generates the magnetic impulses positioned off the left side of the head. Typically, twenty to thirty treatment sessions are given over the course of four to six weeks, with each session lasting less than forty minutes. Anesthesia and sedation are not necessary, and patients can return to work or personal activities immediately.

TMS is prescribed by psychiatrists for adults with major depressive disorder who have not been helped by the proper application of at least one standard antidepressant medication. TMS fits into my integrative psychiatry concept, and I've been impressed by the results. It is worth talking to your psychiatrist about the possibility of TMS treatment.

Although TMS is a large step forward, it and all other new techniques must be used as part of an integrated program based on identifying and treating underlying nutritional deficiencies, for nothing will be successful in the long run unless the problems we've been discussing in this book are remedied.

A New Way

I am passionate about THE ZEEBrA approach: It helps both doctors and patients view depression in a new way and opens the door to solutions that millions have been waiting for.

If you do not ask the questions, how can you find the answers? If you do not look for causes, how do you find the cures? If you understand that you are a unique, biochemical, psychological, and spiritual person, you will understand a new approach is desperately needed for the treatment of depression.

You are in charge of your own health. I hope this book has given you the knowledge and tools you need to begin to heal. I encourage you to engage your health professional in a broad search for factors that may contribute to your depression. Through this search you can find the help you need and the peace of mind you deserve.

Depression is treatable. You will get well.

Epilogue

It's Time

As I finish this book, I ask the same question that prompted me to write the book in the first place. Why?

Why are Vitamin B_{12} and folate levels not routinely checked in every patient who is depressed?

Why are patients who are depressed not routinely screened for celiac disease?

Why are so many psychiatrists so reluctant to explore more deeply the relationship between depression and trace metals such as zinc, chromium, and iodine?

Why do health insurance companies cover memberships in health clubs but not nutritional supplements, even when lab tests reveal a clear nutritional deficiency?

A few years ago I participated in a meeting held in a conference room of one of the nation's largest insurers. The company that developed the rEEG offered to provide this test at no cost to patients who failed to respond to standard psychiatric care for depression. As you will remember, the EEG is a simple test conducted while the patient sits in a chair. There are no possible side effects. Still, the insurer refused to accept the offer to use this promising technology on the grounds that they needed more time to get more results from large research studies.

I am impatient with this kind of decision. We do not have more time. As the chief medical officer of a psychiatric hospital, I regularly see patients in crisis. Too often there is a chart on my desk of depressed patients who commit suicide after shuttling for years between therapies and hospitals, trying one medication after another. The decision to end one's life is their incomprehensible, tragic ending.

The science is available to change the current model of trial-and-error prescribing. The science is available to correct nutritional and metabolic influences on mood. Right now we have the tools we need to identify and improve the treatment of depression.

It's time.

References

Introduction

Berwick, D.M. (2003). Disseminating innovations in health care. *Journal of the American Medical Association, 289*(15), 1969-1975.

Goodwin, J.S., & Goodwin, J.M. (1984). The tomato effect: Rejection of highly efficacious therapies. *The Journal of the American Medical Association, 251*(18), 2387-2390.

Levin, A. (2010). Time to apply cutting edge to the brain, nobelists say. *Psychiatric News, 45*(10), 4.

Part I: Understanding the Problem

Chapter 1: What Is Depression?

Altshuler, L.L., Hendrick, V., & Cohen, L.S. (1993). Course of mood and anxiety disorders during pregnancy and the postpartum period. *Journal of Clinical Psychiatry, 59*(Suppl 2), 29-33.

Bostwick, J.M., & Pankratz, V.S. (2000). Affective disorders and suicide risk: a reexamination. *American Journal of Psychiatry, 157*(12), 1925-1932.

Conwell, Y., & Brent, D. (1995). Suicide and aging. I: Patterns of psychiatric diagnosis. *International Psychogeriatrics, 7*(2), 149-164.

Goldman, L.S., Nielsen, N.H., & Champion, H.C. (1999). Awareness, Diagnosis and Treatment of Depression. *Journal of Internal General Medicine, 14*(9), 569-580.

González, H.M., et al. (2010). Depression care in the United States: too little for too few. *Archives of General Psychiatry, 67*(1), 37-46.

Green, R.C., et al. (2003). Depression as a risk factor for Alzheimer's disease: the MIRAGE Study. *Archives of Neurology, 60*(5), 753-759.

Hellerstein, D.J., et al. (2010). Impairment in psychosocial functioning associated with dysthymic disorder in the NESARC study. *Journal of Affective Disorders*, [Epub ahead of print].

Huang, T.L., & Lee, C.T. (2007). T-helper 1/T-helper 2 cytokine imbalance and clinical phenotypes of acute-phase major depression. *Psychiatry and Clinical Neuroscience, 61*(4), 415-420.

Kessler, R.C., et al. (2005). Lifetime prevalence and age-of-onset distributions of DSM-IV disorders in the National Comorbidity Survey Replication. *Archives of General Psychiatry, 62*(6), 593-602.

Knol, M.J., et al. (2006). Depression as a risk factor for the onset of type 2 diabetes mellitus. A meta-analysis. *Diabetologia, 49*(5), 837-845.

Mark, T.L., Levit, K.R., & Buck, J.A. (2009). Datapoints: Psychotropic drug prescriptions by medical specialty. *Psychiatric Services, 60*(9), 1167.

Sansone, R.A., & Sansone, L.A. (1996). Dysthymic disorder: The chronic depression. *American Family Physician, 53*(8), 2588-2596.

Chapter 2: Depression Can Be Cured

Kennedy, N. & Paykel, E.S. (2004). Residual symptoms at remission from depression: impact on long-term outcome. *Journal of Affective Disorders, 80*(2-3), 135-144.

Mojtabai, R. & Olfson, M. (2010). National trends in psychotrophic medication polypharmacy in office-based psychiatry. *Archives of General Psychiatry, 67*(1), 26-36.

Trivedi, M.H., et al. (2006). Evaluation of outcomes with citalopram for depression using measurement-based care in STAR*D: implications for clinical practice. *American Journal of Psychiatry; 163*(1), 28-40.

Turner, E.H., et al. (2008). Selective publication of antidepressant trials and its influence on apparent efficacy. *The New England Journal of Medicine, 358*(3), 252-260.

Ustün, T.B., et al. (2004). Global burden of depressive disorders in the year 2000. *British Journal of Psychiatry, 184,* 386-392.

Chapter 3: Current Treatments Are Less Effective Than We Think

Bekelman, J.E., Li, Y., & Gross, C.P. (2003). Scope and impact of financial conflicts of interest in biomedical research: a systematic review. *Journal of the American Medical Association, 289*(4), 454-465.

Food and Drug Administration. (2004, March 24). *Worsening depression and suicidality in patients being treated with antidepressants.* Retrieved May 17, 2010 from http://www.fda.gov/Drugs/DrugSafety/PostmarketDrugSafetyInformationforPatientsandProviders/DrugSafetyInformationforHeathcareProfessionals/PublicHealthAdvisories/ucm161696.htm.

Fournier, J.C., et al. (2010). Antidepressant drug effects and depression severity: a patient-level meta-analysis. *Journal of the American Medical Association, 303*(1), 47-53.

Gellad, Z.F. & Lyles, K.W. (2007). Direct-to-consumer advertising of pharmaceuticals. *The American Journal of Medicine, 120*(6), 475-480.

Gregorian, R.S., et al. (2002). Antidepressant-induced sexual dysfunction. *Annals of Pharmacotherapy, 36*(10), 1577-1589.

Kaplan, A. (2010). Antidepressants: how well do they work? *Psychiatric Times, 27*(3).

Moncrieff, J. (2001). Are antidepressants overrated? A review of methodological problems in antidepressant trials. *Journal of Nervous and Mental Disease, 189*(5), 288-295.

Robinson, A.R., et al. (2004). Direct-to-consumer pharmaceutical advertising: physician and public opinion and potential effects on the physician-patient relationship. *Archives of Internal Medicine, 164*(4), 427-432.

Zimmerman, M., Posternak, M.A., & Chelminski, I. (2002). Symptom severity and exclusion from antidepressant efficacy trials. *Journal of Clinical Psychopharmacology, 22*(6), 610-614.

Chapter 4: Depression and Biochemical Individuality

Goldman, E. (2007, June). Hippocampal neurogenesis: Key to antidepressants? *Clinical Psychiatry News, 35*(6), 16.

Mayberg, H.S. et al. (2005). Deep brain stimulation for treatment-resistant depression. Neuron, 45(5), 651-660.

Chapter 5: Genetics, Epigenetics and You

Dolinoy, D.C., et al (2006). Maternal genistein alters coat color and protects Avy mouse offspring from obesity by modifying the fetal epigenome. *Environmental Health Perspectives, 114*(4), 567-572.

Dolinoy, D.C., Huang, D., & Jirtle, R.L. (2007). Maternal nutrient supplementation counteracts bisphenol A-induced DNA hypomethylation in early development. *Proceedings of the National Academy of Sciences, 104*(32), 13056-13061.

Fang, M.Z., et al. (2003). Tea polyphenol (-)-epigallocatechin-3-gallate inhibits DNA methyltransferase and reactivates methylation-silenced genes in cancer cell lines. *Cancer Research, 63*(22), 7563-7570.

Hughes, L.A., et al. (2009). Early life exposure to famine and colorectal cancer risk: a role for epigenetic mechanisms. *PLos ONE, 4*(11), e7951.

Liu Y, et al. (2009). Alcohol exposure alters DNA methylation profiles in mouse embryos at early neurulation. *Epigenetics, 4*(7), 500-511.

Murgatroyd, C., et al. (2010). Genes learn from stress: How infantile trauma programs us for depression. *Epigenetics, 5*(3), [Epub ahead of print].

Maestripieri, D. (2005). Early experience affects the intergenerational transmission of infant abuse in rhesus monkeys. *Proceedings of the National Academy of Sciences USA, 102*(27), 9726-9729.

Sullivan, P.F., Neale, M.C., & Kendler, K.S. (2000). Genetic epidemiology of major depression: review and meta-analysis. *American Journal of Psychiatry, 157*(10), 1552-1562.

Chapter 6: Individualizing Medicine with THE ZEEBrA Approach

Boscarino, J.A., Erlich, P.M., & Hoffman, S.N. (2009). Low serum cholesterol and external-cause mortality: Potential implications for research and surveillance. *Journal of Psychiatric Research, 43*(9), 848-854.

Eby, G.A., & Eby, K.L. (2006). Rapid recovery from major depression using magnesium treatment. *Medical Hypotheses, 67*(2), 362-370.

Hintikka J., et al. (2003). High vitamin B12 level and good treatment outcome may be associated in major depressive disorder. *BMC Psychiatry*, 3, 17.

Levenson, C.W. (2006). Zinc: the new antidepressant?. *Nutrition Reviews, 64*(1), 39-42.

Nemets, H., et al. (2006). Omega-3 treatment of childhood depression: a controlled, double-blind pilot study. *American Journal of Psychiatry, 163*(6), 1098-1100.

Papakostas G.I., et al. (2004). Serum folate, vitamin B12, and homocysteine in major depressive disorder, Part I: predictors of clinical response in fluoxetine-resistant depression. *Journal of Clinical Psychiatry, 65*(8), 1090-1095.

Pope, H.G. Jr., et al. (2003). Testosterone gel supplementation for men with refractory depression: a randomized, placebo-controlled trial. *American Journal of Psychiatry, 160*(1), 105-111.

Su, K.P., et al. (2003). Omega-3 fatty acids in major depressive disorder. A preliminary double-blind, placebo-controlled trial. *European Neuropsychopharmacology, 13*(4), 267-271.

Sublette M.E., et al. (2006). Omega-3 polyunsaturated essential fatty acid status as a predictor of future suicide risk. *American Journal of Psychiatry, 163*(6), 1100-1102.

Tai, S.S., et al. (1999). Promoting physical activity in general practice: should prescribed exercise be free?. *Journal of the Royal Society of Medicine, 92*(2), 65-67.

Young, S.N. (2009). Has the time come for clinical trials on the antidepressant effect of vitamin D? *Journal of Psychiatry & Neuroscience, 34*(1), 3.

Part II: Nourishing the Brain: The ZEEBrA Approach

Chapter 7: T — Take Care of Yourself

Benton, D., Williams, C., & Brown, A. (2007). Impact of consuming a milk drink containing a probiotic on mood and cognition. *European Journal of Clinical Nutrition, 61*(3), 355-361.

Eby, G.A., & Eby, K.L. (2006). Rapid recovery from major depression using magnesium treatment. *Medical Hypotheses, 67*(2), 362-370.

Jacka, F.N., et al. (2010). Association of Western and traditional diets with depression and anxiety in women. *American Journal of Psychiatry, 167*(3), 305-311.

Jacka, F.N., et al. Associations between diet quality and depressed mood in adolescents: results from the Australian Healthy Neighbourhoods Study. *Australian New Zealand Journal of Psychiatry, 44*(5), 435-442.

Koetter, U. et al. (2007). A randomized, double blind, placebo-controlled, prospective clinical study to demonstrate clinical efficacy of a fixed valerian hops extract combination (Ze 91019) in patients suffering from non-organic sleep disorder. *Phytotherapy Research, 21*(9), 847-851.

Poyares, D.R., et al. (2002). Can valerian improve the sleep of insomniacs after benzodiazepine withdrawal? *Progress in Neuro-Psychopharmacology & Biological Psychiatry, 26*(3), 539-545.

Chapter 8: H — Hormones

Almeida O.P., et al. (2008). Low free testosterone concentration as a potentially treatable cause of depressive symptoms in older men. *Archives of General Psychiatry, 65*(3), 283-289.

Aronson, R., et al. (1996). Triiodothyronine augmentation I the treatment of refractory depression. A meta-analysis. *Archives of General Psychiatry, 53*(9), 842-848.

Bloch, M., et al. (1999). Dehydroepiandrosterone treatment of midlife dysthymia. *Biological Psychiatry,* 45(12), 1533–1541.

Lifschytz T., et al. (2006). Basic mechanisms of augmentation of antidepressant effects with thyroid hormone. *Current Drug Targets, 7*(2), 203-210.

Michael, A., et al. (2000). Altered salivary dehydroepiandrosterone levels in major depression in adults. *Biological Psychiatry, 48*(10), 989–995.

Pope, H.G. Jr, et al. (2003). Testosterone gel supplementation for men with refractory depression: a randomized, placebo-controlled trial. *American Journal of Psychiatry, 160*(1), 105-111.

Prange, A.J. Jr, et al. (1969). Enhancement of imipramine antidepressant activity by thyroid hormone. *American Journal of Psychiatry, 126*(4), 457-469.

Schmidt P.J., et al. (2005). Dehydroepiandrosterone monotherapy in midlife-onset major and minor depression. *Archives of General Psychiatry, 62*(2), 154-162.

Chapter 9: E — Exclude

Ciacci, C., et al. (1998). Depressive symptoms in adult coeliac disease. *Scandinavian Journal of Gastroenterology,* 33(3), 247-250.

Elgun, S., Keskinege, A., Kumbasar, H. (1999). Dipeptidyl peptidase IV and adenosine deaminase activity. decrease in depression. *Psychoneuroendocrinology, 24*(8), 823-832.

Hallert, C., & Aström, J. (1982). Psychic disturbances in adult coeliac disease. II. Psychological findings. *Scandinavian Journal of Gastroenterology*, *17*(1), 21-24.

Hole, K., et al., (1988). Attention deficit disorders: a study of peptide-containing urinary complexes. *Journal of Developmental and Behavioral Pediatrics*, *9*(4), 205-212.

Hole, K., et al., (1979). A peptide-containing fraction in the urine of schizophrenic patients which stimulates opiate receptors and inhibits dopamine uptake. *Neuroscience*, *4*(12), 1883-1893.

Lillestol K., et al. (2010). Anxiety and depression in patients with self-reported food hypersensitivity. *Gen Hops Psychiatry*, *32*(1), 42-48.

Ludvigsson J.F., et al. (2009). Coeliac disease and risk of mood disorders – A general population-based cohort study. *Journal of Affective Disorders*, *99*(1-3), 117-126.

Maes, M., et al. (1997). Lower serum dipeptidyl peptidase IV activity in treatment resistant major depression: Relationships with immune-inflammatory markers. *Psychoneuroendocrinology*, *22*(2), 65-78.

Pedersen, O.S., Liu, Y., & Reichelt, K.L. (1999). Serotonin uptake stimulating peptide found in plasma of normal individuals and in some autistic urines. *Journal of Peptide Research*, *53*(6), 641-646.

Reichelt, K.L., et al., (1981). Biologically active peptide-containing fractions in schizophrenia and childhood autism. *Advances in Biochemical Psychopharmacology*, *28*, 627-643.

Saelid, G., et al., (1985). Peptide-containing fractions in depression. *Biological Psychiatry*, *20*(3), 245-256.

Chapter 10: Z — Zinc and Other Minerals

Amani, R., et al. (2009). Correlation between dietary zinc intakes and its serum levels with depression scales in young female students. *Biological Trace Element Research*, *137*(2), 150-158.

Barragan-Rodriguez, L., Rodriguez-Moran, M., & Guerreo-Romero, F. (2008). Efficacy and safety of oral magnesium supplementation in the treatment of depression in the elderly with type 2 diabetes: a randomized, equivalent trial. *Magnesium Research*, *21*(4), 218-223.

Bauer M., et al. (2010). Lithium's emerging role in the treatment of refractory major depressive episodes: augmentation of antidepressants. *Neuropsychobiology*, *62*(1), 36-42.

Beard, J.L., et al. (2005). Maternal iron deficiency anemia affects postpartum emotions and cognition. *Journal of Nutrition*, *135*(2), 267-272.

Cipriani, A., et al. (2005). Lithium in the prevention of suicidal behavior and all-cause mortality in patients with mood disorders: a systematic review of randomized trials. *American Journal of Psychiatry*, *162*(10), 1805-1819.

Crayton, J.W., & Walsh, W.J. (2007). Elevated serum copper levels in women with a history of post-partum depression. *Journal of Trace Elements in Medicine and Biology*, *21*(1), 17-21.

Davidson, J.R., et al. (2003). Effectiveness of chromium in atypical depression: A placebo-controlled trial. *Biological Psychiatry*, *53*(3), 261-264.

De Montigny, C., et al. (1981). Lithium induces rapid relief of depression in tricyclic antidepressant drug non-responders. *British Journal of Psychiatry*, *138*, 252-256.

Eby, G.A. 3rd, & Eby, K.L. (2010). Magnesium for treatment-resistant depression: A review and hypothesis. *Medical Hypotheses*, *74*(4), 649-660.

Jacka, F.N., et al. (2009). Association between magnesium intake and depression and anxiety in community-dwelling adults: the Hordaland health study. *Australian and New Zealand Journal of Psychiatry, 43*(1), 45-52.

Maes, M., et al. (1997). Lower serum zinc in major depression is a sensitive marker of treatment resistance of of the immune/inflammatory response in that illness. *Biological Psychiatry, 42*(5), 349-358.

McLeod, M.N., & Golden, R.N. (2000). Chromium treatment of depression. *International Journal of Neuropsychopharmacology, 3*(4), 311-314.

McLoughlin, I.J., & Hodge, J.S. (1990). Zinc in depressive disorder. *Acta Psychiatrica Scandinavica, 82*(6), 451-453.

Narang, R.L., et al. (1991). Levels of copper and zinc in depression. *Indian Journal of Physiology and Pharmacology, 35*(4), 272-274.

Nowak G., et al. (2003). Effect of zinc supplementation on antidepressant therapy in unipolar depression: a preliminary placebo-controlled trial. *Polish Journal Pharmacology, 55*(6), 1143-1147.

Nowak, G., Szewczyk, B., & Pilc, A. (2005). Zinc and depression. An update. *Pharmacological Reports*, 57(6), 713-718.

Prange, A.J. Jr., et al. (1969). Enhancement of imipramine antidepressant activity by thyroid hormone. *American Journal of Psychiatry, 126*(4), 457-469.

Sawada, T., & Yokoi, K. (2010). Effect of zinc supplementation on mood states in young women: a pilot study. *European Journal of Clinical Nutrition, 64*(3), 331-333.

Siwek M., et al. (2009). Zinc supplementation augments efficacy of imipramine in treatment resistant patients: a double-blind, placebo-controlled study. *Journal of Affective Disorders*, 118(1-3), 187-195.

Szewczyk B., et al. (2008). Antidepressant activity of zinc and magnesium in view of the current hypotheses of antidepressant action. *Pharmacological Reports, 60*(5), 588-599.

Vahdat Shariatpanaahi, M., et al. (2007). The relationship between depression and serum ferritin level. *European Journal of Clinical Nutrition, 61*(4), 532-535.

Chapter 11: E — Essential Fatty Acids and Cholesterol

Borgherini, G., et al. (2002). Serum cholesterol and psychological distress in hospitalized depressed patients. *Acta Psychiatrica Scandinavica*, 105(2), 149-152.

Golomb, B.A., Stattin, H., & Mednick, S. (2000). Low cholesterol and violent crime. *Journal of Psychiatric Research, 34*(4-5), 301-309.

Hibbeln, J.R. (1998). Fish consumption and major depression. *Lancet, 351*(9110), 1213.

Jazayeri, S., et al. (2008). Comparison of therapeutic effects of omega-3 fatty acid eicosapentaenoic acid and fluoxetine, separately and in combination, in major depressive disorder. *Australian and New Zealand Journal of Psychiatry, 42*(3), 192-198.

Lalovic, A., et al. (2007). Cholesterol content in brains of suicide completers. *International Journal of Neuropsychopharmacology, 10*(2), 159-166.

Lehto, S.M., et al. (2010). Low serum HDL-cholesterol levels are associated with long symptoms duration in patients with major depressive disorder. *Psychiatry and Clinical Neurosciences, 64*(3), 279-283.

Lesperance, F., et al. (2010). The efficacy of omega-3 supplementation for major depression: a randomized controlled trial. *Journal of Clinical Psychiatry*, [Epub ahead of print].

Logan, A.C. (2004). Omega-3 fatty acids and major depression: A primer for the mental health professional. *Lipids in Health and Disease, 3*, 25.

Mamalakis, G., et al. (2006). Depression in serum adiponectin and adipose omega-3 and omega-6 fatty acids in adolescents. *Pharmacology, Biochemistry, and Behavior, 85*(2), 474-479.

Mamalakis, G., Tornaritis, M., & Kafatos, A. (2002). Depression and adipose essential polyunsaturated fatty acids. *Prostaglandins, Leukotriens, and Essential Fatty Acids, 67*(5), 311-318.

Morgan, R.E., et al. (1993). Plasma cholesterol and depressive symptoms in older men. *Lancet, 341*(8837), 75-79.

Nemets, H., et al. (2006). Omega-3 treatment of childhood depression: a controlled, double-blind pilot study. *American Journal of Psychiatry*, 163(6), 1098-1100.

Perez-Rodriguez, M.M., et al. (2008). Low serum cholesterol may be associated with suicide history attempt. *Journal of Clinical Psychiatry, 69*(12), 1920-1927.

Stoll, A.L., et al. (1999). Omega-3 fatty acids in bipolar disorder: a preliminary double-blind, placebo-controlled trial. *Archives of General Psychiatry, 56*(5), 407-412.

Su, K.P., et al. (2003). Omega-3 fatty acids in major depressive disorder. A preliminary double-blind, placebo-controlled trial. *European Neuropsychopharmacology, 13*(4), 267-271.

Sublette, M.E., et al. (2006). Omega-3 polyunsaturated essential fatty acid status as a predictor of future suicide risk. *American Journal of Psychiatry, 163*(6), 1100-1102.

Chapter 12: E — Exercise and Energy

Babyak, M., et al. (2000). Exercise treatment for major depression: maintenance of therapeutic benefit at 10 months. *Psychomatic Medicine, 62*(5), 633-638.

Dunn, A.L., et al. (2005). Exercise treatment for depression: efficacy and dose response. *American Journal of Preventive Medicine, 28*(1), 1-8.

Galper, D.I., et al. (2006). Inverse association between physical inactivity and mental health in men and women. *Medicine and Science in Sports and Exercise, 36*(1), 183-178.

Gardner, A., & Boles, R.G. (2008). Mitochondrial energy depletion in depression with somatization. *Psychotherapy and Psychomatics, 77*(2), 127-129.

Goodwin, R.D. (2003). Association between physical activity and mental disorders among adults in the United States. *Preventive Medicine, 36*(6), 698-703.

Kuratsune, H., et al. (1994). Acylcarnitine deficiency in chronic fatigue syndrome. *Clinical Infectious Diseases*, 18(Suppl 1), S62-S67.

Malaguarnera, M., et al. (2007). L-carnitine treatment reduces severity of physical and mental fatigue and increases cognitive functions in centenarians: a randomized and controlled clinical trial. *American Journal of Clinical Nutrition, 86*(6), 1738-1744.

Mizuno, K., et al. (2004). Antifatigue effects of coenzyme Q10 during physical fatigue. *Nutrition, 24*(4), 293-299.

Rezin, G.T., et al. (2009). Mitochondrial dysfunction and psychiatric disorders. *Neurochemical Research, 34*(6), 1021-1029.

Sidhu, K.S., Vandana, P., & Balon, R. (2009). Exercise prescription. *Current Psychiatry, 8*(6), 39-51.

Teitelbaum, J.E., Johnson, C., & St. Cyr, J. (2006). The use of D-ribose in chronic fatigue syndrome and fibromyalgia: a pilot study. *Journal of Alternative and Complementary Medicine, 12*(9), 857-862.

Vaccarino, A.L., et al. (2008). Prevalence and association of somatic symptoms in patients with major depressive disorder. *Journal of Affective Disorders, 110*(3), 270-276.

Wang, C. (2008). Tai Chi improves pain and functional status in adults with rheumatoid arthritis: results of a pilot single-blinded randomized controlled trial. *Medicine and Sport Science*, 52, 218-229.

Woolery, A., et al. (2004). A yoga intervention for young adults with elevated symptoms of depression. *Alternative Therapies in Health and Medicine, 10*(2), 60-63.

Chapter 13: B — B Vitamins and Other Vitamins

Bell, K.M., et al. (1988). S-adenosylmethionine treatment of depression: a controlled clinical trial. *American Journal of Psychiatry, 145*(9), 1110-1114.

Coppen, A., & Bailey, J. (2000). Enhancement of the antidepressant action of fluoxetine by folic acid: a randomized, placebo controlled trial. *Journal of Affective Disorders, 60*(2), 121-130.

Delle Chiaie, R., Pancheri, P., & Scapicchio, P. (2002). Efficacy and tolerability of oral and intramuscular S-adenosyl-L-methionine 1,4-butanedisulfonate (SAMe) in the treatment of major depression: comparison with imipramine in 2 multicenter studies. *American Jounral of Clinical Nutrition, 76*(5), 1172S-1176S.

Fava, M., & Mischoulon, D. (2009). Folate in depression: Efficacy, safety differences in formulations, and clinical issues. *Journal of Clinical Psychiatry, 70*(Suppl 5), 12-17.

Fava, M., et al. (1997). Folate, vitamin B12, and homocysteine in major depressive disorder. *American Journal of Psychiatry, 154*(3), 426-428.

Milaneschi, Y., et al. (2010). Serum 25-hydroxyvitamin D and depressive symptoms in older women and men. *Journal of Clinical Endrocrinology and Metabolism, 95*(7), 3225-3233.

Morris, M.C., et al. (2005). Dietary folate and vitamin B12 intake and cognitive decline among community-dwelling older persons. *Archives of Neurology, 62*(4), 641-645.

Papakostas, G.I., et al. (2010). S-adenosyl methionine (SAMe) augmentation of serotonin reuptake inhibitors for antidepressant nonresponders with major depressive disorder: a double-blind, randomized clinical trial. *American Journal of Psychiatry, 167*(8), 942-948.

Shipowick, C.D., et al. (2009). Vitamin D and depression symptoms in women during the winter: a pilot study. *Applied Nursing Research, 22*(3), 221-225.

Snellman, G., et al. (2009). Seasonal genetic influence on serum 25-hydroxyvitamin D levels: a twin study. *PLoS One, 4*(11), e7747.

Stewart, J.W., et al. (1984). Low B6 levels in depressed outpatients. *Biological Psychiatry, 19*(4), 613-616.

Stewart, R., & Hirani, V. (2010). Relationship between vitamin D levels and depressive symptoms in older residents from a national survey population. *Psychosomatic Medicine, 72*(7), 608-612.

Tiemeier, H., et al. (2002). Vitamin B12 folate, and homocysteine in depression: the Rotterdam Study. *American Journal of Psychiatry, 159*(12), 2099-2101.

Chapter 14: r — referenced–EEG

CNS Response. (n.d.). *Referenced-EEG® (rEEG®): An introductory guide to recording.* Retrieved July 10, 2010, from http://www.cnsresponse.com/doc/CNSR_rEEG_Intro_Guide_to_EEG_Recording_v2.0_Mar2009.pdf.

Debattista, C., et al. (2010). The use of referenced-EEG (rEEG) in assisting medication selection for the treatment of depression. *Journal of Psychiatric Research*, [Epub ahead of print].

Hoffman, D.A. (n.d.) *Referenced-EEG® (rEEG®): A biomarker assessment system to guide pharmacotherapy*. Retrieved from http://cnsresponse.com/doc/CNSR%20rEEG%20 Research%20Summary.pdf.

Worcester, S. (2005). rEEG system helps guide prescribing. *Clinical Psychiatry News*, *33*(2), 1 & 6.

Chapter 15: A — Amino Acids and Proteins

Jin, G., et al. (2009). Changes in plasma and tissue amino acid levels in an animal model of complex fatigue. *Nutrition*, *25*(5), 597-607.

Layman, D.K. (2009). Dietary guidelines should reflect new understandings about adult protein needs. *Nutrition and Metabolism*, *6*, 12.

Levitan, R.D., et al. (2000). Preliminary randomized double-blind placebo-controlled trial of tryptophan combined with fluoxetine to treat major depressive disorder: antidepressant and hypnotic effect. *Journal of Psychiatry and Neuroscience*, *25*(4), 337-346.

Maes, M., et al. (1995). Total serum protein and serum protein fractions in depression: relationships to depressive symptoms and glucocorticoid activity. *Journal of Affective Disorders*, *34*(1), 61-69.

Mauri, M.C., et al. (1998). Plasma and platelet amino acid concentrations in patients affected by major depression and under fluvoxamine treatment. *Neuropsychobiology*, *37*(3), 124-129.

Mitani, H., et al. (2006). Correlation between plasma levels of glutamate, alanine and serine with severity of depression. *Progress in Neuro-Psychopharmacology & Biological Psychiatry*, *30*(6), 1155-1158.

Smith, K.A., Fairburn, C.G., Cowen, P.J. (1997). Relapse of depression after rapid depletion of tryptophan. *Lancet*, *349*(9056), 915-919.

Chapter 16: Laboratory Tests Your Doctor May Order

Almeida, O.P., et al. (2005). Homocysteine and depression later in life. *Archives of General Psychiatry*, *65*(11), 1286-1294.

Lord, R.S., & Bralley, J.A. (Eds.). (2008). *Laboratory evaluations for integrative and functional medicine*. Duluth, GA: Metametrix Institute.

Lukaczer, D., & Schiltz, B. (2005). Assessment and therapeutic strategy—A place to start. In D.S. Jones (Ed.), *Textbook of functional medicine* (pp. 706-708). Gig Harbor, WA: Institute for Functional Medicine.

Part III: Nurturing the Mind

Chapter 17: Beyond Biochemistry

Amen, D.G. (n.d.) ANT Therapy: How to develop your own internal anteater to eradicate automatic negative thoughts. Retrieved September 12, 2010 from http://www.ahha.org/articles.asp?Id=100.

Ananth, S. (2009). Developing healing beliefs. *Explore (NY)*, *5*(6), 354-355.

Andrews, P.W., & Thomson, J.A. Jr. (2009). The bright side of being blue: depression as an adaptation for analyzing complex problems. *Psychological Review*, *116*(3), 620-654.

Broderick, P.C. (2005). Mindfulness and coping with dysphoric mood: contrasts with rumination and distraction. *Cognitive Therapy and Research*, *29*(5), 501-510.

Feldman, G. (2007). Cognitive and behavioral therapies for depression: overview, new directions, and practical recommendations for dissemination. *Psychiatric Clinics of North America*, *30*(1), 39-50.

Lake, J. (2004). Integrative management of depressed mood. *Integrative Medicine*, 3(3), 48-57.

Langer, E.J. (2009). *Counter Clockwise: Mindful Health and the Power of Possibility*. New York: Ballantine Boooks.

Lee Duckworth, A., Steen, T.A., & Seligman, M.E. (2005). Positive psychology in clinical practice. *Annual Review of Clinical Psychology*, *1*, 629-651.

Liebman, J.L. (1946). *Peace of Mind*. New York: Simon & Schuster.

Ray, O. (2004). How the mind hurts and heals the body. *American Psychologist*, *59*(1), 29-40.

Shedler, J. (2010). The efficacy of psychodynamic psychotherapy. *American Psychologist*, *65*(2), 98-109.

Chapter 18: Prayer and Placebos

Bosworth, H.B., et al. (2003). The impact of religious practice and religious coping on geriatric depression. *International Journal of Geriatric Psychiatry*, *18*(10), 905-914.

Fournier, J.C., et al. (2010). Antidepressant drug effects and depression severity: a patient-level meta-analysis. *Journal of the American Medical Association*, *303*(1), 47-53.

Koenig, H.G. (2009). Research on religion, spirituality, and mental health: a review. *Canadian Journal of Psychiatry*, *54*(5), 283-291.

Koenig, H.G., George, L.K., & Peterson, B.L. (1998). Religiosity and remission of depression in medically ill older patients. *American Journal of Psychiatry*, *155*(4), 536-542.

Murphy, P.E., & Fitchett, G. (2009). Belief in a concerned God predicts response to treatment for adults with clinical depression. *Journal of Clinical Psychiatry*, *65*(9), 1000-1008.

Murray, C.J., & Lopez, A.D. (1996). Evidence-based health policy – lessons from the Global Burden of Disease Study. *Science*, *274*(5288), 740-743.

Pollo, A., & Benedetti, F. (2009). The placebo response: neurobiological and clinical issues of neurological relevance. *Progress in Brain Research*, *175*, 283-294.

Shafranske, E.P. (2009). Spiritually oriented psychodynamic psychotherapy. *Journal of Clinical Psychiatry*, *65*(2), 147-157.

Styron, W. (2007). *Darkness Visible: A Memoir of Madness*. New York: Modern Library.

Chapter 19: Letting Go

Bennett, M.P., & Lengacher, C. (2008). Humor and laughter may influence health: III. Laughter and Health Outcomes. *Evidence-based Complementary and Alternative Medicine*, *5*(1), 37-40.

Broderick, P.C. (2005). Mindfulness and coping with dysphoric mood: contrasts with rumination and distraction. *Cognitive Therapy and Research*, *29*(5), 501-510.

Brown, R.P., & Gerbarg, P.L. (2009). Yoga breathing, meditation, and longevity. *Annals of New York Academy of Sciences*, *1172*, 54-62.

Friedman, P.H., & Toussaint, L. (2006). The relationship between forgiveness, gratitude, distress, and well-being: an integrative review of the literature. *International Journal of Healing and Caring*, *6*(2), 1-10.

Kenny, M., Bernier, R., & DeMartini, C. (2005). Chant and be happy: the effects of chanting on respiratory function and general well-being in individual diagnosed with depression. *International Journal of Yoga Therapy, 15*, 61-64.

Krause, N., & Ellison, C.G. (2003). Forgiveness by God, forgiveness of others, and psychological well-being late in life. *Journal for the Scientific Study of Religion, 42*(1), 77-93.

Lawler, K.A., et al. (2005). The unique effects of forgiveness on health: an exploration of pathways. *Journal of Behavioral Medicine, 28*(2), 157-167.

Lund, D.A., et al. (2008). Humor, laughter & happiness in the daily lives of recently bereaved spouses. *Omega, 58*(2), 87-105.

Nolen-Hoeksema, S. (2000). The role of rumination in depressive disorders and mixed anxiety/depressive symptoms. *Journal of Abnormal Psychology, 109*(3), 504-511.

Oman, D., et al. (2009). Meditation lowers stress and supports forgiveness among college students: a randomized controlled trial. *Journal of American College Health, 56*(5), 569-578.

Thompson, L.Y., et al. (2005). Dispositional forgiveness of self, others, and situations: The Heartland Forgiveness Scale. *Journal of Personality, 73*(2), 313-359.

Toussaint, L.L., et al. (2001). Forgiveness and health: age differences in a U.S. probability sample. *Journal of Adult Development, 8*(4), 249-257.

Conclusion: Personalized Medicine

Bhatia, S.K., & Bhatia, S.C. (2001). Childhood and adolescent depression. *American Family Physician, 75*(1), 73-80.

Hamrin, V., & Magorno, M. (2010). Assessment of adolescents for depression in the pediatric primary care setting. *Pediatric Nursing, 36*(2), 103-111.

Jacka, F.N., et al. (2010). Associations between diet quality and depressed mood in adolescents: results from the Australian Healthy Neighbourhoods Study. *Australian New Zealand Journal of Psychiatry, 44*(5), 435-442.

Katon, W., et al. (2010). Depressive symptoms in adolescence: the association with multiple health risk behaviors. *General Hospital Psychiatry, 32*(3), 233-239.

Richmond, T.K., & Rosen, D.S. (2005). The treatment of adolescent depression in the era of the black box warning. *Current Opinion in Pediatrics, 17*(4), 466-472.

Shannon, S. (2009). Integrative approaches to pediatric mood disorders. *Alternative Therapies in Health and Medicine,* 15(5), 48-53.

Whitaker, R.T. (2010). *Anatomy of an Epidemic.* New York: Crown.

Resources

www.JamesGreenblattMD.com serves as a companion and supplement to *The Breakthrough Depression Solution.* A helpful resource, the website contains easy-to-understand information about integrative medicine for depression. It offers:

- Up-to-date research in Integrative Medicine for mental health treatment.
- Regularly updated columns and blogs.
- Dr. Greenblatt's conference and speaking schedule.

Integrative Psychiatry

Comprehensive Psychiatric Resources, Inc. (CPR)
20 Hope Ave, Suite 107
Waltham, MA 02453
Phone: 781-647-0066
Fax: 781-899-4905
www.comprehensivepsychiatricresources.com

Located in Waltham, Massachusetts, Comprehensive Psychiatric Resources (CPR) provides patient-centered, science-based care to individuals suffering from all mental health disorders. Founder and Medical Director Dr. Greenblatt has developed an Integrative Mental Health practice at CPR that specializes in the comprehensive treatment of depression. The staff at CPR understands that because each individual is unique, a person's treatment must be individualized in order to be successful. With that tenet in mind, each patient's genetic, environmental, biochemical, and nutritional status is evaluated. Based on this information, a person's treatment is then tailored specifically for him or her. This integrative approach views the body as a complex network of interacting systems, in which each system can influence the individual as a whole.

To create personalized treatment plans, CPR incorporates the following:

- Referenced-EEG to determine which medication or medications have the best chance of working for an individual, based on the person's distinct brain wave patterns.
- Comprehensive nutritional testing to determine if underlying metabolic disturbances are contributing to an individual's illness and what an individual's nutritional needs are, so that appropriate nutritional recommendations can be made.
- Dedicated staff and clinicians with specialized experience in integrative psychiatry and nutritional biochemistry.
- A focus on restoring optimal physical and mental health and vitality instead of simply reducing symptoms.
- Transcranial magnetic stimulation (TMS), a safe, FDA-approved procedure that uses a magnetic field to stimulate nerve cells, as a treatment too for patients who have failed to improve with at least one prior antidepressant medication trial.

CPR uses an Integrative Medicine approach for the treatment of all mental illnesses, including anxiety, depression, ADHD, chronic pain, OCD, schizophrenia, bipolar disorder, substance abuse, and addictions.

CPR also provides information about quality nutritional supplements, including carnitine, CoQ10, L-methylfolate, ribose, and zinc sync.

Referenced-EEG

CNS Response (Corporate Headquarters)
26895 Aliso Creek Rd, # B-450
Aliso Viejo, CA 92656
Phone: 949-420-4400
Fax: 866-294-2611
www.cnsresponse.com

CNS Response offers information and referral information regarding Referenced-EEG, including information about the nearest treatment providers.

Integrative Medicine Resources

Integrative Medicine for Mental Health: Referral Registry & Resources (IMMH)
www.integrativemedicineformentalhealth.com

IMMH is an organization that provides referral information of integrative medicine practitioners. Resources concerning integrative medicine and mental health treatment can also be found at their website.

American Board of Integrative Holistic Medicine (ABIHM)
5313 Colorado Street
Duluth, MN 55804-1615
Phone: 218-525-5651
FAX: 218-525-5677
www.holisticboard.org

ABIHM is an association that establishes and promotes standards for Integrative Holistic Medicine. ABIHM is also a resource for physicians desiring certification in Integrative Holistic Medicine as well as for those who seek physicians certified in Holistic Medicine.

American Holistic Medical Association (AHMA)
23366 Commerce Park, Suite 101B
Beachwood, Ohio 44122
Phone: 216-292-6644
Fax: 216-292-6688
www.holisticmedicine.org/

AHMA is an association dedicated to the advancement of holistic and integrative medicine in healthcare. AHMA is committed to increasing the awareness and understanding of integrative, complementary and alternative medicine techniques.

American College for Advancement in Medicine (ACAM) Corporate Headquarters
8001 Irvine Center Drive, Ste 825
Irvine, CA 92618
Phone: 1-800-532-3688
Fax: 949-309-3535
www.acam.org

ACAM is a non-profit association dedicated to educating physicians and other healthcare professionals on the latest findings and emerging procedures in complementary, alternative, and integrative medicine.

International College of Integrative Medicine (ICIM)
Box 271, Bluffton, OH 45817
Phone: 866-464-5226
Fax: 610-680-3847
www.icimed.com

The ICIM is a community of dedicated healthcare professionals advancing emergent innovative therapies in integrative and preventive healthcare. They conduct educational sessions, support research and publications, and cooperate with other professional and scientific organizations.

Institute of Functional Medicine
4411 Pt. Fosdick Drive NW, Suite 305
P.O. Box 1697
Gig Harbor, WA 98335
Phone: 800-228-0622
Fax: 253-853-6766
www.functionalmedicine.org

A resource for training physicians and patients about the principles of functional medicine. IFM also provides referrals to functional medicine practitioners.

Natural Medicine Comprehensive Database
www.naturaldatabase.com

Information on natural products for the treatment of a variety of medical disorders. Includes a database of potential interactions between prescription medications and supplements.

Gluten-Free Resources

GFCF Diet
www.gfcfdiet.com

Large online database with answers to many questions about gluten-free and dairy-free living.

GFCF
www.gfcf.com

A good place to start for information on food buying and cooking.

Celiac.com
www.celiac.com

Celiac Disease Foundation
www.celiac.org

Celiac Sprue Association
www.csaceliacs.org

Gluten Free Living
www.glutenfreeliving.com

Gluten Intolerance Group of North America
www.gluten.net

National Foundation for Celiac Awareness
www.celiaccentral.org

Nearly Normal Cooking
www.nearlynormalcooking.com

University of Maryland Center for Celiac Research
www.celiaccenter.org

Dairy-Free Resources

GFCF
www.gfcf.com

A good place to start for information on food buying and cooking.

Go Dairy Free
http://www.godairyfree.org

Online source for shopping tips, recipes, reviews of dairy free products, cookbook guide, and book recommendations.

Nutritional Supplements

Comprehensive Psychiatric Resources
www.comprehensivepsychiatricresources.com

Comprehensive Psychiatric Resources provides information and access to quality nutritional supplements.

Testing Laboratories

Great Plains Laboratory
www.greatplainslaboratory.com

A broad range of nutritional and metabolic testing is offered through Great Plains including opioid peptide testing for casomorphin and gliadorphin.

Doctor's Data
www.doctorsdata.com

Specialists in testing for heavy metal toxicity as well as nutritional and metabolic testing.

NeuroStar TMS Therapy
www. NeuroStarTMS.com

A valuable resource for information as well as available providers for transcranial magnetic stimulation (TMS).

Index

Also Available from Sunrise River Press

Answers to Anorexia

A Breakthrough Nutritional Treatment That Is Saving Lives

James M. Greenblatt, MD This new medical treatment plan for anorexia nervosa is based on cutting-edge research on nutritional deficiencies and the use of a simple but revolutionary brain test that can help psychiatrists select the best medication for an individual. Anorexia is a complex disorder with genetic, biological, psychological, and cultural contributing factors; it is not primarily a psychiatric illness as has been believed for so long. Dr. Greenblatt has helped many patients with anorexia recover simply by correcting specific nutritional deficiencies, and here he explains which nutrients must be supplemented as part of treatment. He finally offers patients and their families new hope for successful treatment of this serious, frustrating, and enigmatic illness. Softbound, 6 x 9 inches, 288 pages. **Item # SRP607**

Taking Antidepressants

Your Comprehensive Guide to Starting, Staying On, and Safely Quitting

by Michael Banov, MD Antidepressants are the most commonly prescribed class of medications in this country. Yet, consumers have few available resources to educate them about starting and stopping antidepressants. Dr. Michael Banov walks the reader through a personalized process to help them make the right choice about starting antidepressants, staying on antidepressants, and stopping antidepressants. Readers will learn how antidepressant medications work, what they may experience while taking them, and will learn how to manage side effects or any residual or returning depression symptoms. Softbound, 6 x 9 inches, 304 pages. **Item # SRP606**

A Practical Guide to Hip Surgery

From Pre-Op to Recovery

M.E. Hecht, MD This book tells you everything you need to know before you undergo hip replacement or resurfacing surgery, directly from an orthopedic surgeon who has performed countless hip surgeries and has undergone a double hip replacement herself! Dr. M.E. Hecht tells you step by step what you'll need to do to before the day of your surgery, and then walks you through the procedure itself so that you know exactly what to expect. Sharing from her own experience as a hip surgery patient, she also discusses issues that can arise during the first few days through first months of your recovery, and includes handy checklists to help you organize and plan for your post-surgery weeks so you can focus on recovering as quickly and smoothly as possible. This book is a must-read before you undergo surgery, and will prove to be a trusted and essential resource during and after your hospital stay. Softbound, 6 x 9 inches, 160 pages. **Item # SRP612**

How to Manage Your Depression Through Exercise

The Motivation to Start and Maintain an Exercise Program

Jane Baxter, PhD Research has proven that exercise helps to lessen or even reverse symptoms of depression. Most depressed readers already know they need to exercise, but many can't muster the energy or motivation to take action. *How to Manage Your Depression Through Exercise* is the only book on the market that meets depressed readers where they are at emotionally, physically, and spiritually and takes them from the difficult first step of getting started toward a brighter future. Through the Move & Smile Five-Week Activity Plan, the Challenge & Correct Formula to end negative self-talk, and words of encouragement, author Jane Baxter uses facts, inspiration, compassion, and honesty to help readers get beyond feelings of inertia one step at a time. Includes reproducible charts, activities list, positive inner-dialogue comebacks, and photos illustrating various exercises. Softbound, 6 x 9 inches, 224 pages. **Item # SRP624**